Inventing a Classroom

Juan
Erica
Larissa
Kyzer
Gina
Marcos
Danny
Michael
Sarah
Joan

Inventing a Classroom

Life in a Bilingual, Whole Language Learning Community

Kathryn F. Whitmore
The University of Iowa

Caryl G. Crowell
Borton Primary Magnet School,
Tucson, Arizona

Stenhouse Publishers
York, Maine

Stenhouse Publishers, 226 York Street, York, Maine 03909

Whitmore, Kathryn F., 1959-
Inventing a classroom : life in a bilingual, whole language learning community / Kathryn F. Whitmore, Caryl G. Crowell.
p. cm.
Includes bibliographical references and index.
ISBN 1-57110-002-4
1. Language experience approach in education—Arizona—Tucson—Case studies. 2. Education, Bilingual—Arizona—Tucson—Case studies. 3. Language arts (Primary)—Arizona—Tucson—Case studies. 4. Multicultural education—Arizona—Tucson—Case studies. 5. Borton Primary Magnet School (Tucson, Ariz.) I. Crowell, Caryl G., 1949- . II. Title.
LB1529.U5W45 1994
372.6′09791′776—dc20 94-29656
CIP

Cover and interior design by Joyce C. Weston

Interior photographs by Joel Brown

Typeset by TNT, Merrimac, MA

The quilt on the cover was created by the members of the Sunshine Room during the 1992–1993 school year.

Manufactured in the United States of America on acid-free paper

99 98 97 96 8 7 6 5 4 3 2

Contents

To my parents for their trust in my abilities, their respect for my determination, and the time they share with my family. And to my children, Martin, Monica, and Kaeli, who fill me with wonder as they teach me about learning every day.

— Kathy

To all the children and staff of Borton Primary Magnet school, my thinking-learning community; and to my family for supporting me as I pursue my dreams.

— Caryl

Acknowledgments

We must begin our thanks with the people who are the characters in this book. This is a true story. None of the real names of the people, places, or events have been changed or omitted, because the children and adults involved in this story are proud of their participation and what we've learned together. We especially thank the students from the Sunshine Room and their parents, who have entrusted us with permission to work with and write about their children. These children's names are scattered throughout these pages. In addition, we want to acknowledge with affection our colleagues in Tucson who have been crucial to our project: Bob Wortman, the principal of Borton Primary Magnet School; Halie Pence, the teaching assistant in the Sunshine Room; Carmen Bejarano, the community representative in the school while we were involved in the study; Tom Birdseye, who pushed us to remember our audience; and Joel Brown, who supplied the photographs. Thanks also to our mentors: Ken Goodman, Yetta Goodman, Luis Moll, Teresa McCarty, and Kathy Short. Thank you for your trust in our inventions.

We also wish to thank the people who took part in the development and production of *Inventing a Classroom* at the University of Iowa, who read and responded, provided secretarial assistance, and kept up Kathy's spirits as the deadlines approached: Cathy Roller, Linda Fielding, Jean Hammonds, Mark Ceilley, Lori Norton-Meier, Gayle Bray, Cecelia Saddler, Erma Statler, Beth McCabe, Sandie Hughes, and Val Dentino. And thanks to Paula Baltes and her staff for compiling the Middle Ages bibliography.

On a more personal note, we want to acknowledge our gratitude to Philippa Stratton and Tom Seavey, whose enthusiasm has enabled us to reach a dream we've shared since this project began. Philippa and Tom have exhibited many of the qualities we find so important in Caryl's classroom. Most important, they've held high expectations for our work (and our time!), but while they've supported us as writers, *we've* maintained control of our own writing process. Just like the children in the Sunshine Room, we've found such an authentic literacy event to be a pleasurable and rewarding experience that has invited us to reach our potentials. We've invented this book, within the conventions of a commercial publication process, thanks to our working relationship with Stenhouse Publishers.

And our most endearing thanks to those most special to us: Martin, Monica, Kaeli, Dennis, David, and Benjamin.

Inventing a Classroom

THE EGYPTIAN
CINDERELLA
BIENVENIDOS

1

Stories Are So Important
An Introduction

IT'S THE first day of school, in a classroom in Tucson, Arizona. It's hot, still in the 100s in late August. A crowd of twenty-five eight- and nine-year-old third graders has gathered on a carpet in the group meeting area. The kids look with wide eyes at their teacher, Caryl Crowell, who sits calmly in front of the group. But I can hardly keep still in my seat in the back: I can't wait to witness and record what will happen in the next few minutes. The air is thick with anticipation. Caryl and I exchange looks, wondering what the day will bring.

I study the children in the room. Some sport the latest fashions, their feet adorned with dazzling new Nike Air Jordans; others wear clothes and shoes that, though clean, are obviously not new. Blond and brunette heads show off new haircuts (Randy has a symbolic sun "carved" into his hair), and each child wears a fresh new name tag: Marco, Daniel, Jesus, Colin, Aaron, Lolita, Antonia, Stephanie, Seaaira, Angelica. While I scramble furiously to write down everything I see and hear, the kids regard each other cautiously. They greet old friends in hushed tones, probably wondering who will become their special friends this year. Caryl's reputation as a teacher in this school precedes her eventual relationships with her students. She's carried out some very memorable activities in other years, and the children are respectfully quiet—at least for this first morning.

Several moms hover in the background, equally curious. Colin's mom keeps one eye on her wandering toddler, listens attentively to Caryl, and keeps tabs on Colin as well. Some children urge their moms to leave, eager to be on their own, while others nestle close for a few more moments of familiar security.

"Every day in the Sunshine Room starts with a story because stories are so important," Caryl says, as she opens a picture book, *Knots on a Counting Rope,* written by Bill Martin, Jr., and John Archambault and illustrated by Ted Rand. The children listen silently. She points out the valuable autograph she collected from Bill Martin, Jr., over the summer: it dedicates the book to this class. Caryl tells them about the book's original copyright date—1966. Then, through Caryl's dramatic voice, the story about stories begins. And so does the year . . .

Each fall children and teachers everywhere find themselves in classrooms, beginning new shared experiences that will continue for the next nine months. This book is the story of how one classroom develops as a community of readers, writers, and learners over the course of an academic year. It describes the complicated process of "becoming" that occurs in all classrooms, as unique individuals are placed into a single social unit.

All children, teachers, and parents have personal objectives and goals for a school experience. Some kids may be intent on writing a chapter book, learning long division, or making a new best friend. Parents perhaps hope that their child's particular talent will be nurtured or that a new ability will emerge, that she will be perceived as normal and healthy and part of the group. Teachers may resolve to try a new technique or method or to organize their assessment program differently.

Besides their individual goals, the members of a classroom community bring to school individual backgrounds, personalities, and interests: a love of the environment or music, maybe, or a special collection of baseball cards or sparkling rocks; a cultural and family history; stubbornness, leadership, or shyness.

This uniqueness notwithstanding, parents, teachers, administrators, and children share a common educational purpose: the academic, social, physical, and emotional growth and development of the students. Although this purpose is played out in widely varied behaviors and is nuanced by different expectations, the hope is always for children to succeed: to learn, become socially capable, physically adept, independent, responsible, and better equipped to make sense of—and contribute to—their world.

The process of how personal differences and mutual goals are reconciled in one classroom is the meat of this story. It's not a particularly new issue. John Dewey, in *The Child and the Curriculum* (1990) writes:

> The fundamental factors in the educative process are an immature, undeveloped being; and certain social aims, meanings, values incarnate in the matured experience of the adult. The educative process is the due interaction of these forces. Such a conception of each in relation to the other as facilitates completest and freest interaction is the essence of educational theory. (p. 182)

Our goal is to reveal Dewey's "essence of educational theory" through the events and relationships in a third-grade bilingual whole language classroom. Our analysis of these events and relationships suggests the following perspective: during the process of becoming a community of learners, a whole language classroom *invents itself.*

This book is based on research I conducted in Caryl's classroom, which the members of the community call the Sunshine Room, between 1989 and 1992 while a doctoral candidate at the University of Arizona. It is a qualitative ethnographic study of a classroom as a system and uses the exemplary teaching of Caryl Crowell, my coauthor, to broaden the theory of whole language learning at the "chalk-face" (K. Goodman 1990). In our study, Caryl and I demonstrate how whole language learning can be explained as a tension between personal invention and social convention.

For two years I was a participant-observer in Caryl's classroom at least once, often several times a week. I interviewed the students; Caryl and her assistant, Halie Pence; the principal of the school; the community representative; and the parents of four target children. I collected samples of what the children wrote, and I taped and transcribed literature study group discussions. Analysis of the data lasted another year.

Caryl participated in each of these components of the research process, while maintaining her own research agenda as well. We reviewed data individually and together, we wrote independently and as a team, and we talked frequently—formally and informally—with our colleagues about what we were learning. We invented a process of collaborative interpretation that enabled our work together.

We present our experiences as a story for many reasons. First, this was our shared real life for several years as we became colleagues, collaborators, and friends, so we want to tell it as it happened, to include the nitty-gritty of kids, learning, and researching. But more important, the telling of stories has value to us as educators, researchers, theorists, and women. We enjoy stories and we value the power narrative has to communicate ideas. We applaud the current movement to present the results of educational research in language all professional educators can share. We want other teacher researchers to recount stories, to discover their emotional and academic value. We hope that you enjoy our story, that you will grow as a result of listening to it, and that you will be encouraged to tell your own.

An Overview of the Study: Critical Events

I was interested in how the participants in the Sunshine Room invent negotiation, curriculum, oral language, and culture, so I identified and described certain events that highlight these parts of classroom life. Education ethnographer David Bloome tells us how events fit into our notion of classrooms as junctures between the individual and the social:

> Events are social and communicative; people acting and reacting to each [other] as they construct group or community and establish public definitions for what is happening at that time, for what is being accomplished, and who each other is within that group. . . . When people engage each other in face-to-face interaction, they need to construct a shared framework for how each other is to be understood and how they are to signal their intentions. (1986, p. 3)

I intentionally developed the term *critical event* to capture the importance of the pieces of this story that we selected to describe. Whether a daily routine or an unexpected occurrence that alters or changes a routine, a critical event is a glimpse into the complex system that is the classroom. It sheds light on the power structures of a classroom from a political perspective, a perspective that intentionally situates the event in the broader context of a triadic relationship between literacy, schooling, and the sociocultural complexities of our real world.

The critical events narrated in this story are the relatively small elements that nevertheless exemplify an amount of time, type of activity, or set of behaviors descriptive of daily life in the Sunshine Room community. The four critical events are:

- The process of negotiating curriculum for the year.
- The creation of a theme cycle about the Middle Ages.
- A vicarious experience of war through children's literature and discussion.
- A friendship between two children from different cultures.

Embedded in these four events, but never discussed overtly, is another important critical event: the development of a sense of genre through process writing, reading, and learning.

As I interpreted each of these events during data analysis, four specific issues emerged as the most salient:

- A high level of intellectual expectation.
- Symmetric power and trust relationships.
- Authentic language and literacy events.
- Additive bilingualism and biliteracy.

A description of the process through which these categories emerged is included in Chapter 8. Figure 1-1 shows how the critical events and specific issues are webbed or woven together to give a clearer understanding of Ken Goodman's (1988) theory of invention and convention.

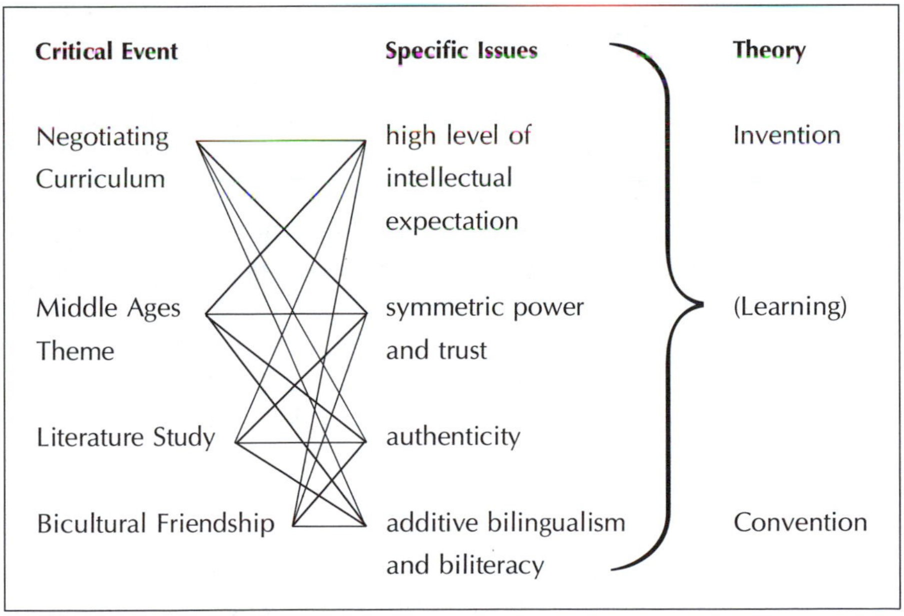

Figure 1-1. A synthesis of the research project.

Chapter-by-Chapter Preview

Chapter 2 introduces the members of the community of the Sunshine Room: the children, the teachers, and the staff members of the school. It also describes the setting for the story. The Sunshine Room is part of Borton Primary Magnet School, a court-ordered desegregated school in Tucson, Arizona, that provides a bilingual program in about half of its classrooms (one per grade level). The neighborhood that surrounds the school, the physical context of the classroom, and my role in daily classroom life are also described.

Chapter 3 moves forward from that first morning when Caryl reads *Knots on a Counting Rope.* During the first week of each new year, the children in Caryl's class negotiate the curriculum for the rest of the year, and this process is detailed and explored from beginning to end.

Chapter 4 provides more descriptive contextual information about the Sunshine Room and how literacy instruction is organized. It explains the typical routine of the literacy block, a daily period of time during which the children and the adults focus on oral and written language events. Drop Everything and Read (DEAR), writing workshop, and literature studies are illustrated.

Chapter 5 reveals how the children in the Sunshine Room, along with Caryl, develop a meaningful curriculum for themselves during a theme study about the Middle Ages. We see them write about their questions and ideas, read about Cinderella, and work with other fairy tales in literature studies. The complete theme study highlights the process through which their learning experiences progress from questions about the history of the world to the presentation of their knowledge to their peers and school community.

Chapter 6 tells what occurs in the Sunshine Room when war breaks out in the Middle East. It illustrates the power of children asking their own questions and recognizes the value of natural conversations in school. There is dramatic talk about war, peace, quality literature, and the naïveté of childhood.

Chapter 7 describes the relationship that develops between Seaaira and Lolita, two students in Caryl's classroom during the second year of the study. Seaaira is a monolingual English speaker from a white middle-class family that chooses to send her to Borton; Lolita is bilingual and lives in the Spanish-speaking Mexican American barrio in which the school is located. These girls share a strong affection for one another, and their relationship provides them with a fascinating bicultural experience.

Finally, Chapter 8 summarizes our story and makes sense of it for other settings, characters, and plots. We believe strongly that our knowledge of educational theory is extended by better understanding exemplary practice in whole language classrooms around the world. Without generalizing, we claim implications for other teachers and researchers from what we have learned. We also discuss how our collaborative relationship has benefited our classroom research and present our views about the collaborative classroom research movement.

Caryl and I have known each other for six years and have worked together for five in one stage or another of qualitative educational research. Together, we've deepened our knowledge about literacy and biliteracy development, educational theory and practice in whole language, and the research process. We've also followed our colleagues' recent discussions regarding teachers as researchers and relationships between public school and university faculty members; Caryl has written about her role as a teacher-researcher (Crowell 1993). We have examined how our relationship and the time we spend together in the classroom contributes to what we learn from the data that the classroom provides.

In November of the second year of our study, Lucy Calkins came to Tucson to speak to the annual Teachers Applying Whole Language Conference. Talking to Lucy at a social gathering afterward, I explained Caryl's and my goals for our study, particularly the process we call collaborative interpretation, which enables us to view each other's analysis of the same raw data.

She listened thoughtfully and then posed an idea that has lingered in my thinking ever since: "I wonder if the two of you are coming closer together in your views of the classroom and the learning process." She held her arms out widely at her sides. "I wonder if at the beginning you looked at an event very differently, and slowly, as you work together, you are coming to see events through each other's eyes, knowing how the other will interpret as it happens." Lucy drew her arms closer together in front of her body. "I wonder if at some point you'll come together and see things as the same."

In hindsight, although Caryl and I came to predict many of each other's interpretations and to learn in depth from each other, our perspectives haven't yet merged. Through the study, we exchanged knowledge, ideas, and language. We expanded our early personal research questions to accommodate the other's interests. We came to know each other more personally and involved each other in our families' lives. But we never reached the synonymous stance that Lucy's extended arms suggested. We still see classrooms, children, learning, and language through our own personal backgrounds and interests, knowledge, and experiences.

So, we've complicated our story (although we hope we've made it more real and more comprehensible) by attempting to maintain our separate though very similar voices. My outsider's voice narrates the events, although Caryl has contributed responses and additions to these sections. Then I analyze each event against the theoretical foundation that gives the event significance for me. My analysis appears in a different font, like this. Each time this voice begins, it is prefaced by a sun icon, like this: . Caryl's insider's voice continues this analysis as she makes sense of her key role as the teacher in this process. ***Her interpretation is represented in italics, like this. Her voice is also marked with a sun icon:*** . Although the two are tightly meshed, each analysis can also be read independently. Practicing teachers may enjoy reading Caryl's interpretation before mine, for example. Each has equal value in understanding the Sunshine Room, and each orients the reader within the larger context and provides a frame to add analytic substance to the stories. It is also possible to read only the narratives of each chapter. Parents and the general public may want to approach the book this way. For these readers, Caryl's and my analyses may nevertheless help answer questions prompted by the narratives or may provide interesting additional explanations.

To illustrate, we return to the beginning of our collaboration as each of us comments on our early goals for this study.

The questions that drove my part in this research project changed considerably over the course of my four-year doctoral program. I began with fairly specific yet burning questions about how children develop a sense of genre in their writing. I had observed my oldest child, Martin, when he was writing at home and had analyzed his writing with him during his first-grade year. It included numerous genres, all easily distinguishable according to conventional standards. I had also encountered various forms of children's writing from kindergarten through third grade in my own teaching and consulting and was repeatedly presented with children's seemingly intuitive knowledge of genre. I was convinced that children develop a conventional sense of genre during sustained periods of process writing and reading, when topics and forms are unassigned, a real purpose and audience are available, and meaning guides evaluation. I was sure, and still am, that practicing the parts of a letter that will never be mailed, writing arbitrary arguments and reports without a cause, or completing other contrived instructional exercises are not necessary to ensure genre development.

My attitude contrasted strongly with new ideas emerging from a group of linguists in Australia. Jim Martin, Joan Rothery, and others continue to posit that children, particularly those in marginalized circumstances, need to be directly instructed in the conventional forms of writing (Collerson 1988; Derewianka 1990; Littlefair 1991; Martin 1991). They contend that these children need to be taught "genres of power." They also suggest that the process writing characteristic of the work of Don Graves (1983), Nancie Atwell (1987), Lucy Calkins (1986), and others prohibits children from accessing the powerful genres, thus perpetuating marginalized children's disempowerment. (For a fascinating critical review of the "genre debate," see Barrs 1991/92, Cairney 1992, and Cambourne & Brown 1987.)

Having seen otherwise in my informal kidwatching (Y. Goodman 1978), I visualized a study that would counter the theorists' argument. I wanted to demonstrate that young children can produce a wide variety of written forms, especially during holistic language and literacy events in a classroom. I set out to find a classroom where I could document this process.

Meanwhile, I was fortunate enough to be a member of the research team, led by Luis Moll, Carlos Vélez-Ibáñez, and James Greenberg at the University of Arizona, that conducted the well-known collaborative study between departments in education and anthropology called the Community Literacy Project (CLP). The study worked toward understanding "funds of knowledge" in the community and in bilingual elementary classrooms in South Tucson (see Chapters 5 and 7 for elaborations of this concept). I was a classroom ethnographer for the project, regularly observing several fourth-, fifth-, and sixth-grade bilingual classrooms.

Toward the end of my first year with the CLP team, Caryl Crowell's third-grade classroom was added to our list of research sites. I had met Caryl in a graduate course and was familiar with her reputation as an innovative whole language teacher. Her comments during class discussions piqued my curiosity. I eagerly volunteered (nearly begged!) to observe her room.

Once there, I was delighted to find a classroom where there was real writing going on—an abundance of it. Children were developing their own topics and working through the writing process as real authors. Caryl's role in her elementary classroom, although I didn't understand it in depth at the time, was similar to how I perceived my role in my own teaching. Her classroom was far different from the majority of classrooms in which I had spent time. I realized very quickly that I wanted to spend more concentrated time understanding how and why this classroom "looked" so different, how bilingualism functioned in it, and especially what genres were being used by children and how they developed.

My time with Caryl and her students was eye-opening. Although I held on to my specific interest in genre development, it didn't take me long to realize that the gold mine of events in the Sunshine Room extended far beyond my original question and now included the ways children talked to each other and their teacher, the types of curricular studies the class was involved in, the self-run feeling I had about classroom routines, the interactions during math centers, and the ever-present mix of cultures and languages.

All this fit within my understanding of whole language. I believed at the beginning of this project, and still do, that whole language is a philosophy of teaching and learning built on sound theories of language and literacy development, understood through rigorous empirical research. In practice, whole language classrooms put learners, their experiences, needs, futures, and interests at the heart of learning. Whole language teachers work knowledgeably and professionally to ensure that all learners are supported in their quests to find meaning in the world and to reach their potentials in the classroom setting.

As a result, whole language learning often looks more like learning outside of a classroom than like typical school learning. The learners (of any age) are more actively involved in their experiences, teachers are less visible (although no less important), and there is a natural flavor of conversation, activity, movement, and exchange of ideas. Readers who are less familiar with the notion of whole language teaching and learning may want to sample the wide resources available for teachers, researchers, parents, and other interested individuals. Our bibliography refers to readings that have influenced Caryl's and my thinking previous to and throughout our writing of this work. For newcomers, we especially recommend *What's Whole in Whole Language* and *The Whole Language Catalog.*

While I spent time in this whole language setting, I also read ethnographic accounts of other classrooms and settings in which literacy learning occurs. These studies changed my view of education and the role of literacy in the world, and helped me focus my unresolved questions. Many dealt with communities outside the classroom (Taylor & Dorsey-Gaines 1988; Heath 1983). Others described special components of classroom life but not the whole picture (Newkirk 1992; Dyson 1989) or presented classrooms that operated under a transmission model (Philips 1983). I read Tracy Kidder's *Among Schoolchildren* (1989) at this time, and was angered by both its form and content. Kidder describes, in a readable and novelistic way, a classroom characterized by rote teacher-directed instruction (albeit by a teacher who cares and works hard) where the purpose is to transmit conventional knowledge to children. This transmission orientation and its accompanying (and frightening) deficit view of children, particularly Puerto Rican children, their families, their culture, their language, and their intellectual abilities, maintains the status quo for educational settings. Kidder presents this grim view of life in school without a word about how he acquired his intimate knowledge of the children, their teacher, or their school. His account contributes tellingly to the negative image of education and public educators that blinds the public to stories of success. It perpetuates the myth that our students and our school system are failing.

A third influence on my thinking at this point, nudged on by my two mentors, Ken and Yetta Goodman, was my growing knowledge about theories of language learning. I spoke continually with Ken about his theory of language development as a tension between the forces of personal invention and social convention. Ken's own words best describe this process:

> Each human being creates language, a means of representing the world and his or her experiences with it. But each human being does that within a social context and makes use of the linguistic resources in that social environment. Eventually, the personal language of each individual comes safely within the social language: the symbols, the grammar, the ways of representing the world for the individual are

> those of the society in which that individual functions. But the creative force never diminishes and it plays a dual role in all subsequent language development. So in a real sense personal language is the product of society and social language is the product of the individuals who speak it. Neither ever loses its dynamic quality; both personal and social language change to meet the functional needs of their users. (1988, p. 3)

These ideas were influencing my thinking in profound ways as I observed Caryl and her students.

I was also reckoning with a growing understanding of the influences of the political context of our society and the purposes of school and the activities that occur in it. Luis Moll's (1990b) explication of Vygotskian theory helped me formulate a new concern for the social realm of learning, and his discussions of the complexities of education for Latino students led me to read Peter McLaren (1994), Paulo Freire and Donaldo Macedo (1987), Jean Anyon (1980, 1981), Pedro Pedrazza (1981), and Denny Taylor and Catherine Dorsey-Gaines (1988), all thinkers who bring the political ramifications of schooling sharply into focus.

As I mulled these issues around in my head, I gradually became acquainted with the routines of a whole language bilingual third-grade classroom. My expectations were challenged regularly, and my conversations with Caryl fueled my questions rather than answered them. Ken's theory of invention and convention embraces all the political realities of schooling in this country as well as the developmental and instructional realities. It succinctly explains for me much of what I observe and celebrate in my own children's language learning and that of numerous students over the years. As I observed Caryl's kids learning and thinking without the restraints of a transmission orientation, I came to recognize the power of the metaphor of invention and convention.

My goals slowly changed until I realized that I wanted to understand *how* and *why*. *How* this classroom, exemplary in the minds of many, came to be itself. And *why* this classroom's make-up led to products of learning, *in two languages,* that were far more advanced and intellectual than were evident in many fourth-, fifth-, and sixth-grade rooms.

The research questions came into focus as all the influences from my studies, my mentors, and my observations began to connect. It took a long time, and the questions I ended with could never have been written before the research began. This is one of the joys and the frustrations of qualitative, active classroom research. Nonetheless, the questions provided a frame for organizing my learning and making sense of it against the rest of the professional literature available. They offered a way to express the how and the why of the Sunshine Room.

My purposes for this research are best described through two basic goals. First, I want to offer a description of a bilingual whole language classroom that provides evidence contradictory to the growing mistrust of public education rampant in our communities and nation. I want to tell the story of a group of children and their compassionate, hard-working, knowledgeable teachers who belie our predictions by engaging the eight- and nine-year-old children from a bilingual working-class community in intellectual rigor. My hope is that through this story and others, we can rally support for a celebration of our nation's children, teachers, and schools.

Secondly, I want to clarify for other teachers and researchers, as well as for myself, an example of how learning can happen in school when the process of invention is valued and nurtured in young children. This story illustrates Ken Goodman's belief that language is invented by children within the dynamics of the conventions of the language as expressed by the society and culture. It goes beyond language development, however, to show how all learning occurs in the dynamic tension between invention and convention. And it explains my focus on the invention and convention process that includes individuals but highlights groups in schools.

The Sunshine Room, over the time of a year, invents its own conventions for behavior, language, teaching, and learning. My goal is to demonstrate that process through the telling of the story.

I had only recently come to regard myself as a researcher. It wasn't until I began studying with Ken and Yetta Goodman, Kathy Short, and Luis Moll that I began to see a new role for myself as a classroom teacher. My mentors at the university felt strongly that classroom teachers have significant contributions to make to the body of knowledge regarding teaching and learning. As I studied the research of others, building a theoretical framework for what had been rather intuitive practice, I looked to my own classroom experience as a frame of reference for my learning and as the place where I could conduct my own research. To their credit, these university professors allowed me to pursue my own questions, even if my questions fell somewhat outside the syllabi for their courses. They also encouraged me to share my new understanding and my more informed teaching through conference presentations and professional articles.

Always, the questions that I pursue are connected to my classroom, my teaching, and my students, but I usually can't come to those questions easily or quickly. Ruth Hubbard and Brenda Power (1993), two university researchers who work closely with classroom teachers, refer to finding research questions as a process of "wandering through wonderings." I certainly spend a lot of time doing both. I tend to collect the artifacts of children's work that demonstrate to me that the children are learning, those "Ah-ha!" moments, along with the pieces that show frustrations and at times despair. I wander through them as I wonder why and how, and my questions seem to evolve in the process. Often they change as I see things in new ways.

When Kathy came to the Sunshine Room, I was cleaning up the final draft of what was to be my first published article, the results of a year-long effort to find an appropriate way to capture the second language literacy growth of my bilingual students. The hierarchical, highly structured practices of most commercially developed ESL programs are an uncomfortable fit with the Sunshine Room's whole language philosophy and practice. Such programs are typically organized into leveled categories of vocabulary and grammar, implying a linear progression of language development from simple phrases to more complex structures. Oral competency is established as a prerequisite for second language reading and writing. Furthermore, the programs' assessment strategies, by failing to make use of current knowledge about language learning, perpetuate the myth of second language learners as limited.

In my own classroom, I routinely observe learning behaviors that other researchers also document. My students are acquiring literacy in their second language while they are attaining oral proficiency, as Rosalinda Barrera (1981) contends. Some children are acquiring two languages simultaneously, just as Ken and Yetta Goodman and Barbara Flores (1979) describe. Every day, my students demonstrate the developmental nature of second language literacy through the purposeful reading and writing experiences that Carole Edelsky (1982, 1986) and Sarah Hudelson (1981, 1984, 1986, 1987) advocate.

I find support for maintaining our classroom's authentic language learning opportunities in the work of these researchers and of others such as Steve Krashen (1982, 1985) and Jim Cummins (1986) and, more recently, David and Yvonne Freeman (1992). I also find ways to reflect the tremendous potential and intellect of my students by using miscue analysis (Goodman, Watson & Burke 1987), writing samples of various genres, and direct observations. These strategies provide convincing evidence of the children's abilities, and I have documented the results of my study in writing (Crowell 1991).

In the meantime, as a result of university coursework and my reading of Louise Rosenblatt (1978, 1982), Margaret Meek (1988), Kathy Short and Kathryn Mitchell Pierce (1990), and others, I became involved in developing literature discussion groups as part of the literacy focus in my classroom. The first groups were tentative, but I was encouraged to continue striving for "grand conversations" by the work of Maryann Eeds and Ralph Peterson (1990, 1991). As the groups steadily improved, my students and I enthusiastically explored fairy tales as a genre. Having never before thought these tales to be much more than idle entertainment, I was motivated to consider them as essential literature for children through my contact with the thinking of Northrup Frye in Glenna Sloan's The Child as Critic *(1984) and the writing of Jane Yolen (1981) and Joseph Campbell (1988, 1990).*

By the time Kathy watched our groups for the first time, I was already transcribing our tape-recorded literature study conversations, a strategy I discovered through my reading of Maryann Eeds and Deborah Wells (1989). In this way, I was able to analyze my own role in the groups and learn more about how the children were expressing their understanding of what we had read. Kathy was immediately captivated by what was transpiring, with the discussions themselves and my analysis of them.

At this point, we began to work together for the first time. Although our questions remained separate, we made use of the same data, discussed our interpretations of it, and shared our different ideas about what was occurring. I think this was the first time we realized that perhaps evaluation and research are more alike than we have been led to believe. The very artifacts that I collect to evaluate my students, myself, and our curriculum, Kathy uses as data for her own work.

Throughout Kathy's years in my classroom, I continued to explore questions related to literature study and discussion, always pushing myself and the children beyond where we had been. The literature study group that arose during the Gulf War was astonishing in its depth and impact. I regard it as the finest experience I've ever had with children, and it's discussed in detail in Chapter 6. Gradually, Kathy and I began to consider each other as more than coinformants for our individual studies. We took interest in each other's questions and learned both cooperatively and collaboratively. We even use each other's words in the many presentations we give about our work. Although there are some questions we share, we continue to maintain our individual interests.

The children who joined Kathy and me in this study were not exceptional, as has been suggested by some people who have listened to us talk about our time together. They were no brighter, no better behaved than any other group of students either one of us has ever taught. However, I know they were affected by the research going on in the room. Perhaps they saw their learning as especially significant since two adults were consummately interested in almost everything they did and snatched up almost every piece of writing they produced. Perhaps they were so successful as learners because they came to regard themselves as worthy of the attention. Perhaps I was a better teacher that year because someone was studying me, too. These are lingering questions that I allow myself to wander through from time to time.

There is no doubt in my mind that I will continue to engage in classroom research, although I certainly do not have the time to report formally on every issue I investigate. I'm sure there will be no shortage of questions in the future, because I continue to be amazed and awed by children and their learning.

When Kathy first came into my room as part of Luis Moll's CLP, I had mixed feelings about her presence. Normally, I welcome the teachers, university students, and others who visit to learn more about whole language classrooms. Their questions force me to become articulate about my teaching and learning, to bring to the surface the theoretical framework that underlies what often appear to be intuitive decisions.

On the other hand, I was somewhat suspicious of university researchers. A number of years earlier, a researcher had spent time in Borton classrooms collecting data for a time-on-task study. Although he had appreciated the activities that occupied the children, he had seen their talking as time off-task, and suggested that I change my practice. Needless to say, I did not receive his advice warmly. His narrow view of the classroom ignored its bilingual focus and the understanding that to learn a second language, one must hear it and speak it for real purposes.

Kathy quickly assured me that she was not in my classroom to carry out some experimental design, but rather to observe what she had been told was a successful bilingual whole language classroom. I did not need to become a part of her study, although she hoped I would become an informant, responding to field notes and talking about my work in the same way I had been accustomed to doing for visitors. I was free to follow my own agenda with regard to my classroom decisions and my own research. Kathy felt that practice could lead theory, and with that auspicious beginning, we began our story together.

2

Meet the Sunshine Room

The role of *context* is increasingly important in educational research and theory building. Our recent collaboration with anthropologists and other social scientists has broadened our appreciation for cultural meaning and ethnographic methodology. The increased value we have given to natural learning and authentic settings for research has helped us see how complicated learning is for children, especially in school. We realize that research has often oversimplified learning through contrived experimental designs and isolated variables. Qualitative, interpretive researchers caution themselves not to overlook complex relationships and influences outside their immediate research question, the location in which the research takes place, or the expected result of the research.

For example, Ofelia Garcia and Ricardo Otheguy (1987) describe a revealing experience wherein their most significant finding was the irrelevance of their research questions regarding bilingual education for Cuban American children. The contextual influences of the community and parents were key components of their final understanding of this particular school setting.

In this chapter, we introduce the context of our study by describing Borton Primary Magnet School, the Sunshine Room, the children, and the adults—Caryl, the teacher, Halie, the teacher assistant, and me, a classroom ethnographer. These are the central, most visible components of our immediate context. We begin, however, with a description of the community/neighborhood, which is also a key part of the personality of the school. Then we move through the school, into the classroom as a system, and finally to the individual children and teachers (see Figure 2-1). My role as an "outsider" is described too.

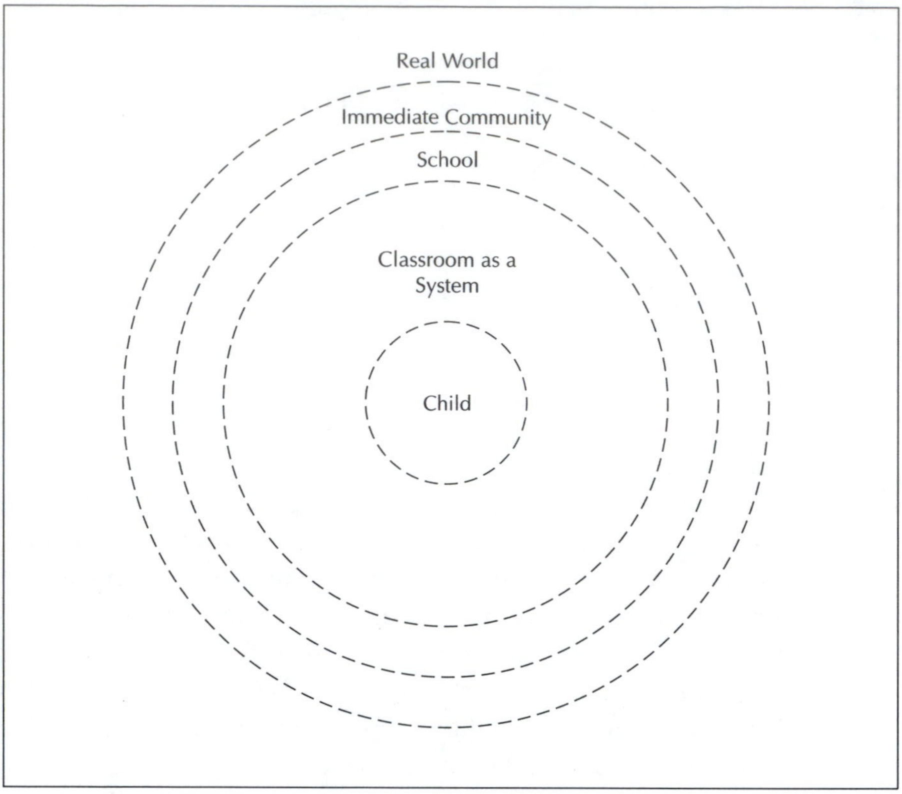

Figure 2-1. The context of the classroom.

The Context of the Classroom

The diagram of nested contexts in Figure 2-1, which you should picture as three-dimensional, represents the design of the research study. It places the classroom as a sociocultural system within the tension between the invention of the individual student and the conventions of the formal educational setting and the real world. The relative sizes of the layers in the figure emphasize our focus on the classroom. Movement from the classroom level toward the center signifies a closer, more microethnographic examination of the individuals and smaller groups present in the classroom; movement from the classroom level outward signifies a broader, more macroethnographic examination of the institutions, individuals, and groups that impact the classroom.

Thus, the classroom exists within the realities of the historical, cultural, and political contexts of its school and community. Notice, however, that the design concurrently maintains an awareness of, and an appreciation for, the ongoing development of the individual. It acknowledges the commonly recognized purpose of school—to educate individual children—but places that purpose in its surrounding context, which includes a history, a culture, and a political reality. Seen this way, the classroom rests in a zone where the tension between the forces of the social and personal is clearly visible. It is only in this nested perspective that we can appreciate the complexities of the process of inventing a classroom community.

The Community

The neighborhood surrounding Borton Primary Magnet School is predominately industrial and not particularly inviting to look at. The school sits on a major Tucson thoroughfare, so much of the heavy traffic passing by is industry related. The school grounds are bordered by several aluminum recycling collection centers, a Coors beer distribution center, and a manufacturing plant for construction materials. Auto resale businesses, parking lots, metal processing plants, and a restaurant supply company are within blocks, and each of these industrial sites is surrounded by unkept, barren fields and vacant lots. These buildings are regularly marked with graffiti, although the school is rarely touched. A nearby city park offers homeless people a place to congregate, especially since it's close to a neighborhood soup kitchen.

So on first glance, the neighborhood around Borton appears uninhabited by residents with regular lives. On closer look, however, significant things are happening just blocks away.

Like other desegregation and Chapter I schools in its district, Borton has a community representative on the staff, Carmen Bejarano, who is a liaison between the neighborhood and the school. Carmen has a personal connection with the families and businesses in the Borton community, and she visits homes frequently. Groups of University of Arizona preservice teachers completing a methods block at Borton are fortunate to be led through the community by Carmen each spring. On the tour are stops at the Tucson Urban League, the Quincie Douglas Neighborhood Center, the Housing Authority, and the Community Food Bank. At each of these stops the university students are greeted by staff members, volunteers, and clients who tell stories of hard work, survival, and triumph against the realities of their community. Borton sits amid this often quiet and unrecognized struggle, where successes *do* occur, as well as amid the more visible littered streets, graffiti, homeless families, poverty, and industry.

Following the period of this study, Borton began its own community project at the initiation of some of the Borton teachers and parents. Currently, Borton is in the second year of developing an urban bird sanctuary in a vacant lot behind the playground. The project moves the school curriculum outside the walls of the school and the fences of the playground as children participate in planning the sanctuary, developing it, and maintaining it.

The neighborhood immediately surrounding Borton is divided into three natural sections, marked on three sides by major streets, industrial dividers, and railroad tracks. The area to the west of the campus is largely Hispanic and bilingual. Most of the residents of this section are low-income families, living on welfare and in government-subsidized housing. Two large housing projects are located in this area, as well as multiple-family motels and small apartment complexes. Carmen explained to me on one tour that many of the families in this section of the community depend on a neighborhood free kitchen for at least one meal each day. The homeless population that frequents this area and lives in the nearby park is a source of controversy. Recently gangs have become a problem, especially since gang-related incidents have involved students as young as those in kindergarten. Many of the children in the Sunshine Room live in this section of the neighborhood.

To the north of the campus is another section bordered by busy main streets and railroad tracks. There are fewer families from this area with children at Borton, because it is made up predominantly of businesses and industrial sites. The families that do live here tend to be Mexican American and bilingual; according to Carmen, most of them have an extended history in the neighborhood. One girl from the study lives here.

The third area of the barrio is located to the east of the campus. The majority of the few African American families who attend Borton live in this area, as do many recent arrivals from Mexico. This area has a history of drug dealing, especially around the Quincie Douglas Neighborhood Center and in the park where it is located. However, a determined group from the center has successfully transformed it into a thriving provider of elderly recreation and low-income preschool care and city police now patrol regularly.

Their work has included an artistic restoration of the facilities and a renewed enthusiasm for hope, survival, and pride. This area consists primarily of single-family rental homes, although many extended families live together in these homes and lengthy visits from relatives who live in Mexico are frequent. Several children in the Sunshine Room live in this section, too.

Borton School draws from an unusual community for an elementary school. The community represented by the student population includes both the barrio immediately surrounding the school and the wider district. The children who are from the local barrio come from one of the three distinct geographic areas just described, each approximately one-third of the barrio's size. These children are primarily from a lower-socioeconomic, parallel-culture population (Crowell, Crites & Wortman 1991).

The remainder of the three hundred kindergarten-through-third-grade children that attend Borton do so voluntarily, and live in nonminority and working- or middle-class neighborhoods all over the city. These families are usually monolingual English speakers. The children are bused from their homes and participate fully in all of the benefits awarded magnet programs in the district. Together with the neighborhood population, the children at Borton represent a "wide range of cultural, socioeconomic, and linguistic backgrounds" (Crowell, Crites & Wortman 1991, p. 15).

The map in Figure 2-2 illustrates how Garth, a child from the volunteer community, gets to Borton on his school bus. His journey begins at his house, on the left, and he travels to Lineweaver Elementary School where he transfers to a second bus. From there, he continues to Borton. The trip is approximately ten miles each way and takes roughly an hour. Notice how Garth represents the significant points on his way, but recognizes that he hasn't represented distance according to scale.

Like most parents, the parents from all the Borton neighborhoods are caring and hardworking. They do not fit into the negative stereotype of poor, minority, non-English-speakers unconcerned about their children or their children's successes at school. Rather, these parents are generally very supportive of the Borton curriculum, its teachers, and the school as a community. They volunteer at school in the library and classrooms, they participate in programs especially geared for them by the community representative (such as English as a second language and adult literacy), and they support

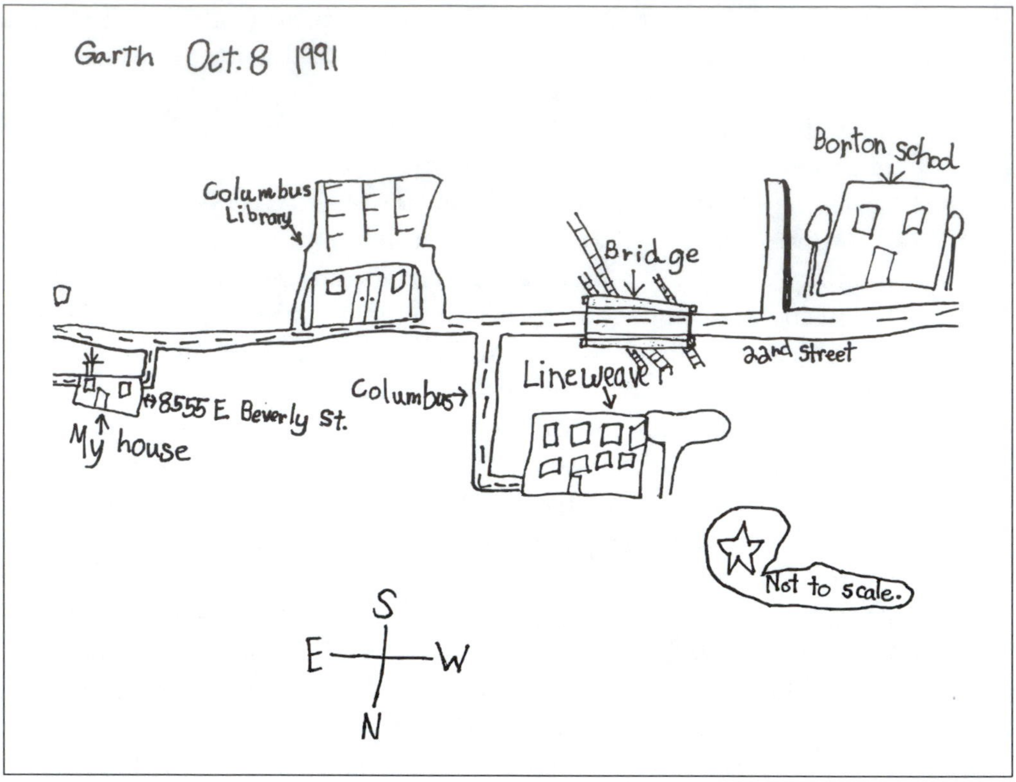

Figure 2-2. Garth's map of his route to the Borton neighborhood.

their children's school successes at home as best they can. Parents frequently tell the teachers and staff how much they value the special attention and innovative programs their children receive in this school. Their support is evident in high levels of participation at school functions like open house and parent-teacher conferences, and the annual Cinco de mayo fiesta. Parents all along the continuum of geographic, socioeconomic, and linguistic backgrounds in the Borton community contribute to the working of the school.

Borton Primary Magnet School

Borton Primary Magnet School is in the largest school district in Tucson, Arizona. It is an unimposing red brick and white stucco building with a red tile roof, constructed in the Southwest style common to public schools built in Tucson in the late 1920s. The classrooms of the main building are built around a square courtyard or patio area, with doors opening to an elevated covered walkway.

There is only one hallway in the school, in a wing that includes the school offices, library, computer laboratory, and one classroom. Additional portable classrooms extend along the south side of the school, accommodating a growing population that exceeds the original size of the site. (See the floor plan in Figure 2-3.) Upon arrival, guests to the main section of the school are greeted by the colorful displays of children's artwork that are plastered on the walls from the kindergartners' eye level on up to the high ceilings. Recently published children's books being promoted and displayed by the principal, Dr. Bob Wortman, beckon from a table in the hall. The exterior walls display artifacts of exciting curriculum and accomplishments. They also remind students of appropriate behavior, share knowledge with the greater community, and remind families and students of upcoming events.

The heart of the school and its philosophy are represented by the central patio. It is a well-used area that offers an attractive

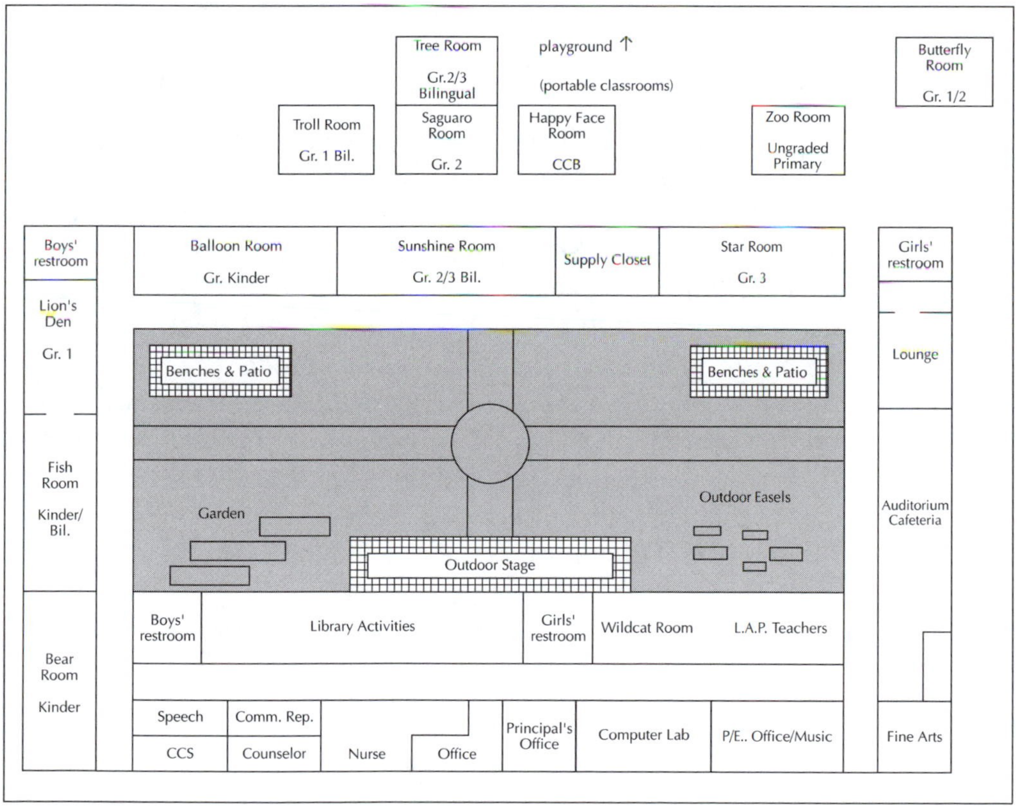

Figure 2-3. Floor plan of Borton Primary Magnet School.

respite from the surrounding impersonal blocks of the neighborhood. Art easels, water and sand tables, a stage, small caged animals, and an assortment of brightly painted picnic tables invite children and teachers to extend their learning activities outside their classrooms. Tall trees block the hot desert sun and pathways entice visits between classrooms.

The entire school community meets ritualistically every morning of the year in the patio. Here, adults and children share greetings and announcements, recite the Pledge of Allegiance and sing a song or two before they begin their day. Some children eat lunch in the patio, and parents frequently meet their children here after school. Community members have recently sanded and painted wooden benches and planted aloe plants at the perimeter. The attention of children is evident in the garden, protected by a scarecrow and tended by the kindergarten classes. Cement walkways crisscrossing the area are permanently etched with names of former students, families, and staff, written into the fresh wet cement when the walkways were originally laid. These names remind the community that each of these families and individuals donated the funds to pay for the concrete for this project. The labor was donated as well.

Our Community Pledge was instituted on the first day of the first year that Borton came under the court order to desegregate, in 1979. As an early childhood magnet, we wanted our school to have a comfortable, homelike atmosphere, where our young students would feel at ease with all the adults and where all the adults would take responsibility for all the children. We were fortunate to have a central area large enough to accommodate our entire school population at one time. Being able literally to see ourselves as one community and to have shared experiences as a school contributed to the sense of belonging that has persisted ever since. We've been meeting in the patio for Community Pledge almost every day for the last fifteen years. When it rains, we meet in the cafeteria. Each week, a different class is responsible for conducting the proceedings. Our fine arts teacher makes sure that everyone is familiar with the same core of songs in English and Spanish, although it's not unusual for the sponsoring class to use the pledge time to teach the whole school a new song.

Borton's popularity in the district is attested to by the lengthy waiting list of children from the volunteer community whose parents would like them to attend. Many parents place their children on this list at birth, in part because of the school's exceptional reputation. In 1986, the National Council of Teachers of English recognized Borton as a Center of Excellence. The Arizona State Board of Education commended Borton as an A+ school in 1987, and in 1988 Borton became one of the first schools in Arizona to be identified as an early literacy site (Crowell, Crites & Wortman 1991, p. 15). More recently, the International Reading Association named Borton the winner of its 1991 Exemplary Reading Program Award.

Borton also enjoys an excellent reputation in the minority community, particularly in the neighborhoods that surround the school. Since minority children may attend Borton only if they reside within the area the school is designated to serve, parents will sometimes resort to listing false addresses in efforts to enroll their children. Because our building is antiquated and our classrooms are small, we cannot be sure of being able to invite enough volunteer students to balance any surge in the neighborhood minority population of young children. As a result, we must verify neighborhood addresses by requesting rent receipts, utility bills, or other documents that can prove a family lives within the school boundaries.

The ethnic backgrounds of the children represent the two separate types of communities that attend Borton. Approximately half are nonminority, and slightly more than half represent parallel-culture populations—in one recent year this broke down specifically as 37 percent Hispanic, 9 percent African American and 8 percent Native American.

Borton was designated a desegregation school for the district by a federal court order in 1979 (Crowell, Crites & Wortman 1991). The implication of this status is that the school does not enroll a high enough percentage of low-income children to qualify for any federally funded programs, even though the neighborhood population qualifies.

Borton is well known in the district and across the nation as an active whole language school. Bob Wortman is an invited speaker and writer on whole language education, as are many faculty members. Both the bilingual and monolingual programs at Borton are recognized as innovative, holistic, process-oriented, and successful. This reputation brings scores of local, national, and international visitors to the school each year to observe and learn from the skilled staff. Borton is so frequently visited, in fact, that the children and faculty are often unaware of visitors in their classrooms as they proceed with their routine activities. They are also fairly accustomed to stopping for a moment to explain what they're doing and why.

The highly qualified staff includes a variety of support personnel, as well as regular classroom teachers. There is a full-time fine arts teacher, physical education teacher, and librarian. The Child Study Team, as in all the district schools, deals with concerns for specific children. It includes a speech and language therapist, a school psychologist, and a counselor, who serve other district schools as well. Full-time teacher assistants are in every room of the school, and resource teachers include a part-time teacher of gifted children, a Spanish teacher, and a Literacy Assistance Project teacher. These resource positions are funded variably by district, state, or magnet monies. There are annual guest artists, such as painters and dancers, who have been invited to collaborate with teachers and students, and other guests present puppet shows, give concerts, teach safety concepts, and so on.

Although Borton has just recently been recognized by the district as a fully functioning site-based decision-making school, the faculty and staff have always worked together to make decisions that affect the school community as a whole. School goals and plans for achieving them, some budgetary decisions, operational procedures, building-use plans, and behavior norms have traditionally been established through consensus. Also, every year, a schoolwide theme is selected and each classroom develops some aspect of that theme and shares its work with the rest of the school community.

The resources for a before-and-after-school program are provided at no expense to Borton families: it includes snacks, crafts, and outdoor recreation. The extended day staff has also created a readers club for the children. University support is available through student teaching programs, and an on-site preservice methods block focusing specifically on whole language teaching is conducted on the Borton campus (Crowell, Crites & Wortman 1991).

Borton has some extraordinary materials, which have been acquired through several sources, including a special two-year federal magnet school grant awarded to the district. There is a computer lab, as well as individual computers and printers in each classroom. Cultural arts materials, such as a collection of African musical instruments, support the excellent fine arts program. Each classroom has an audiovisual center that includes a stereo, VCR, and television. The library has a large collection of resources in English and Spanish. The significance of the library in Borton's overall program is evident in the circulation of almost 2,500 books per month (an average of eight per pupil), approximately 43 percent of which are nonfiction (Crowell, Crites & Wortman 1991).

Although some of these materials and opportunities are provided by magnet funds, teachers are to be credited with securing additional funding through grants and by making requests to the community. Caryl, for example, bought her students personal calculators with one year's grant money, and in the year following our study, she received funding to help her students build a room-size playhouse for the patio as part of their learning about construction and shelters. The fine arts teacher, with a minigrant from the Educational Enrichment Foundation, developed cultural fine arts backpacks for children to borrow and take home. They include thematically organized materials such as musical recordings, art prints, sculptures, and books.

The Sunshine Room

Each of the classrooms at Borton is referred to by a name that was selected by its original class. The name frequently reflects an aspect of the classroom—the Zoo Room, for example, is home to a vast array of animals who live in cages and aquariums and who provide a source of curriculum as well as a strategy for developing community and responsibility. Names like the Sunshine Room, the Zoo Room, the Bear Room, the Lion's Den, and the Fish Room eliminate having to call classrooms by the teachers' names or by complicated characteristics like combination grades, bilingual versus monolingual classes, and special education sites. Perhaps most important, the classroom names contribute to the uniqueness of the school, each adding its own personality and flair to the larger community.

When Borton first opened its doors as a magnet school we wanted to establish ourselves as a child-centered site. Knowing that our oldest students would be nine years old and about four feet tall, we decided to mark our classrooms with logos on the doors rather than with numbers that were too high for the children to see. At a previous school, my classroom door sported a poster of a smil-

ing sun and a child's words, "Mamí, no te preocupes. Estoy en la escuela." (Mommy, don't worry. I'm at school.) That so captured the feeling of trust that I wanted parents to have when they sent their children through my door, that it was the first thing I put up when I arrived at Borton. My classroom immediately became identified as the Sunshine Room. My mother added a second sun logo, a framed needlepoint design depicting a winking sun. Over the years, students and their parents have presented me with sun art of one type or another—rubber stamps, posters, ceramic and wooden wall hangings, and the like. I own sun earrings, sun pins, sun T-shirts, and whatever else I find that identifies me as the Sunshine Room teacher.

At the beginning of each school year, as you will see in Chapter 3, our class spends the first week or so establishing ourselves as the Sunshine Room. We each design individual sun logos that are used to decorate writing folders and journals, bulletin boards, and some years, T-shirts. We read books about the sun and learn sun songs, like "The Sunny Side of Life." Since everyone else in the school refers to us as the Sunshine Room, it doesn't take long for my students to claim that identity for themselves.

The classroom is on the south side of the school, with two entrances that open to the covered walkway and central patio and let in the breeze. At a first look, I recognize that the room is functionally organized. There are several large tables that, along with a large section of carpeted floor, provide work space for the children and adults. There are cubbies and cupboards for children to store their personal belongings, but the school supplies (pencils, paper, crayons, and so forth) are shared by the classroom community. They are all within easy access for the children and are clearly labeled in Spanish and English. A study carrel, loft, and the teacher's hidden desk give children important places to hide away to work, read, and visit.

I usually make changes in the physical arrangement of the classroom yearly, not because it didn't work out the year before, but more likely because I want to accommodate some new routine, my changing interests, or possibly a new piece of equipment. During this year, I needed to accommodate an audiovisual cabinet with a TV, VCR, and stereo, a sizable piece of equipment funded by our magnet school grant. Also, I wanted students to take more responsibility for managing their own papers and files. So I purchased file crates and hanging folders and set aside some space in the room for this new filing system. (Figure 2-4 is a floor plan of the room.)

The Sunshine Room most noticeably immerses children in print in both English and Spanish. Walking through the room at any given time, one is sure to see the children and the adults using print to complete activities and "live" successfully in the room. One of my favorite times to enter the Sunshine Room is when the children and Caryl aren't there. Then I can soak up the activities that go on through the artifacts they've left behind. Through the trail that they've left, I can predict what I might encounter when they return.

Books of every type imaginable are everywhere. The books that are shelved near the group meeting area and that cover the window-sill are categorized in bins according to topic, to be used for ongoing theme studies. Twelve categories are incorporated into a Native American theme, for example. These books range from Byrd Baylor's and Paul Goble's picture books to Aliki's cartooned information books

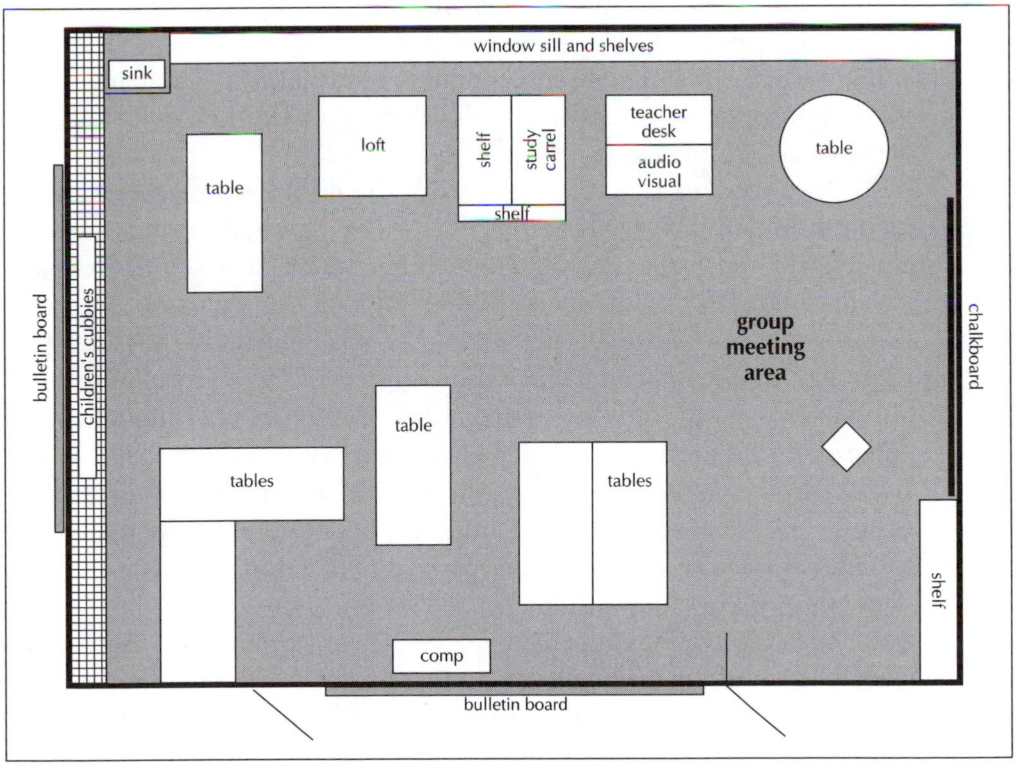

Figure 2-4. The physical arrangement of the Sunshine Room (approximate and not to scale).

to adult nonfiction and coffee table books. They not only are sources of information, in English and Spanish, for the thematic work, but they are frequently chosen by the children for free reading during DEAR (Drop Everything and Read) time. The children help categorize them, wrapping a different color of yarn around the spine of the books in each group. In this way, they begin to focus on the various genres in the collection and take responsibility for managing the shared and borrowed materials.

Still more books can be found elsewhere in the room. The children's selections from the library are in a labeled box, waiting to be exchanged at their next visit. A peek into the children's cupboards that extend along one end of the classroom reveals books they are taking home to continue reading and books they are bringing from home to read and share with others. Some books are on reserve for upcoming literature circles and themes and are temporarily "off limits."

Other functional print in many genres fills the environment. Two alphabets hang in the room, one in English and one in Spanish. Negotiated behavior norms, scripted in calligraphy and agreed upon and signed dramatically by the children, Caryl, and Halie, are framed and posted near the door. Schedules that remind participants of activities, such as guitar lessons and time in the loft, are near the related work areas.

It is evident that this community values written communication: there are notes and messages from one student to another, and from students to teachers and vice versa; letters to parents, in Spanish and English, from the teacher, the teacher assistant, and the school are waiting to be delivered when school is dismissed. The daily schedule is changed each morning and referred to by everyone (including visitors) throughout the day. Evidence of group learning, recorded on charts and other public documents, includes webs representing brainstorming sessions, data collected during math and science experiments, and ongoing records of thematically organized activities (lists of questions children generate at the outset of each new theme, for example).

In short, it is impossible to *keep from* reading in this room. Reading is not a subject, but it is of necessity used (and enjoyed) by everyone for a variety of authentic purposes. Functional written language frequently takes the place of speech.

I believe children are readers and writers when they enter my classroom, and I strive to support and enhance their continued development and success. With some children, I work constantly just to let them know that they can be learners. I try to surround the children with print and good books, giving them lots of time to read.

The students at Borton expect to have real books and quality children's literature in their classrooms. For example, one of the trails of artifacts Kathy notes in our classroom quite literally wraps its way around us. On the wall above the doors and chalkboards is a strip of adding machine tape that lists the books we have read aloud since the beginning of the year. It's a visual record of our shared history as a community of readers. By the end of the year, there will be at least 250 stories that we have all heard together. When I look at the strip I can pick out the topics that we have been studying from the strings of books with common topics or themes. It's a highly dramatic and visible way of recording our experiences. Although it is an awkward system and could be improved, it symbolizes the value of reading books in the Sunshine Room. At this school, and in our classroom, reading and writing share an authentic relationship in the classroom curriculum instead of being separated or isolated for instruction.

Daily Schedule

In keeping with a whole language philosophy, the daily schedule in the Sunshine Room is organized around blocks of time and subjects integrated across the curriculum. The classroom schedule Caryl has designed for the year is provided in both English and Spanish so that it will be accessible to all students and parents in the class (see Figures 2-5 and 2-6). Of course, the schedule changes from year to year and sometimes from day to day. My observations in the classroom, however, confirmed that these schedules are predictable and reliable.

The Children

The Sunshine Room is a third-grade bilingual classroom. During the first year of the study, the class comprised twenty-seven children, twelve boys and fifteen girls, sixteen from the barrio surrounding the school and eleven from other neighborhoods. During the second year, there were twenty-four children, eleven boys and thirteen girls, thirteen from the barrio and eleven from other neighborhoods.

Here, because of our status as a desegregation magnet school, we have a tremendous range of students. The children in my class from the barrio that surrounds the school generally come from families that are struggling to get by. In some, both parents work and they are able to meet most of their needs. Other families are absolutely destitute. I have a few students that do not have jackets; some of the children's families need food boxes periodically. The children who come from the volunteer community tend to be mostly middle class. Often, both parents work, but they are not especially affluent. There's a fair number of single-parent families among both groups. The variety of children is delightful and it's wonderful to see how well they get along in a situation that encourages them to work together.

As is common in bilingual classrooms, there is considerable diversity in the children's language and literacy abilities. The bilingual and biliterate abilities of the children involved in one year of

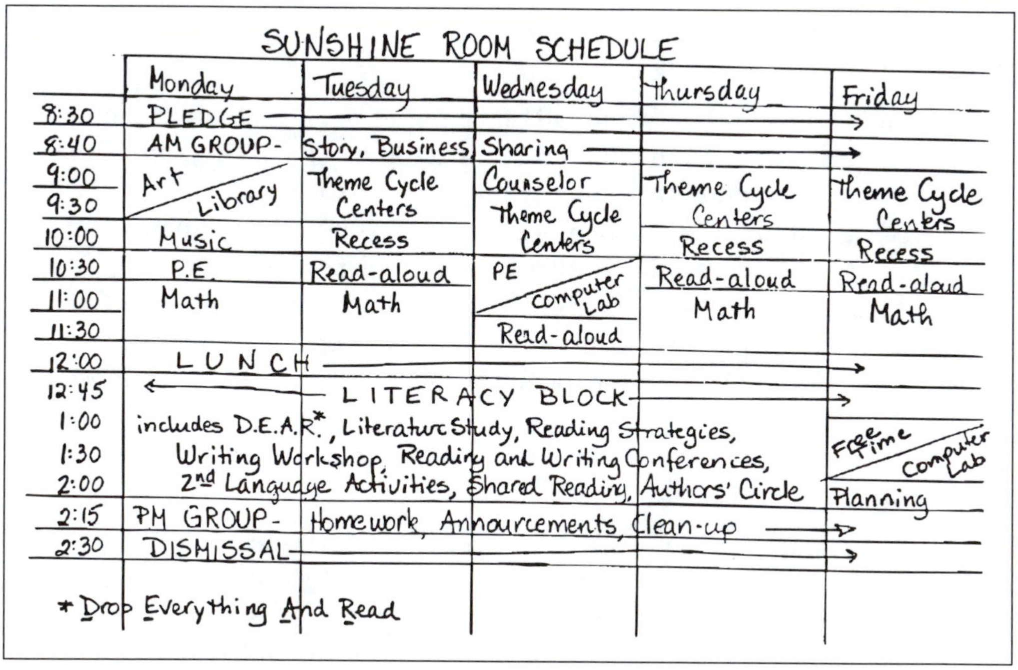

SUNSHINE ROOM SCHEDULE

	Monday	Tuesday	Wednesday	Thursday	Friday
8:30	PLEDGE →				
8:40	AM GROUP-	Story, Business	Sharing →		
9:00	Art / Library	Theme Cycle Centers	Counselor	Theme Cycle Centers	Theme Cycle Centers
9:30			Theme Cycle Centers		
10:00	Music	Recess		Recess	Recess
10:30	P.E.	Read-aloud	PE / Computer Lab	Read-aloud	Read-aloud
11:00	Math	Math		Math	Math
11:30			Read-aloud		
12:00	LUNCH →				
12:45	← LITERACY BLOCK →				
1:00	includes D.E.A.R.*, Literature Study, Reading Strategies,				Free Time / Computer Lab
1:30	Writing Workshop, Reading and Writing Conferences,				
2:00	2nd Language Activities, Shared Reading, Authors' Circle				Planning
2:15	PM GROUP-	Homework, Announcements, Clean-up →			
2:30	DISMISSAL →				

* Drop Everything And Read

Figure 2-5. Sunshine Room schedule in English.

HORARIO DEL SUNSHINE ROOM

	lunes	martes	miércoles	jueves	viernes
8:30	CEREMONIA DE LA BANDERA →				
8:40	GRUPO - Cuento, Anuncios, Compartir →				
9:00 9:30	Arte / Biblioteca	Centros	Consejera Centros	Centros	Centros
10:00	Música	Recreo		Recreo	Recreo
10:30	Educ. Fis.	Cuento	Educ. Fis. / computadoras	Cuento	Cuento
11:00 11:30	Matemáticas	Matemáticas	Cuento	Matemáticas	Matemáticas
12:00	ALMUERZO →				
12:45 1:00 1:30 2:00	ARTES DE LENGUAJE incluye D.E.A.R.* Estudios de literatura, Estrategias de lectura, escritos, conferencias de lectura y escritura, estudios de 2º idioma, círculo de autores				Tiempo Personal / Computador Planear
2:15	GRUPO - Tareas de casa - anuncios - limpiar →				
2:30	SALIDA →				

*Drop Everything And Read - Dejamos todo para leer.

Figure 2-6. Sunshine Room schedule in Spanish.

the study are represented in Figures 2-7 and 2-8. Fifteen of the children in each class (year one and year two) are monolingual English speakers and readers. Of these, two children during the first year and one child during the second year are learning to speak, read, and write in Spanish. One girl during the first year is learning Romanian. One child during the first year and two children during the second year are English-dominant bilingual speakers. Nine children during year one and six during year two are bilingual.

Within the label "bilingual," there is still variability. Some children, like Lolita and Antonia, read and write in both languages equally well; others read mostly in one language or the other. Jaime and Azucena during year one and Marisela during year two are monolingual Spanish speakers who arrived in the United States during their respective third-grade years. Each of these children is moving toward bilingualism and biliteracy and doing some speaking, reading, and writing in English by the end of the year. While they learn English, the children continue to develop as Spanish speakers, listeners, readers, and writers. As the bilingual and biliteracy abilities of the children are relatively similar from year to year in the Sunshine Room, the bilingualism/biliteracy continuums in Figures 2-7 and 2–8 are representative.

Clearly, the children vary in their oral skills in each language and in their level of and ease with biliteracy. The children's success in advancing their oral language and literacy development in a second language is a credit to Caryl's acute knowledge of the children's individual abilities. Children are not limited by simple descriptions such as "English speaking" or "Spanish speaking," nor are they labeled with deficit terms such as "limited English proficient" or "semilingual." Caryl describes her students as individuals with varied abilities, interests, experiences, and needs.

Interestingly, it's the bilingual-biliterate children in our room who enjoy the most prestige. They are the ones who always know what is happening no matter what language is being used. Through their ability to interpret, they control access to knowledge for those who are monolingual. Since the adults in our class defer responsibility for translation to the children, these bilingual children

ORAL LANGUAGE

English only	Bilingual	Spanish only
Mark Gabriel	Cathy Daniel Antonia	Marco Marisela
Cari Seaaira	David Lolita Judith	
Angelica	Carolina	
Aaron		
Paul		
Elizabeth		
Michelle		
Trevor		
Stephanie		
Randy		
Colin		
Thomas		
Elliott		

Figure 2-7. Continuum of oral language abilities of children in the second year of the study.

WRITTEN LANGUAGE				
English only		**Biliterate**		**Spanish only**
Daniel	Seaaira	Lolita	Marco	Judith
David		Antonia	Carolina	Marisela
Mark				
Angelica				
Elliott				
Colin				
Thomas				
Aaron				
Paul				
Cari				
Elizabeth				
Michelle				
Trevor				
Stephanie				
Randy				
Cathy				
Gabriel				

Figure 2-8. Continuum of written language abilities of children in the second year of the study.

are often sought out as resources and their contributions to the classroom are recognized by all.

I recall a math investigation where the children were asked to find ways to share equally fewer paper cookies than there were members in their groups. They were to cut up the paper cookies and label the fractional parts. Randy's group had no difficulty deciding how to share two cookies among four people, but three cookies was causing some problems. When Marisela, a monolingual Spanish speaker, finally sketched out a solution, Randy was duly impressed and remarked, "Gee, it must be great to be smart in Spanish!"

The notion that bilingualism and biliteracy is problematic is perpetuated in the labeling of these children. Even the bilingual education community refers to them as limited English proficient, or LEPs, an acronym that makes being bilingual sound like a disease. I prefer Luis Moll's classification of everyone else as "limited to *English proficiency." I spend considerable effort making sure my students know that I have my teaching position because I am bilingual and that speaking a second language has enriched my life and expanded my opportunities and view of the world. I frequently remind them that by nine years of age, they are well on the way to accomplishing something that most people can't do in a lifetime—they will be able to speak, read, and write two languages. One year, a publisher at a conference was handing out buttons that read, "Quien sabe dos lenguas vale por dos." (One who knows two languages is worth double.) I wear mine proudly.*

The Teachers

My colleague, Caryl, is a knowledgeable and experienced professional. She moved to Arizona from the midwest twenty-two years ago. She received her bachelor's degree in Spanish, later added an elementary bilingual education certification and a master's degree in bilingual education, and as a graduate student is currently working toward an education specialist degree at the University of Arizona while considering a doctoral program. I regard Caryl as energetic and concerned, both as a teacher and as a person. She uses her classroom for her own learning purposes, as well as the children's, by conducting research there for her graduate courses, by increasing her understanding of children and education, and by addressing topics within the curriculum that she herself wants to learn more about.

During the course of the 1989–90 school year, for instance, Caryl studied reader response to children's literature in the fall and author studies in children's literature in the spring. Both of her studies were conducted to meet requirements of advanced children's literature courses and graduate seminars and the results have been published (Crowell 1993; Whitmore & Crowell 1992). She also led the children in an in-depth study of astronomy, building on her own interest and knowledge in the field.

One of the aspects of elementary school that I enjoy most is being able to teach all subject areas. I can get my fingers messy with clay and paint, build flashlights and electric circuits, read children's books, and do a million other things that help me hold on to the child within me. I am curious about a wide range of topics, some that are new interests and some that have persisted since childhood. I also know that all of us learn best when learning is connected across disciplines to real-life contexts. I could never teach an isolated subject; it would be too confining.

Caryl's teaching experience extends from early childhood through college, and she is frequently asked by her district, the university, and national professional organizations to share her expertise with her colleagues and preservice teachers. Her continued education provides her with current information from both theoretically and practically oriented sources. Caryl's continuous and visible role as an active learner is crucial to the development of the classroom as a community.

Caryl is a role model for teachers and other professional women. She maintains several agendas simultaneously, and thereby impacts not only her own classroom but the thinking of her school's and the district's faculty as well. Her ideas about authentic assessment have been put into action at the district level, she is a board member and officer of the local Teachers Applying Whole Language group, and she serves on a multiorganization task force on integrated curriculum. In addition to these ambitious professional activities, Caryl and her husband are raising two teenage boys and managing a household.

Caryl is supported in her teaching by Halie Pence, who has been the teacher assistant in the Sunshine Room for ten years, and by occasional students from the university methods block and student-teaching program. Halie has a purposeful role in the class as a team teacher with Caryl, participating and interacting with children in planning, developing, implementing, and evaluating activities. She is a native Spanish speaker who immigrated from Mexico many years ago. Although she holds a master's degree in bilingual education she chooses to work in an assistant position. Her actions show that she strives to emulate Caryl in her teaching practice and she is fully supportive of the program and curriculum developed in the Sunshine Room.

My Place in the Community

The technical term for my role in the Sunshine Room is "participant observer." During my time in the classroom, I was what James Spradley (1980) calls a moderate participant. I sat with the children as they read, wrote, and talked with one another. I took field notes, chatted casually with the children, and helped them or commented on their work whenever they asked.

My presence in the classroom became gradually more participatory as the study progressed over the course of the two years, however. I realized at the beginning of the study that I hoped to remain in the classroom for an extended period, perhaps several years. Since Caryl and I didn't know each other, I began as an observer, but my goal was to be involved in a truly collaborative relationship with Caryl as a co-researcher, or parallel researcher. Thus I became a much stronger participant in the classroom as the study progressed.

During my first year with Caryl and her students, I maintained the attitude and the appearance of an outsider. I participated enough to be accepted by the group and to peek into an insider's role, but I did not become an active or full participant. I concentrated on my research needs for field notes, remaining in the background.

During the second year, my role became considerably more active (Spradley 1980) as I filled in, at Caryl's request, as an instructor with small groups, sought personal relationships with individual students both in and out of school, and occasionally suggested curriculum. For example, I led discussions or read aloud when Caryl was absent or needed to attend to things outside the classroom. I handled disciplinary situations if I needed to. I conferred with students as they read, wrote, and researched. I invited Marco, a student during the second year of the study, to my house several times to play with my son and to interact with my family. And I arranged for a group of students to perform their bilingual play at another elementary school.

My gradual progression from an observer during the first year of the study to more active participation in the second year was intentional. I think it was also successful, for three reasons. First, my early role as observer ensured that I was able to attend carefully to my observations and note taking. My memory doesn't "hang on" to specific details and verbatim speech once they've occurred. Other ethnographers, especially anthropologists in culturally diverse settings, report they can hurry from a research site and record details into a notebook, but I knew I couldn't do that unless I had no alternative. Along the same line, I was keenly aware of my limited experience with the process of classroom ethnography, so copious notes were very helpful. I found that my concentration on the written record of the events of the classroom reminded me to be explicitly aware of my social surroundings. As a result, I developed a workable procedure for taking notes and analyzing them, and I came to understand the underlying framework of the classroom as a system. Taking time and patience with my role and my developing system served as a strong foundation for the next year of more in-depth and experienced research.

Second, limited participation during the first year ensured that my presence did not intimidate Caryl. I did not want Caryl to get the inaccurate impression that I was an evaluator, judging her teaching abilities, or a consultant, showing her the "right" or "better" way to teach. Caryl and I slowly developed a collaborative relationship that was built on successes and founded in my honest belief that she is an exemplary whole language teacher. I developed this participatory relationship with her over time, however, and whenever I doubted the value of my participation in terms of the relationship I was building with her, I remained passive or neutral, observing rather than influencing. Judging from Caryl's remarks in Chapter 1 about how suspicious she was of outside researchers when I entered her classroom, this decision proved to be crucial to our success. Caryl and I gradually began to work more collaboratively, and she eventually contributed valuable additional data through collaborative interpretation. This is clear in each of her contributions in this book.

Third, and perhaps most important to my professional development, my early observer role ensured my self-perception as a researcher. I already considered myself an educator and a teacher. In my new role in a classroom setting, I was consciously concerned about self-monitoring; I wanted to learn the language and the culture of this classroom with as little influence from my expectations as possible. I felt deliberate observation was the best way to discover the acceptable language and behavior in this particular classroom and thereby to know its culture and language *as it is* rather than as I *expected it to be* (Goodenough 1957). In other words, through my attention to my role as observer, I increased the level of what Spradley (1980) calls "introspection." My need to be conscious about this phenomenon never left, but its intensity certainly decreased as my participation increased and as I became more comfortable in my researcher role.

After each visit to the Sunshine Room, I transferred my handwritten field notes to the computer. The computerized field notes have two components. The first is a detailed description of everything that I observed and recorded, in the order of when it happened. In the second section, I analyze the data as it pertains to oral language, written language, culture, and curriculum. For every hour I spent observing in the classroom, I spent two or three hours expanding my field notes on the computer.

In addition to taking field notes, I interviewed adults and children, audiotaped classroom conversations, collected writing samples, talked with Caryl (face-to-face or in writing), and visited the homes of a few of the children. Each of these activities is better described within the relevant critical event in subsequent chapters. And Caryl and I reiterate our views of collaborative research in Chapter 8.

During Kathy's first few visits to the Sunshine Room, she sat on a child's chair at the edge of the group and silently observed, taking notes in what was to be the first of many spiral-bound notebooks. The children paid her no more attention than they gave to any other visitor—and we had many during the course of the year. As all of us became more accustomed to her presence, the children began to ask her why she was in the room. They wanted to know why she came back regularly and what the study was about. They asked what she was writing in her notebooks and were always interested and pleased to see their own names there. They also asked personal questions about her family and the baby she was carrying at the time. Kathy answered openly and returned their queries with similar questions of her own. Bit by bit, we all began sharing pieces of our personal lives and our classroom work.

Following any particular visit, Kathy would usually ask me things about what she'd observed. At first, these were typical visitor questions about the classroom organization, the curriculum, and the materials. Knowing how busy I was, she kept these sessions brief. I did not regard her work as an intrusion, because I was familiar with the CLP and relished the opportunity to showcase a successful bilingual education classroom. As time went on and our research paths began to converge, we became a two-person thinking community. Our discussions did not always focus on the purposes of Kathy's study. Instead, we began to share what we knew and hypothesize about what we were each discovering as we went about our work.

A whole language classroom is a busy place where students are often engaged in a variety of individual and small-group pursuits. Even the best, most energetic teacher would have a difficult time following the development of every student every day. During the time that Kathy was in the Sunshine Room, I was devoting a lot of attention to discussions with literature study groups, leaving just enough time during our literacy block to touch base with most of the students about their writing. When Kathy began asking questions about individual students, about their work on a particular task, or about a comment they had made, I realized that she had something to offer me as well. The student activities that captured her interest and made their way into her field notes were the kinds of learning behaviors that I valued. Kathy brought an additional pair of teacher eyes into the room and she was eager to share what she was seeing. Moreover, Kathy was frequently able to spend extended periods watching and interacting with a particular student or eavesdropping on the work and conversation of a small group. Through her field notes and our follow-up discussions, I was able to learn more about my students and their learning.

I recall very clearly the day I first noticed that Kathy had became a participant in our classroom. It was during the spring of her first year in the room, when some students and I were studying the work of children's author William Steig. We had read as many of Steig's books as we could obtain and were attempting to make some connections across the body of his work in an effort to characterize his writing and illustrations. The children and I were seated in a circle on the floor; Kathy was in the circle, but up until then had only been an observer, as she had been in previous sessions with this group. As we struggled to construct a web that might show the connections between the stories we read, Kathy was drawing in her notebook. When we realized that our web was becoming too complicated to work effectively, Kathy showed us the Venn diagram she had been trying to construct in lieu of taking field notes. In the end, the Venn diagram did not work well either. But from that point on, Kathy was regarded as a member of our class. She had been willing to share her thinking with us, a risk-taking step that generally indicates a desire to enter our community as a fellow learner.

Together, the children, Caryl, and Halie are the regular cast of characters in the daily-unfolding story of the Sunshine Room. I watch and participate as they bring personal and unique experiences to the classroom to be challenged by the needs of the group as a whole. Each individual, as demonstrated by the nested circles in Figure 2-1, is situated in the larger contexts of classroom, school, and community. Each is a member of several communities, in fact—families, neighborhoods, social groups, and cultural groups. The story of the tension between these children and adults as individuals and the community they become during an academic year is the subject matter of this study.

This work
ready to go
home and share
with family.
Measuring
Object

3

Inventing Negotiation
The Year Begins

THE FIRST day of school in the Sunshine Room is a day to get acquainted. Before the bell on the first day, there is a steady stream of excited and nervous parents and third graders. Caryl introduces herself, shakes hands, and answers questions, primarily in Spanish. Parents ask about free and reduced-price lunch, they inform Caryl of their plans to pick their children up after school, they introduce their children.

Marco and his mom, Gloria, arrive a few minutes before the bell rings. As Gloria is telling Caryl that Marco is a Spanish-speaking child new to Borton, Gabriel sticks his head into the room.

"He doesn't only speak Spanish," Gabriel offers.

"Well, that's great," answers Caryl, "because this is a bilingual classroom and that means two languages." She ushers everyone outside as the bell signals the beginning of the day.

The entire Borton community meets in the central patio of the school to start the day. Bob Wortman, the principal, greets families and children: "Good morning everybody. Please find your teachers and stand with them." There is a shuffle of children, moms and dads, and others, as they move to their appropriate places while Bob leads a boisterous rendition of the song "Bingo." The crowd quiets. A teacher welcomes everyone to Borton and Bob shares announcements about the after-school program and expectations for behavior at the school. He says there are three rules at Borton: that children keep themselves safe, keep others safe, and keep property safe. The classes are then dismissed, and the new Sunshine Room class moves indoors.

The first of many critical events in the Sunshine Room occurs the first few days of school as the community members negotiate their curriculum for the year. (Remember, critical events are activities, procedures, relationships, or interactions that are of special illustrative significance to the classroom.) Caryl, Halie, and the children in the Sunshine Room begin each year not knowing the curriculum, learning activities, or topics of study for the next nine months. These key elements are determined during the first week of school, as the children brainstorm ideas and questions they have about the world and democratically vote for a curriculum. Caryl contributes her ideas in this process, but they have the same value as any child's contributions.

This process demonstrates Caryl's philosophy and ideology to children and parents right away. The symmetric power relationships between her and Halie and the students emerge. Caryl's value of authentic questions and her practices regarding literacy, language, and learning in English and Spanish are immediately evident. Above all, the stage is set for an unusually high intellectual expectation for the children. Therefore, we give curriculum negotiation considerable attention as a preface for the story of the year.

The children find name tags, say good-byes to parents, and settle in at the group meeting area on the floor where Caryl reads *Knots on a Counting Rope.* She tells them the schedule for the day and then opens the floor for questions. I watch from a table in the back of the room.

"Can we call you Caryl?" asks Seaaira.

"If you speak my name with respect, it doesn't matter which name you use," Caryl responds. She lets the children know they may decide what names to use for herself and Halie: "Can you make that decision for yourself?"

The children respond yes, negotiating the first of many decisions about how to relate with one another in school. Interestingly, the name convention changes from class to class. Some years Caryl's students have called her by her first name. During the study, children overwhelmingly called Caryl and Halie by their surnames, Ms. Crowell and Ms. Pence.

For the remainder of the morning, the children are involved in a variety of experiences. They design sun prints to enliven the room's decorations, select books from a library collection and read silently, and learn a new song titled "The Sunny Side of Life."

When they return to the room after lunch, they conduct interviews to get to know one another. Caryl suggests that the children partner with someone they don't know very well, and she tells them she has written out some suggested questions in both Spanish and English.

To demonstrate, Caryl and Halie interview each other in front of the children. Caryl interviews Halie in English, taking notes on the chalkboard. Then Halie interviews Caryl in Spanish and writes notes on a piece of paper.

"When you are doing your first drafts, you don't need to spell everything correctly. You may invent your spellings. And it's up to you to choose the language you want to use. You can interview in Spanish or English. Whichever is more comfortable for you." The kids find partners and receive the written questions, in Spanish or English.

There is a bilingual buzz of conversation as the children disperse to all areas of the room and get to know each other. Daniel and I squeeze into a space on the floor under the study carrel. I find that Daniel is bilingual, a very competent English speaker, and rather hesitant to participate. In the next few days Caryl and I will continue to monitor Daniel's apparent disinterest in school. Although he is clearly not excited by our task, Daniel does tell me about his family and that he often goes to Mexico.

When the children return to the whole-group meeting area about fifteen minutes later, Caryl shows them how to file their writing materials in their personal writing workshop folders and the group prepares for lunch. The next day the students will write up what they learned in these interviews.

On the second day of school, the children brainstorm topics of study for the rest of the year. The process begins individually and quietly, as the children sit at tables with long strips of lined paper and list ideas. Caryl begins by talking with the children.

"What could you put on these papers?" she asks.

The children suggest rhymes, a spelling test, a very short story, and so on.

"Could you put a list on it?"

"Yes."

Caryl explains that a list could go on this type of paper because it is just one word under another word. She adds, "You're the only person who'll need to read it so don't worry about the spelling."

She asks them to put their names on the top, and the date, which she reminds them of in Spanish and English. She wants the children to sit quietly and think and compose their own lists of what they want to learn about during the year, what themes they hope the class will study. They'll have a chance to talk about their ideas soon.

Some children write fast and furiously. Seaaira, who is gratefully enthusiastic about being able to spell for herself, generates a long list with no apparent problem. (Her list appears in Figure 3-1.) A very few children, like Daniel, are lost in terms of ideas or what to write. With great difficulty and after some supportive encouragement from me, Daniel eventually writes invented forms for animals and Mexico. Most children, however, given some reassuring comments from their teachers, create a list of five or six ideas without difficulty, in whatever language they prefer. Lolita's list (see Figure 3-2) is an example of a bilingual child's thinking and writing in both Spanish and English.

After about ten minutes of individual brainstorming, the children share their lists in small groups. Each child in the small group reads his or her personal list while a group recorder writes everything down on a large piece of lined chart paper. This way, the final product includes all their ideas. The children who serve as recorder

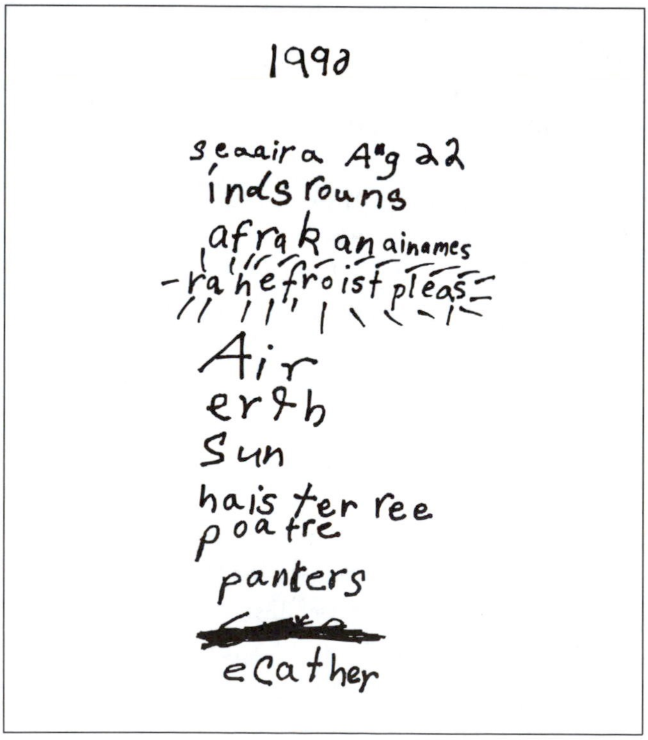

Figure 3-1. Seaaira's individual brainstorming list: Indian ruins, African animals, *rain forest please,* air, earth, sun, history, poetry, painters, equator.

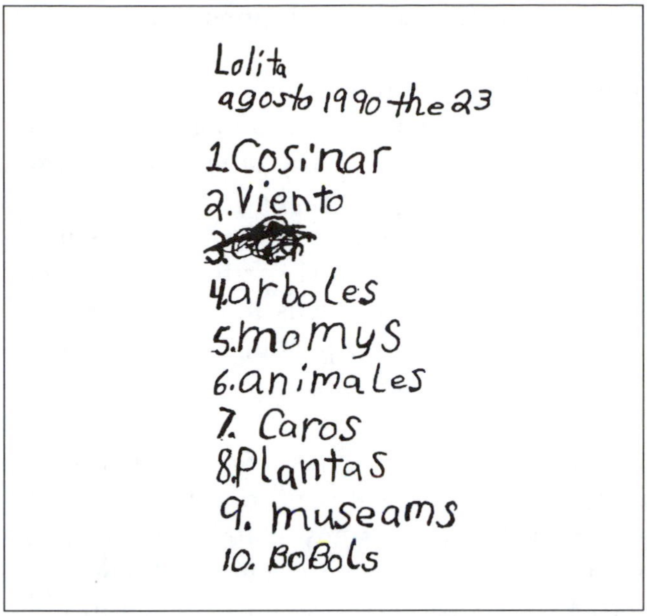
Lolita
agosto 1990 the 23
1. Cosinar
2. Viento
3.
4. arboles
5. momys
6. animales
7. Caros
8. Plantas
9. museams
10. BoBols

Figure 3-2. Lolita's individual brainstorming list: cocinar (to cook), viento (wind), árboles (trees), mummies, animales (animals), carros (cars), plantas (plants), museums, bubbles.

invent spellings. Some children add new ideas to their personal lists based on the ideas shared by others.

About twenty minutes later, Caryl announces that the children have sixty more seconds. The warning sparks a flurry of talking and activity. The activity in the room has increased exponentially over time; as the children understand the process and hear about other children's interests they create more possibilities for themselves.

As the small-group phase ends, the children come together in the class meeting area.

"Brainstorming is like an explosion because ideas suggest more ideas," Caryl says. "Since there is no way we can study all of these ideas in one year, tomorrow the class will rank the list from most favorite to least favorite. You're going to leave the year with more questions than you start with—at least I hope so, because if not, I'm not doing my job."

Caryl then reads the small-group lists out loud. The students interpret their invented spellings when she needs help, and they talk about classifying some of the topics into groups. We all laugh about some of the ideas, and the kids share their backgrounds as they go, talking informally. The suggestion raised by Seaaira, to study "the middle ages," which she defines for Caryl as, "You know, when the girls wore poodle skirts and stuff," is greeted with humor and pleasure.

"This day is the funnest day of third grade so far," murmurs Travis. His voice is filled with a sense of satisfaction and expectations of more "fun days" to come. He, like the other children (and me), leans forward with interest. It is quiet as the reading continues. Two of the small-group lists provide a flavor of the children's interests, and we share them below. (The original spelling is preserved; conventional spelling and English translations follow in parentheses.) These lists document the wealth of possibilities available for investigation when children are invited into the curriculum development process.

Carolina, the recorder for her group, has written: the sea; hiking; Amozom (Amazon); fiar (fire); yo ciero estudiar matematic (yo quiero estudiar matemática: I want to study mathematics); space; doenesors (dinosaurs); trees; me gustaría tener jugetes (I would like to have toys); babols (bubbles); snaecs (snakes); nachr (nature); me gustaria tener lentes (I would like to have glasses); jau too maec cartoons (how to make cartoons); roks (rocks); fonges (fungus); peopole (people); me gustaría tener un carro (I would like to have a car); bokonos (volcanoes); anamoles (animales: animals); me gustaría tener una casa (I want to have a house).

Seaaira has recorded these ideas for her group: Insrons (Indian ruins); baterfly (butterfly); spas (space); dinasorns (dinosaurs); afraken anamels (African animals); sains (science); palse (plants); raine forist ples (rain forest please); u.f.o.; sloer stam (solar system); air; erth (earth); sun; fuol (fuel); sea; poatre (poetry); book riteers (book writers); gavad (gravity); dsert (desert); anamall (animal); babels (bubbles); manes (magnets); elttsat (electricity); tacing (unknown); art; rokit caligen (rocket challenger); haisterree (history); pasatorikitim (prehistoric times); in the 50 (in the 50s); vikins (vikings); air plans (airplanes); danter (dinosaurs); unvers (universe); sime caapen (unknown); food; nike case (knights and castles); malteagsa (middle ages).

The lists are read for the entire class in preparation for a democratic process in which the children categorize the ideas and rank their top ten choices, assigning ten points to their most favorite, nine points to their second choice, and so on. Caryl then calculates the point totals for each theme. This provides a group consensus for the decisions about the year's topics. It ensures that everyone's voice counts equally. Seaaira's list in Figure 3-3 shows her rankings, and

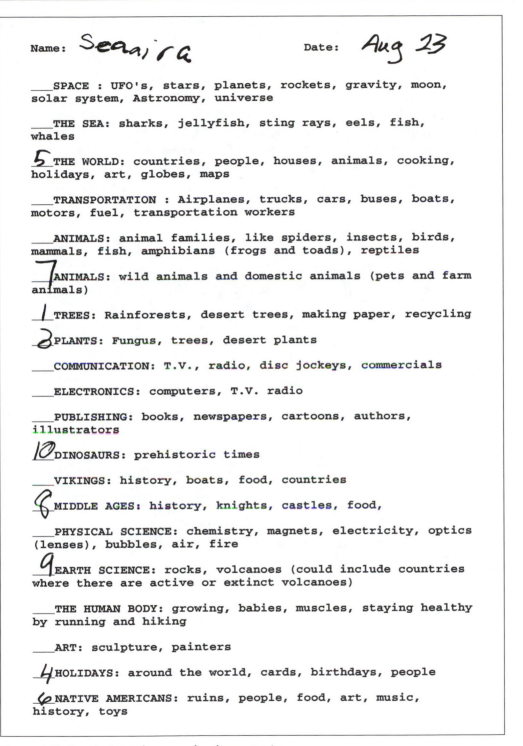

Name: Seaaira **Date:** Aug 23

___SPACE : UFO's, stars, planets, rockets, gravity, moon, solar system, Astronomy, universe

___THE SEA: sharks, jellyfish, sting rays, eels, fish, whales

5 THE WORLD: countries, people, houses, animals, cooking, holidays, art, globes, maps

___TRANSPORTATION : Airplanes, trucks, cars, buses, boats, motors, fuel, transportation workers

___ANIMALS: animal families, like spiders, insects, birds, mammals, fish, amphibians (frogs and toads), reptiles

7 ANIMALS: wild animals and domestic animals (pets and farm animals)

1 TREES: Rainforests, desert trees, making paper, recycling

2 PLANTS: Fungus, trees, desert plants

___COMMUNICATION: T.V., radio, disc jockeys, commercials

___ELECTRONICS: computers, T.V. radio

___PUBLISHING: books, newspapers, cartoons, authors, illustrators

10 DINOSAURS: prehistoric times

___VIKINGS: history, boats, food, countries

8 MIDDLE AGES: history, knights, castles, food,

___PHYSICAL SCIENCE: chemistry, magnets, electricity, optics (lenses), bubbles, air, fire

9 EARTH SCIENCE: rocks, volcanoes (could include countries where there are active or extinct volcanoes)

___THE HUMAN BODY: growing, babies, muscles, staying healthy by running and hiking

___ART: sculpture, painters

4 HOLIDAYS: around the world, cards, birthdays, people

6 NATIVE AMERICANS: ruins, people, food, art, music, history, toys

Figure 3-3. Seaaira's preferences for theme topics.

the resulting class totals are presented in Figure 3-4, with the circled numbers indicating the ten most preferred topics for the whole class.

From this final list, Caryl determines which of the class choices will fill the year's curriculum and the order in which they will be presented. Controlling the order allows her to sequence topics logically. It also ensures that she has time to gather materials and prepare each new topic. By the end of the first week of school, Caryl, Halie, and the students have a sense of the shape of their future curriculum.

Then, as each theme begins over the course of the year, the brainstorming process is repeated. Typically, the children participate in the following steps as they study each theme:

1. Brainstorm and web their previous knowledge about the topic.
2. Create questions about what they want to learn.
3. List possible activities, centers, and projects that they could do.
4. Explore the topic through a wide range of experiences and materials.
5. Present their learning in a form that is generated during the learning phase.

(This process is explored in detail in the example of a theme about the Middle Ages in Chapter 5, which focuses on curriculum.)

In order to examine what is special about how this third-grade year begins, and to understand what makes this event *critical,* the four issues that surface repeatedly throughout the descriptions of this classroom need to be explored. These four issues are a high level of intellectual expectation, symmetric power and trust relationships between teachers and children, authentic language and literacy events, and additive bilingualism and biliteracy. Caryl's and my voices are represented in different fonts throughout our interpretation.

High Level of Intellectual Expectation

The education that is unveiled for me during the first few days of school in the Sunshine Room contradicts my expectations, which are based on how many schools and communities describe educational practice for minorities and working-class populations. Here, children are challenged to think about their questions about the world and to pose those questions as topics for study for themselves and their classmates. This sharply contrasts with work children are asked to complete in many school settings.

Many of the studies about education for minority and working-

(3) 126 SPACE : UFO's, stars, planets, rockets, gravity, moon, solar system, Astronomy, universe

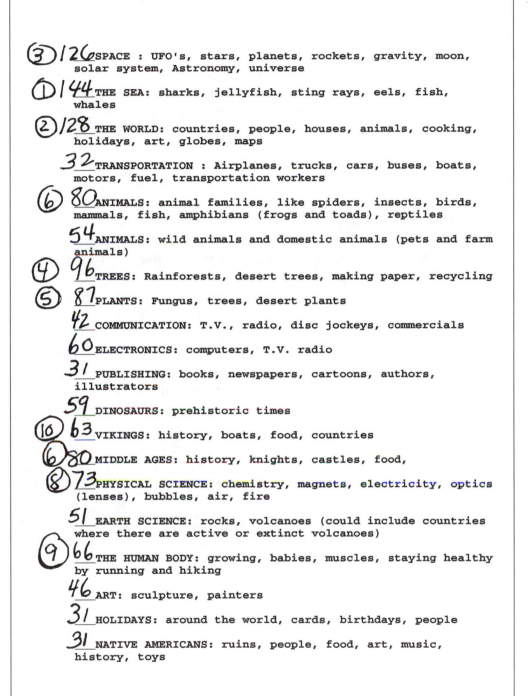

(1) 144 THE SEA: sharks, jellyfish, sting rays, eels, fish, whales

(2) 128 THE WORLD: countries, people, houses, animals, cooking, holidays, art, globes, maps

32 TRANSPORTATION : Airplanes, trucks, cars, buses, boats, motors, fuel, transportation workers

(6) 80 ANIMALS: animal families, like spiders, insects, birds, mammals, fish, amphibians (frogs and toads), reptiles

54 ANIMALS: wild animals and domestic animals (pets and farm animals)

(4) 96 TREES: Rainforests, desert trees, making paper, recycling

(5) 87 PLANTS: Fungus, trees, desert plants

42 COMMUNICATION: T.V., radio, disc jockeys, commercials

60 ELECTRONICS: computers, T.V. radio

31 PUBLISHING: books, newspapers, cartoons, authors, illustrators

59 DINOSAURS: prehistoric times

(10) 63 VIKINGS: history, boats, food, countries

(6) 80 MIDDLE AGES: history, knights, castles, food,

(8) 73 PHYSICAL SCIENCE: chemistry, magnets, electricity, optics (lenses), bubbles, air, fire

51 EARTH SCIENCE: rocks, volcanoes (could include countries where there are active or extinct volcanoes)

(9) 66 THE HUMAN BODY: growing, babies, muscles, staying healthy by running and hiking

46 ART: sculpture, painters

31 HOLIDAYS: around the world, cards, birthdays, people

31 NATIVE AMERICANS: ruins, people, food, art, music, history, toys

Figure 3-4. The final class tally for theme topics.

class populations, referred to as parallel cultures by Rudine Sims Bishop (1982; Y. Goodman 1992), show that the type of educational experiences children typically receive differs considerably according to the socioeconomic status of their community and the languages spoken in their homes. Children from minority populations, economically poor homes, and non-English-speaking homes (like roughly half of the students at Borton) receive different content and types of learning experiences than do children from majority, middle- or upper-class, and English-speaking homes (Anyon 1980, 1981; Moll 1988; Moll & Díaz 1987; Oakes 1985; Wilcox 1982; for a review of research dealing specifically with reading instruction, see Shannon 1992). Jeannie Oakes, for example, in her book *Keeping Track* (1985) finds that "poor and minority students are most likely to be placed at the lowest levels of the school's sorting system" (p. 67). And yet Caryl's working-class and minority students are participating and being challenged without a tracking system in their classroom or school.

Jean Anyon's research (1980, 1981) on the relationship between social class and intellectual work in school has had a key influence on my analysis. Anyon conducted participant observations in fifth-grade classrooms in five schools with contrasting social-class communities and compared the intellectual work across social-class categories. She observed instruction, analyzed and compared textbooks and instructional materials, and interviewed students and teachers in communities and schools that she labeled "working class," "middle class," "affluent professional," and "executive elite." Her work in classrooms evolved into a description of school work as it compares to social class. Anyon proposes that each social-class community receives varied types of work in school, as summarized in Figure 3-5.

Anyon's descriptive phrases depict how the quality of children's school work improves with elevation in social class in the United States, so as I watch Caryl and her students and read and reread my field notes, I compare these first days with Anyon's descriptions. When Caryl invites children into the curriculum planning process, I recognize how her expectations for her children are so different from those of the teachers Anyon observed and describes. Working-class children typically receive an education characterized by memorization and the completion of photocopied worksheets and copying exercises. Children have no role in the organization of curriculum or the decision-making processes that affect their lives at school. In middle-class schools, children typically follow directions and procedures that require more independence

Social-class Community	School Work
Working-class school	Following the steps of procedures
Middle-class school	Getting the right answer
Affluent professional school	Carrying out creative activity independently
Executive elite school	Developing one's analytical intellectual powers

Figure 3-5. Anyon's comparison of social class communities and school work. (Summarized from Anyon 1980.)

and decision making, but answers are limited to a single correct response. All of the students in the Sunshine Room fall into one of these two social classes that would typically receive rather dull intellectual work or none at all.

The affluent professional school in Anyon's work provides children with more creative activities that focus on children's involvement in expression and application of ideas and concepts. Individuality is a goal and is accomplished through writing creatively, illustrating social studies ideas, and originating math problems.

At the top of the social-class continuum, the executive elite school wants children "to produce intellectual products that are both logically sound and of top academic quality. . . . School work helps one to achieve, to excel, to prepare for life" (Anyon 1980, p. 83). Current events, the history of civilization, research reports, and essays are typical topics and assignments, and children are given primary responsibility for learning and for behavior.

According to Anyon's findings, the work in the Sunshine Room is unexpectedly intellectual, rigorous, and interesting given the children's social-class backgrounds. For Caryl to involve students in the construction of curriculum is unusual; for her to center the academic work of the class around their unique and personal questions is extraordinary.

The children in the Sunshine Room are not only working class, many of them are bilingual and some are Spanish-dominant or monolingual Spanish speakers. For about half the class, English is not the first language. Luis Moll and Stephen Díaz (1987) claim that curriculum is reduced for children who represent linguistic minorities in classrooms, particularly when children are also working class. Their research highlights what they consider to be a

> major problem in the schooling of the working-class Latino students, indeed in the schooling of working-class children in general: the practice of reducing or "watering down" the curriculum to match perceived or identified weaknesses in the students. (p. 301)

In a study that informs my interpretation of Caryl's classroom, Moll and Díaz observed bilingual students in both English and Spanish reading and writing classes in San Diego. They found that expectations are lowered for the Spanish-dominant children while reading in English:

> Even students who were among the better readers in Spanish were treated in English as low-level readers. . . . We have suggested that because the children decoded in English with an obvious Spanish accent, as second-language readers are bound to do, and because accurate pronunciation is the best index of good decoding, the students never quite sounded right to an English monolingual teacher. (p. 303)

Teachers in this study measured Spanish-dominant children's reading abilities against an expectation for accurate decoding and pronunciation for native English readers. When children mispronounced words or made omissions or substitutions in their oral reading, their miscues were judged to be errors. In reality, the children were incapable of meeting their teachers' unrealistic expectations, given the dominance of Spanish in their oral language.

The interesting part of this study occurs when Moll and Díaz define reading differently and hold reasonable but challenging expectations for the children's biliteracy. They begin with the assumption that all the children, with varying ability, can comprehend written Spanish as they read, thus elevating their expectations for what children can accomplish. Next, they provide the children with bilingual zones of proximal development by giving them opportunities to display their comprehension of written English during reading discussions in Spanish. When the same children experience a new social structure for reading and the evaluation of their reading is meaning centered rather than decoding centered, they exhibit much stronger reading comprehension abilities. The results illustrate how crucial the instructional arrangements and intellectual expectations are for high or even adequate performance for children in school. As Moll and Díaz say, they took advantage of the children's Spanish language, rather than perceiving it as an impediment to intellectual engagement.

The issues that are explored by critical theorists relate very directly to the Sunshine Room when the level of intellectual expectation for the students is scrutinized. A critical-theory approach tells us, for example, that "the differentiated curriculum has served to reinforce the racial and socioeconomic stratification of society" (Oakes 1985, p. 153).

It is clearly not a simple matter to change the practice that perpetuates status quo expectations in schools given that our acceptance of the stratification of individuals and groups is rooted in U.S. tradition and history. Hegemony, or the process through which "the dominant culture is able to exercise domination over subordinate classes or groups" (McLaren 1994, p. 182) occurs in the practices, forms, and structures of our schools. I think hegemony is compounded by a shared mythology about the strength of education to "equalize" (McLaren 1994) that has entrapped rather than empowered many minority groups. Frank Smith (1989) speaks to the additional myth that literacy itself can eliminate poverty, unemployment, crime, and other ills of society. To counter these deep traditions and hegemonious beliefs, learners must share experiences that provide personal purposes and values in school as a way to establish an awareness of the power of learning.

Many descriptions of typical schooling graphically depict groups of young learners as incapable of, or disinterested in, intriguing intellectual work. In contrast, the expectations in this third grade are that student participation will be highly intellectual. There is no ceiling on the possibilities that can "erupt" during the "explosion" of brainstorming, for example. Children are not hindered by language constraints or community backgrounds; rather, such differences in personal knowledge are capitalized on. Perhaps more important, the class as a whole is not limited by specified, mandated curriculum from the school or district, so that children are encouraged to be curious, to ask questions, and to challenge themselves, each other, and their teachers. The ground rules for a very high level of intellectual expectation are laid now, as the year begins. They are carried out as the children investigate their topics over the course of the year.

This process immediately invites children to be inventive, creative, and responsible. It makes what they are curious about important and serious. No one's ideas are rejected and all ideas are validated as they are shared and prompt additional shared thinking. The themes are constructed from real questions, involve rich content and advanced academic processes, and integrate skills and content in real experiences. Opportunities for such an atypically high level of intellectual expectation begin the first day and week of school; they are repeated time and again as children explore different topics, processes, and materials, maintaining the quality of their experiences throughout the year.

"Brainstorm" provides such a wonderful metaphor for this process of negotiating curriculum. There is never a shortage of ideas. Some children write furiously, hardly able to keep up with the surge of possibilities. Angélica has over forty items on her list. By compiling the results of the entire class, we identify the categories that have been rated highly by the majority of us, and thus define the content of the year's curriculum. Since the children's individual lists offer so many points of connection to the ten class choices, everyone has at least some of their interests addressed. Moreover, the children can easily see how powerful group participation can be. As a group, they always know more than any one individual. Brainstorming goes a long way toward building a sense of community in the classroom. All participants, including adults, have input, and we arrive at decisions for our intellectual work by consensus, making us all winners.

No limits are placed on the topics that children offer or the questions that they ask. No child is ever told, Sorry, you can't learn that. It's too difficult for you. In the Sunshine Room, we believe that if children can ask a question, they are ready to search for an answer, even if that means reaching a partial understanding, an approximation, or a new question.

Traditional curriculum guides place limits on what children can learn by assigning different topics to different grade levels. They control access to learning and deny children an opportunity to explore what may be relevant and meaningful. Unfortunately, even those curriculum guidelines are controlled by players outside the school district. Sometimes, the curriculum for any particular grade is not necessarily what even a school district committee decides is appropriate for their children to study, but rather, what happens to be included in the textbook that is adopted. Lately, that seems to be everything that any single-issue group with political clout demands to have included. My son's current high school texts are so all-encompassing that in order to cover everything with equal weight in five hundred pages or less, the Holocaust has been reduced to a three-paragraph entry. Grant Wiggins (1989) calls these curriculums a series of "TV sound bites" that reduce teaching and learning to a game of Trivial Pursuit.

I want the focus in the Sunshine Room to be on the kind of activity that helps students develop the habits that will make them lifelong learners and the wisdom to understand that the more they learn, the more they will realize how much they don't know. Wiggins describes such a curriculum as having the potential to

> *(1) Equip students with the ability to further their superficial knowledge through careful questioning; (2) Enable them to turn those questions into warranted systematic knowledge; (3) Develop in students high standards of craftsmanship in their work irrespective of how much or how little they "know"; and (4) Engage students so thoroughly in important questions that they learn to take pleasure in seeking important knowledge. (p. 57)*

Our questions repeatedly invite children into the learning community by centering our curriculum around their truly important questions about their world. Our work becomes that of finding the answers to these questions and, usually, generating new ones. I often let the children know that if we don't have new questions by the time we come to the end of a particular theme cycle, we haven't done justice to our study.

Other teachers often ask me what I do about the required curriculum. In my mind, the only required curriculum is the one my students and I create. I keep the adopted texts in my room and we use them as resources, along with the books we check out of the library. I am aware of the district's expectations for students at the grade level I teach, and I keep these in mind as my students and I plan the activities that support our inquiry.

Fortunately, in Arizona, there has been a shift at the State Board of Education to modernize curriculum by relieving it of the traditional scope and sequence charts for discrete areas of knowledge in different disciplines. Instead, school districts and classrooms have been mandated to ensure that students gain control over learning processes that are the same across grade levels, becoming increas-

ingly more complex as a student moves from elementary to middle school and on to high school. Unfortunately, these have been identified as "Essential Skills," and I'm afraid this may lead some people to assume that the "skills" can be taught devoid of any content. The students in the Sunshine Room come to use these "Essential Skills" (for example, being able to locate information in an encyclopedia or reference book by using an index) through content that is meaningful and important to them.

These first few days of school are concerned with organization. We spend time learning the routines that will be used throughout the year and setting the expectations for learning. Within the first week, the children are exposed to brainstorming, stories, reading, writing, talking, and learning, all within a strongly social context. They hear repeatedly that they are expected to control their own behavior and assume responsibility for their own learning. They begin to see that reading, writing, and talking are purposeful and involve language choices that they are empowered to make. They are shown routines that will keep themselves and their work organized. Most of all, we work at becoming a community of learners at the same time that we allow each one of us to be an individual within that community.

Symmetric Power and Trust Relationships

During my observations the first few days of school, I watch Caryl repeatedly demonstrate to the children that there is a mutual trust between her and them. This relationship of trust is only beginning, yet it begins dramatically. The process of selecting theme-cycle topics demonstrates to the children, and to observers like me, Caryl's trust in children's abilities to learn and to have valid questions that are worthy of study. She trusts their decisions about how to call her by name, and she trusts that they have important curiosities about the world. The amount of control Caryl believes is necessary for them to have valuable learning experiences is evident in the process of negotiating.

We know, however, that teachers usually control the majority of what goes on in elementary school classrooms, even more so in working-class schools, as Anyon's work shows. Much of what I read and observe in classrooms confirms that teachers hold an asymmetrical amount of power over students in terms of decision making, controlling the floor for discourse (Philips 1983), assigning tasks (Y. Goodman & Wilde 1992), and determining activity and single correct answers (Board 1982). Teachers' desks may symbolically face the desks of the children, for example, and the children's desks may be lined up respectfully and submissively. I recently watched children gather at the front door of an elementary school to start the day. The bell rang, the children lined up, and a teacher appeared on the top step. She held one hand up in the air for attention and pressed the other hand to her lips, shushing the children as they marched across the threshold. All components of typical classrooms support the power structure, although some are more obvious than others. Peter McLaren (1994) tells us that knowledge and activities in school are more likely to be meaningful to the teacher than to the students.

The power of the authority of any teacher is revealed in how curriculum is developed for learners. Typically, teachers, not children, make all important decisions about what learning experiences will be shared by the class. McLaren defines curriculum as "an introduction to a particular form of life; it serves in part to prepare students for dominant or subordinate positions in the existing society" (p. 191). This type of curriculum development unfortunately perpetuates the notion that the rich (or smart) get richer (or smarter) and the poor (or less smart) get poorer (or less smart) (Shannon 1992).

The issue of teachers' power and control fits well with our past beliefs about how learning occurs. Asymmetrical power relationships develop from the behavioristic belief that children enter school empty or void of knowledge and wait to be taught by their knowledgeable (thus, powerful) teachers. They also assume there is a one-to-one relationship between what a teacher teaches and what a child learns. They assume that because a teacher *teaches* the rules for sentence construction or the life cycle of an insect that children will *learn* the content as it is presented to them. These beliefs permeate curriculum development, interactions between participants, expectations for outcomes, oral and written language use, and learning itself, so that students and teachers alike maintain their asymmetrical power relationships as they move through the educational system. This asymmetry prepares all participants for their place in a stratified society.

On the other hand, Caryl intentionally fosters a relationship that places her and other adults in a more symmetric relationship with the children than is typical. I believe that her behavior and language during the first week of school demonstrate that she is a teacher like McLaren advocates. She is knowledgeable about students' voices, not as mere reflections of their worlds, but as constitutive forces that both mediate and shape reality. Children's voices are trusted as significant and as representative of themselves as able learners. This view is in keeping with the principles of whole language.

When we are choosing our theme-cycle topics, my own agenda takes a back seat. I do have things I would like to do during the year—new strategies I want to try or a new topic that I would like to explore. Often, I've discovered some fantastic new book that would be just perfect for a particular theme study. However, I know I won't be successful, even with the most wonderful ideas, if the children don't share my interest and desire or if my ideas don't connect to something they already know or want to learn. I'm confident enough in my own knowledge of teaching and learning to know I can at least fit in the strategies, no matter what we study.

Learning to trust each other in a classroom community means being willing to take risks. For myself as a teacher, it implies trusting children as capable learners and demonstrating that trust openly and often. As I share my beliefs about learning with the students, I tell them that I know all of them can learn but that I know they will not all learn the same things at the same rate at the same time in the same way. However, my words alone are not enough. I accept my students' decisions about what questions to pursue and respect their ideas about how to go about that inquiry. I allow them opportunities to choose how they will spend their time, what books to read, what to write about, who to work with. Sometimes the children make worthwhile decisions; sometimes they do not, and logical, somewhat unpleasant consequences result. We all know that on another day there will be another chance.

It's hardest but perhaps most important for me to show this trust to the students who worry me the most. The child who struggles to read or who chooses not to read must still be treated as a reader. For these children, I hold onto my high expectations, create a support network, and honor a zone of proximal development that will encourage them to try together with another child or with an adult. Then I pull back. Most of these children have been observed, assessed, and fretted over until they no longer see any reason to trust themselves as capable human beings. I stand aside, choosing not to test their learning at every step. Only when they recognize that their teacher assumes they can take responsibility for their own learning will they begin to take the kinds of risks necessary to succeed. Often, it means months of patient waiting.

In order for our classroom to be a community, I must also earn the children's trust. I must show them that I am a learner and a human being. I never hesitate to reveal that I am ignorant about many of the things they want to know. When the children ask to study the Middle Ages, I know I'll have an opportunity to learn along with them. I contribute my own questions to our web, study with the children, and then share what I learn. I also express my satisfaction with my own learning.

In addition, I must be willing to risk revealing my innermost feelings. The last time I read aloud Robert Munsch's book Love You Forever, *I had to ask Halie to take over after two pages. My grandmother had just moved to Tucson after leaving the hospital. Although she was trying hard to adjust to losing her independence, I sensed she would not be with us much longer. The book struck a response in me that I could not contain. The children left me alone at my desk to dry my eyes, although later they expressed their concern for me. My grandmother died the next day and I have not read that book since. Now, when my students ask me why I won't read it, I simply explain the connection it makes for me, and they understand. These moments serve to develop the trust and concern for each other that allows us to maintain a strong community of learners.*

The quiet and easy cooperation of that first day are never seen again during the year. Once the students accept the power and responsibility to control discussion and learning in the classroom, I will never get it back, even when I think I would like to have it, if only for a moment. From this point on, we will have to trust each other as learners and community members, and negotiate the activity and processes that take us all forward together.

Authenticity

In the Sunshine Room, learning and literacy experiences are authentic right from the beginning. This is a high priority according to the ideology that underlies everything that Caryl plans for children. For me, "authenticity" means that the literacy, language, and learning events use real, whole materials and are directed to real audiences for real purposes rather than instructional ones.

Other writers and whole language thinkers influence my personal definition of authenticity. Carole Edelsky and Karen Smith (1984) investigated the authenticity of literacy events in Smith's classroom. They indicate that in authentic writing the graphophonic, semantic, syntactic, and pragmatic systems of language must all interact and operate interdependently to produce meaningful texts. In authentic writing, the purpose of language use is varied and the information used is unique and incorporates private information.

In his own dissertation research, Bob Wortman (1991), Borton's principal, initially defines authenticity as "the degree to which the physical, social and emotional environment supports a writer in creating purposeful text for a specific audience" (p. 33). He later modifies his definition "to reflect the purpose of the *individual child* as the overarching element" so that "authenticity is reflected in the *individual's choice* to create and share meaningful and purposeful text for a self-selected audience" (p. 311, emphasis added). Bob's research was conducted in his own classroom when he taught at Borton before becoming the school's principal.

Michael Breen's work (1985) emphasizes the social nature of authenticity, also giving the learner the primary control over determining the authentic nature of texts and functions for texts in classrooms. He says the criteria for selecting authentic texts, whether written or spoken, must be found in the learners rather than in the texts. The purposes for learning tasks must

> require the learners to communicate ideas and meaning and to metacommunicate about the language and about the problems and solutions in the learning of the language. . . . Tasks can be chosen which involve the learners not only in the authentic communication with texts and with others in the classroom, but also about learning and for the purpose of learning. (p. 66)

The classroom is a unique social context where individuals meet for the express purpose of learning: "Perhaps one of the main authentic activities within a language classroom is communication about how best to learn to communicate" (p. 68).

I find it helpful to consider the concept of authenticity as it relates to the functions of language. Michael Halliday (1975) and Frank Smith (1977) discuss functions for language, but I appreciate the connection between the theoretical and the pragmatic outlined by Ken Goodman in *What's Whole in Whole Language* (1986). Goodman describes language as having one of five social functions: environmental, informational, occupational, recreational, or ritual. There is a sixth function for language, though, that is found in schools, the instructional function. When language is used only for instructional purposes, without also having, or being embedded in, a real-world function, it becomes inauthentic. Goodman describes how the inauthentic nature of typical language use in schools is found in classrooms centered around a skills approach to language education:

> Carole Edelsky says schools break the link between authentic language and natural speech and literacy events [in the home]. They turn language into abstraction and essentially destroy it. This decontextualization makes it hard to learn language. You will not be surprised to learn that a successful whole language program consists, to the fullest extent possible, of authentic speech and literacy events. (p. 21)

Inauthentic school events are those that isolate components of language and learning for the single purpose of instruction. They ask children to look for dictionary definitions for arbitrary words, to memorize geographic information unrelated to their personal lives or questions, to write letters of argument without an opinion. They separate instruction from real use and are therefore far less meaningful to language users and learners.

All of the language and literacy events of the first days of school have purposes in the life of the classroom community. Interviewing each other builds early relationships. Brainstorming is the first step in defining the class's work for the year. These literacy events are surrounded by lively and natural conversation. As the curriculum in the Sunshine Room continues to unfold, the children's learning will repeatedly comprise authentic materials and events.

Caryl recognizes, though, that being offered an authentic experience such as this is new for some of the children, especially those who haven't attended Borton before. So while the children brainstorm and discuss possibilities, she kidwatches, especially the children who appear to lack ideas or questions. She worries about children who don't demonstrate the curiosity she feels is a natural development in childhood. And Caryl is very conscious of assuring them a year of authentic language and learning events.

In my mind, classroom learning is authentic when it capitalizes on the language, experiences, and interests that children bring to school with them and when it reflects the world outside the classroom. When we learn outside of school, as children or adults, we identify what it is we need to or want to know, from tying our shoes to changing the spark plugs in our cars. Then we develop proce-

dures for learning the new knowledge or ability. A child might ask someone who already knows how to tie shoes for help. The adult might check out a repair manual from the public library. The first time the child ties his or her own shoes, they might come untied very quickly; the adult might need a skilled mechanic to adjust the timing once the spark plugs have been changed. Learning outside of school is always purposeful. It is initiated by the learner, who is free to develop his or her own procedure or consult with others who are more experienced. It makes use of real texts as resources, and something less than perfection still indicates learning. I want classroom learning for my students to take place in much the same way. I want the children to have a voice in determining what will be learned and how we will go about learning it. We will use the processes and procedures that learners use in real contexts outside of school. We will read and write real texts for purposes that we determine and use the conventions of real conversations to talk about our work.

When the students select the topics, it gives them ownership in their learning process and also the responsibility that comes with it. No one can say, We're only doing this because the teacher wants to. Now they have to say, We're doing this because I want to. It makes a big difference in what happens the rest of the year.

When the children choose a topic that is not within the realm of my current knowledge, I take advantage of the opportunity to reveal myself as a learner in my own classroom. This creates another layer of authenticity that gives the children a valuable demonstration of what it means to be learner and how I go about taking charge of my own learning.

At the beginning of the school year, I worry about the children who don't have any questions or don't know how to ask questions that will lead to inquiry. Most of these children are new to Borton School and have never been in a classroom where they have a real voice in determining the curriculum. I imagine they are accustomed to being the recipients of questions, not the initiators. Courtney Cazden (1988) finds that in most classrooms, teachers control the discourse, deciding who gets to speak, about what topic, and when the speaker or subject of discussion will change. In these kinds of classrooms, it's a sure bet that the children are not invited to invent the curriculum as equal partners with the teacher.

Ray McDermott (1988) suggests that there are occasions in which even the most fluent speakers are at a loss for words. He postu-

lates that these "occasions in which people are left without words are systematic outcomes of a set of relations among a group of persons bound in a social structure" (p. 38). These children are capable of carrying on extended conversations, covering a wide range of topics, with their peers. Yet in the presence of an adult, especially in a school context, they have nothing to say about their interests. They have come to see themselves as powerless, and, finding themselves in a new situation of being expected to generate their own learning questions, they respond by not responding.

I put forth extra effort to help these children find a way to enter conversations and to see their ideas come to fruition. By fostering a highly social climate in the classroom, one in which everyone, including the listeners, has a role to play, I hope to encourage these reluctant children to take ownership in the process that is beginning. It's a critical step that will make it easier for them to be involved in their own learning and the learning of our community throughout the year.

Additive Bilingualism and Biliteracy

Bilingual education in the United States has been marked by a range of goals and programs for children of non-English-speaking homes learning English. The varieties of bilingual education in the United States evoke controversies and emotional reactions about what bilingualism is, who should receive special programs, what the purpose of bilingual programs should be, and how these programs should be conducted and evaluated. A short summary of bilingual education policy and practice will place further discussions of bilingualism and biliteracy in a historical and theoretical context. Readers who are interested in these issues are referred to more complete and critical reviews by Kenji Hakuta (1986), Richard Ruiz (1984), Richard Otheguy (1982), Jim Cummins (1986), and Lilly Wong Fillmore and Concepción Valadez (1985), among others.

Much of bilingual education philosophy and practice in the United States is termed *transitional,* and this reflects overarching bilingual education policy goals (meaning the term is pervasive at all levels of the system). The goal of transitional programs is to help children become competent users of English for learning in school. Although content instruction in the early or primary years may occur in a child's first language, that instruction continues only long enough to enable the child to make a transition to English. Then the child has successfully met the goals of the bilingual education program and can continue school in an English-only setting. In this type of program, success is defined as having gained the ability to speak, read, and write in English.

Another type of program in this country is referred to as *maintenance.* In maintenance programs, competence in the first language of the speaker is to be maintained as the child learns a second language. In such programs, children become capable in the English language while they continue to use their first language for functional and real purposes at school. An important component of maintenance programs is that children learn to read and write in both languages, so that a goal of maintenance programs is for children to become both bilingual and biliterate.

The design and organization of bilingual programs, regardless of their purpose or type, also vary. Some bilingual programs use each language in some alternating sequence. For example, children might speak English on Monday, Wednesday, and Friday, and their first language on Tuesday and Thursday. Or the alternation may be based on subject matter—math occurs in English and science occurs in Spanish, for instance. At times, children may even move to another classroom or work with another teacher for "Spanish reading" or "English language arts," as was the case in the classes Moll and Díaz visited. In each of these situations, the choice of which language to use is determined by the teacher, the program, or the day's schedule.

Maintenance bilingual programs are more in keeping with a whole language philosophy than are transitional programs (K. Goodman, Y. Goodman & Flores 1979). In whole language classrooms, language is used for real reasons, according to the audience for the language and the purpose for which it is being used. A bilingual program structured according to a regimented schedule or an arbitrary decision by a teacher or policy maker is inauthentic, so it contradicts a basic tenet of the philosophy of whole language. Likewise, the typical design of transitional programs is transmission oriented, which also isolates instructional functions from the authentic functions of language in the real world. Even more important, whole language classrooms build on the strengths of learners. In a bilingual situation, the child's native language is her strength, and a maintenance program builds on that first language.

In the Sunshine Room, the children and the teachers use Spanish and English for natural, authentic, and functional purposes. Lolita interchanges her choice of language on her list of ideas to study. Even her writing of the date, "agosto 1990 the 23" shows the blend of languages always accessible to her. She also "codeswitches," or changes between languages, according to how words or concepts are familiar and comfortable to her. So, she represents "bubbles" and "mummies" in English, and her other ideas in Spanish.

All participants in the classroom use both languages at various times of the day or year, although the Spanish-dominant children are far more likely to speak English than the English-dominant children are to speak Spanish. Regardless, as I observe the class, I consistently see children choosing the language they will use based on the audience, the materials, and their purpose.

Bilingualism and biliteracy are viewed by the members of this learning community as resources for learning. This is therefore in opposition to a transitional view, and more proactive than a maintenance view. The view of bilingualism and biliteracy taken in the Sunshine Room is *additive* (Cummins 1989; Moll & Whitmore 1993): development of more than one language and culture is a philosophical and pedagogical goal of the community.

During the critical event of negotiating theme topics, the children write and speak in either Spanish or English, depending on their abilities, interests, and available linguistic knowledge. Children like Lolita alternate the languages to express themselves. Other children, like Carolina, use their knowledge of Spanish phonology and orthography to write in English. Carolina represents the meaning *how to make cartoons* like this: jau to maec cartoons. She incorporates her knowledge about Spanish orthography, the sound of */h/* marked by a *j,* into her written representations in English.

As the group comes together following their brainstorming sessions, they use both languages to read and discuss the topics presented. Caryl and Halie codeswitch appropriately and translate when necessary. They take advantage of teachable moments to share information about the differences and similarities between languages, like comparing the spelling of words across languages. For example, when reading Carolina's representation of the word "volcanoes" as "bokonos," Caryl points out that the /v/ sound may be represented with either a *b* or a *v* in Spanish. In these ways, the bilingual and biliterate abilities provided by the children in this classroom are valued and capitalized on, not viewed as problems to be eliminated. A goal is for bilingualism and biliteracy to be shared and celebrated as resources.

We've already discussed the level of prestige enjoyed by the bilingual children of the Sunshine Room by virtue of their having access to all of the language that is used. That power arises when their native language, an important but still minority language in the community, is accepted in the classroom as a language of literacy and learning.

Whole language classrooms such as the Sunshine Room provide children with authentic contexts for enhanced development of their native language and for second language learning. Research by Cummins (1978, 1986, 1989), Krashen (1982), Flores (1982), Moll (1988) and others has shown us that both first and second languages are acquired globally, not linearly, with the emphasis on the message and function of language rather than the form. We know that we need to provide real opportunities for meaningful talk and work with authentic texts in both languages if the children are to become truly bilingual and biliterate. The children and adults in the Sunshine Room have opportunities to make choices about which language to use in the same ways those choices are made in the larger community. We consider the audience, the message, the social context, and the relationship among individuals.

The Sunshine Room is not a quiet place. The children are encouraged to talk with each other and with adults as a way of learning. We surround ourselves with print in both English and Spanish and make use of any materials or person that might help us find answers to our questions. Both languages enjoy equal status as resources for learning. At times, that means we need to read to children, interpret from one language to the other, or find alternative ways of helping children make use of the available resources. We want to be sure that language is not an impediment to learning.

At the same time, we recognize the developmental nature of language learning. We no more expect children to wait until they control every aspect of their second language before they try to use it purposefully than we expect our own toddlers to wait until they can carefully articulate "Mommy, I would like a cookie" before begging for an Oreo. The children's approximations are expected and celebrated as developmental moments in their developing bilingualism and biliteracy.

Reading English texts that children write with Spanish phonology is one of my favorite pastimes. Invariably, the children are effective in producing a meaningful text. One just needs to know Spanish in order to read what has been written. Carolina's written language sample, "jau to maec cartoons," shows us that she has been attending to English print as well as her native Spanish. Her spelling of "to" is English, instead of the Spanish, "tu," and she uses a consonant sound to end "maec" that you would not find at the end of a Spanish word. Moreover, "cartoons" is spelled conventionally, indicating her awareness of some English print reference in the room. This is not a phenomenon, but a regular feature of bilingual environments that other researchers also observe (Edelsky 1986; Hudelson 1984, 1986). Most bilingual children, when writing in their second language, will use what they know about both languages to help them, and a combination of spelling patterns from both languages in the same utterance is typical. It's actually a sign of growth, being a step further along the continuum from complete use of Spanish phonology toward writing with English spelling patterns.

Examples like these abound in the Sunshine Room. Each day throughout the year, children read in one language and discuss their reading with someone who speaks the other language. They write for different audiences in different languages, and they combine the two when it suits their purposes. Eventually, they come to control these choices, not by accident, not because one language is more dominant than the other, but consciously, by design. Examples of this manner of selecting language will resurface as we describe the critical events of the next three chapters.

So, as the year begins in the Sunshine Room, the children and teachers join each other in curriculum negotiation by sharing personal goals and interests. They engage in building a mutual history by sharing past experiences, home backgrounds, and languages, as well as by acquiring new experiences, texts, and relationships. A groundwork is laid for the symmetric power relationships between the participants, and a high level of intellectual expectation is set forth for future work. Spanish is valued and encouraged alongside English, and there is an emphasis on meaning as opposed to parts of language. These specific issues are unveiled gradually but repeatedly over the course of the year, as the following chapters show.

ROALD DAHL
DIRTY
BEASTS

4

Language and Literacy Events in the Sunshine Room

AT APPROXIMATELY 12:45 each afternoon, the children in the Sunshine Room return from their lunch-time break on the playground to reconvene at the meeting area and move into a block of language and literacy experiences. The block consists of DEAR (Drop Everything and Read), literature study groups, and writing workshop. Often, while Caryl, Halie, or a student teacher who is apprenticing in the Sunshine Room meet with two of the literature study groups, the other children meet independently in their own literature study groups or "do DEAR." Writing workshop follows these reading-oriented activities. This chapter describes the routine of these literacy events and examples of literacy strategy lessons, in order to better contextualize the critical events of the other chapters. Caryl provides comments on these descriptions.

DEAR

DEAR time in the Sunshine Room means a minimum of fifteen minutes and usually about thirty minutes daily spent reading any material of choice. A period of silent reading is common in many classrooms. It is sometimes referred to as sustained silent reading (SSR) or uninterrupted sustained silent reading (USSR), when children and adults are all engaged in a required period of reading silently. Caryl prefers the DEAR label over these others because she feels it more accurately represents what happens during this period of the day. She changed the name when she realized she did not expect, or even want, children to be "silent" while they read.

In some classrooms, a silent-reading period is the only time during the school day that children transact with real, whole texts. In the Sunshine Room, DEAR time is one of many opportunities for children to experience real books of varied types.

Sometimes, the children and adults all read at once; always, the reading materials are extensive and varied in type, topic, and language. For her personal silent reading, Caryl frequently selects a piece of adolescent literature for her children's literature courses at the university, in either Spanish or English. Newspapers are usually Halie's choice, and the student teacher's. They share articles with each other, chatting as they would over the breakfast table. Stephanie, one of the girls in the class, often shares the paper with these adults, reading the department store ads as her first choice. I use DEAR time to review my field notes, once I've briefly recorded what everyone else is doing. I also enjoy leafing through and reading children's books I notice in the classroom that I am not familiar with.

DEAR time allows the third graders an extended period for personal reading, thus encouraging children to invent their personal reading styles, preferences, and habits. Children can become experts in particular types of literature, certain authors, or favorite illustrators. They read magazines, chapter books, books made by groups of students or by the whole class, picture books, comic books, poetry, and nonfiction books. They settle in with friends or alone, finding niches under the loft or piano or lying on the floor. DEAR time is not silent, although it is quiet. Music sometimes plays in the background, and children share information and illustrations as they read. Some children read out loud to themselves or to a friend. The pleasure of the reading experience is punctuated by laughter. The children's sighs when DEAR time ends illustrate their involvement in personal reading.

At DEAR time, there are always children who readily and easily engage in reading activities, silently and by themselves. Wilson scans the shelves or boxes, picks out a book that he thinks will interest him, and reads the blurbs on the back or the first page to confirm his decision. Often, he becomes absorbed in his reading so quickly that he doesn't even move from the spot where he has found the book. Twenty minutes later, he will still be there, sitting on the floor, or perhaps still standing or crouching, still reading. Trevor describes himself as "really connectable to books." Keeping his mind on his writing is frequently an overwhelming task, but when he lies down on the rug to read, nothing disturbs him. Children and adults come and go, stepping over him on their way across the room, but Trevor reads on. When it's time to put the books away, someone needs to tap him on the shoulder to tell him DEAR time is over.

Some children are not comfortable enough with their own self-image as readers to choose a book quickly and then read to themselves for an extended period. Also, some children so enjoy reading with a special friend that they cannot help but share their favorite parts and comments. Encouraging buddy reading and reading aloud legitimatizes their needs in ways that still meet the goal of DEAR time—to enjoy reading. Monica loves to read aloud and will even do so by herself, her book held "teacher-style." But more often than not, she has an audience, usually children who do not engage easily with text. Her joy of reading is observed by all who join her as she surreptitiously expands their understanding of stories. Etched permanently in my mind is a memory of Ethan and Jason, scrunched under the piano, reading Mrs. Frisby and the Rats of NIMH. *As they begin each day, one of them says to the other, "Don't forget to stop at the end of the chapter and we'll talk." The discussion about what they read is so much a part of their reading that they hold their own literature study group during DEAR.*

The buddy-reading strategy the children employ is one way that I deliberately teach my students to support each other as readers. We spend about a week near the beginning of the year learning to buddy-read in a variety of forms: choral reading, taking turns, and silent reading with a partner.

I ask the children to choose their own partners for buddy reading, both when we practice these reading strategies and when they buddy-read on their own. Pairing experienced readers with less-experienced readers isn't necessarily successful. Even two inexperienced readers, like Marco and Gabe, whom you'll meet in Chapter 5, build more meaning together than either could alone. The passages I give them to learn buddy-reading strategies are usually short stories taken from an anthology or even an old basal reader. I do consider literary merit, since I'm asking the children to talk with each other about the story as they read. Every set of partners gets a single copy of the story, with several places in the text marked with an asterisk as "say something" spots, a technique suggested by Jerry Harste, Kathy Short, and Carolyn Burke in Creating Classrooms for Authors *(1988).*

On the first day of buddy reading, I pick a student and together we demonstrate how to read together chorally, making our two voices sound as much like one as possible. I show them how one reader can trace a finger under the line of text to set the pace, reminding them that faster readers need to slow down a bit and slower readers need to speed up. When they come to an asterisk, they are to stop and "say something" to each other, whatever is on their minds. When everyone has finished reading, we come together as a whole group to share feelings about reading with a partner. We also discuss the different kinds of things the buddies said to each other.

The next day, we use a different story, this time taking turns reading aloud as partners. Everyone still has to stop and "say something" when they arrive at an asterisk. On the third day, the partners each read a single text silently, using an unvocalized, unobtrusive signal to let each other know when to turn the page. Once again, the partners stop to discuss the story at the asterisks, and later the whole group discusses the process.

The children's comments about buddy reading are almost unanimously positive. "It's fun to read with a partner," "I could read faster and easier with my buddy," and "When I got stuck I didn't have to go looking for someone to help me" are typical statements. By the end of the three days, our list of "say something" topics includes predictions, questions about plot, requests for clarification, comments on characters, personal connections, connections to other stories, and personal likes and dislikes.

Throughout the year, the children choose to buddy-read for a variety of reasons. Some need support as readers in order to be able to participate in the literature study group of their choice. However, I find that most of them buddy-read for the sheer pleasure of sharing a book with a friend. Whatever the reason, buddy reading puts literature within everyone's grasp.

Buddy reading is also particularly supportive of children who are beginning to read their second language. Often, bilingual children begin to read their second language before they control it orally. Although I know they are still capable of constructing meaning on their own, they benefit from the extra support provided by a reading buddy who will help with unfamiliar vocabulary and talk with them about the story.

Literature Study Groups

Literature study groups make up a large part of the Sunshine Room reading program, providing frequent social reading experiences. Literature studies are fashioned after the notion of literature circles (Short 1986; Harste, Short & Burke 1988; Short & Pierce 1990). In literature circles, or literature study groups, children read quality pieces of literature and meet in groups to discuss their reading, reactions, and responses.

> Talking about a piece of literature with others gives readers time to explore half-formed ideas, expand their understanding of literature through hearing others' interpretations, and become readers who think critically and deeply about what they read. Readers need to understand that a variety of interpretations exist for any piece of literature and that they can collaboratively explore their interpretations with one another to reach new understanding. Literature circles help readers become literate. (Harste, Short & Burke 1988, p. 293)

The children select literature study groups according to their reading preferences. This includes preferences for topics, titles, genres, authors, and illustrators, as well as for the language (Spanish or English) in which to read. Children also base their selections on other children's choices, because they often like to be in groups with their friends, regardless of the topic of the book group. Negotiation sessions between friends are a part of the book group selection process.

When new literature study sessions begin, Caryl gives a book talk about each of the available selections. Then the children rank their choices and justify them in writing to Caryl. Caryl gives each child her or his first choice whenever she can, but if too many children select the same group or if copies of a particular book or set of books are limited, she makes sure that children at least receive their second choice. Different groups may study the same selection.

Each literature study group meets about two times a week with an adult member, and at other times without an adult's participation. Caryl and Halie join particular groups, or rotate through various groups, depending on the circumstances and the needs of the students.

In these groups, the children might read a single title, or they might read a text set, a group of books (usually picture books) centered around a certain concept, author, illustrator, genre, style, or subject. During literature study groups, children extend their reading into writing through literature logs and other writing projects. They also analyze plots and illustrations and create story maps. Children studying a text set by a selected author might learn biographical information about the author, compare the books in the text set, or write letters to the author. An example of a text set organized by genre is described in Chapter 5, when literature study groups concentrate on fairy tales in connection with a theme about the Middle Ages.

The extension experiences that accompany the reading and subsequent discussions are generated within the context of the group or are suggested by individual children. Often, these experiences become vehicles through which the children present their learning to themselves or their classmates—for example, a group may present a play about a book or post a comparison chart in the classroom.

A literature study of children's author Byrd Baylor offers a look at how the children negotiate presenting their experiences to their classmates, Caryl's respect for negotiation in building curriculum, and her expertise in helping her students meet their negotiated goals. This author study occurs in conjunction with a theme about Native American people and culture.

After several days of reading from a set of Baylor's books, Ilinca, Rita, Mariah, and Caryl meet to discuss their impressions of the books, the commonalities across texts, and how they might share their reading with the class.

Ilinca begins. "All the books are deserty. They all have to do with the desert—mostly the plants and animals."

"All the desert scenes look like they were painted with watercolors," notices Mariah while she flips through pages of one book.

Rita adds, "What I liked best was the lettering, the print. It was like in poetry. It doesn't have anything to do with poetry. Well, maybe a little. It sounded like poetry."

"Poetry doesn't have to rhyme. It's more a way of expressing feelings and describing things," Caryl interjects. "Do you think Byrd Baylor was expressing her feelings about the desert?"

Rita answers, "I can tell she's a gentle person. It sounds like she cares about the desert and doesn't want it destroyed."

"I read about Byrd Baylor in that newspaper article," says Mariah. "She lives in the desert. Her house is kind of Indian style."

At this point, Ilinca has an idea. "Maybe we could write about the desert, a plant, or animal, and make it look like poetry like Byrd Baylor does. I like being in the desert. Could I write about being in the desert?"

"Yes, of course. That sounds like a wonderful way to share what you have learned with the rest of the class," Caryl answers.

"And we could make pictures like the books, too," adds Mariah.

The group then spends time studying Peter Parnall's illustrations more carefully, noticing how he uses simple lines and little color, and how only some parts of the plants and animals are detailed.

The children are not sure how to go about writing in a style similar to Byrd Baylor's. Caryl suggests that first they simply write something about the desert that expresses their own feelings. She does the same, and then breaks her prose into shortened segments to establish the rhythm that identifies it as more poetic. The children are very pleased with the results when they participate in the process. Jon and Sarah, other members of the group, compose the following examples:

The coyote
eats by day,
the coyote howls
by night.
The coyote
goes out in the
middle of the
night to find
his prey. At
the time of
dawn, he comes
home, with good
things to eat.
The mother
says (in coyote
words) I was
worried.—Don't worry,
be happy.
I thought
you got
caught. Who me?
Never.
—by Jon

I love
to watch the hawk soar
through the sky

and the coyotes howl
at night
The rabbits hop
from cactus to cactus.
—by Sarah

Writing Workshop

"Writing workshop," Caryl announces quietly as she turns out the lights following literature studies and DEAR time.

"Awww," the children murmur, but they put their reading material away in cubbies and retrieve writing folders. After this period of transition, they become equally absorbed in their writing. Materials and work partners change and quiet talking about reading becomes active discussion about writing projects, illustration, and publication.

A glance at the chalkboard shows me several choices the children have to work on: (1) pen pal letters, (2) stories, (3) journals.

But Caryl reminds the children of a previous conversation. "We said we would negotiate the rest of the afternoon. It needs to be something with language. So how about this. You can do anything with reading or writing, and I can live with that."

In response, the children involve themselves in a variety of ways. They write letters using Sunshine Room stationery (designed and printed by the class during a previous project), write notes to each other, make pop-up books, keep diaries, write to businesses listed in *Free Stuff for Kids* (Lansky 1989), create cards for family members, and read books and other printed materials.

When it's time for writing workshop, children scatter throughout the room alone, in small groups, or in pairs. Each child is at a different point in developing writing projects, but most are following a process approach to writing. After they select a topic, children sometimes create a web of ideas, they write first drafts, they read their drafts to friends, they revise and edit, they confer with adults and other children, and eventually they publish most of their writing in some form. This process could be completed in a single writing workshop period or over the course of months of prolonged attention. It varies according to the purpose and appropriate form of the writing. I like to wander around the busy room and check in with children on their projects, helping when I can and frequently serving as a sincerely interested reader and listener.

Collaborative pieces, when two or more children complete the writing process together, are popular. At the piano bench, Rachel and Lupita confer with the student teacher about spelling and then return to the publication process. Rachel, a monolingual English speaker, had approached Lupita on an earlier day and invited her to join her in a project so that they could produce a bilingual book, Lupita being strongly bilingual and biliterate. Their joint story concerns a young English-speaking girl who encounters a monolingual Spanish-speaking girl and the problems they face as they develop a relationship.

"Lupita, you know what we should do?" Rachel says, suggesting a minor revision of adding a rhyming dialogue.

"No, that won't sound good," counters Lupita.

"Okay, you're right." Rachel is copying an edited page into final form. "I'm not good at the Spanish, Lupita," she says, insinuating that copying is harder when you don't understand the content or meaning of the print.

"You're not? Then just copy the letters."

Their book becomes a cherished part of the classroom library when it is completed.

Jason and Evan are stretched out on the floor, a sea of papers spread out around them. They're working on two separate science-fiction stories. Jason's piece, an elaborate comic book about characters called Griffins, has been evolving for several months. He has written the text and separately drawn illustrations in comic-book style. Now that he is in the final stages, Caryl is his collaborator: she is copying the text into the illustrations at his direction because Jason can't print small enough to fit his words into the speaker balloons.

Jaime and Roberto are nestled under the loft, busy writing letters in Spanish. The letters are headed across the room to David and Raymundo, who are scrunched under the study carrels. "Hey guys," I ask, "Why are you writing letters today?"

"Because they don't want to be our friends and we want them to," explains Roberto.

Lolita and Seaaira are planning a special weekend together, a joint trip to Mexico with Seaaira's family, so they huddle together on the loft and giggle and talk as they make lists of what to bring. Each girl keeps her own list, written in English, to use while they pack at home. Seaaira's list is shown in Figure 4-1.

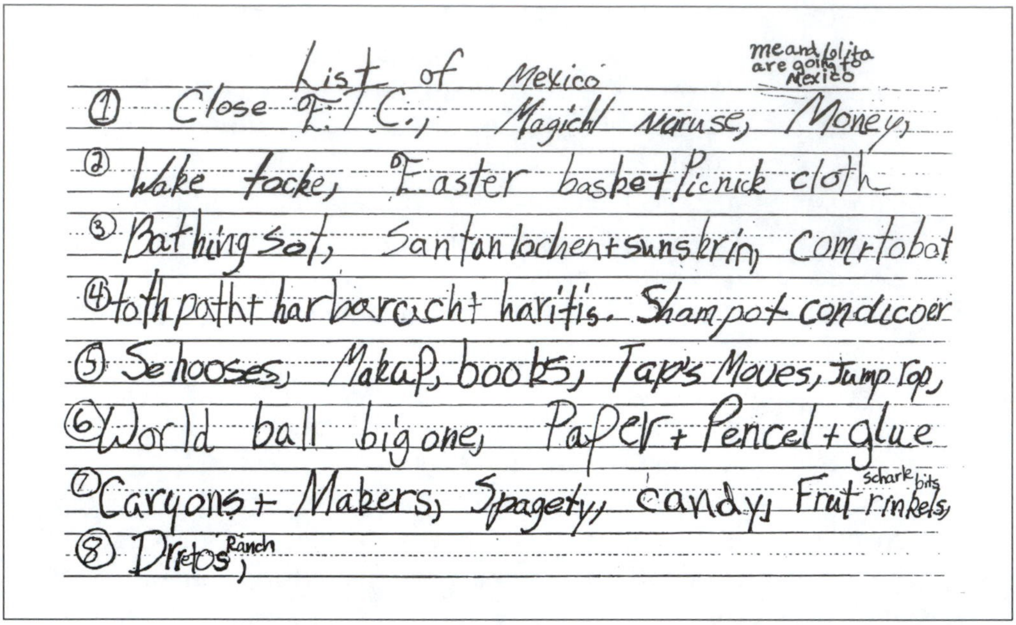

Figure 4-1. Seaaira's list of packing items for Mexico: Clothes, etc., magical nursery, money, walkie talkie, Easter basket, picnic cloth, bathing suit, suntan lotion & sunscreen, comb, toothbrush, tooth paste & hairbrush & barrettes. Shampoo & conditioner, sea horses, makeup, books, tapes, movies, jump rope, world ball big one, paper & pencil & glue, crayons & markers, spaghetti, candy, fruit wrinkles, shark bites, doritos ranch

Shelley and Sarah sit at a round table, deeply absorbed in their writing. They have been working on one project for an extended period, a collaborative choose-your-own-adventure (CYOA) story about time travel. It began as a complex skeletal outline, created on two long sets of taped-together papers, one for each girl. At each step of the outline, the reader (an active character in the story) makes a decision and the decision alters the plot of the story. Shelley and Sarah have finished their outline and are now working on transforming it into readable text on note cards. Caryl, as consultant, helps them invent a workable process for formatting their complicated text. (This is a difficult new process for all three participants.) Caryl also helps by putting the lengthy book on the word processor, saving the girls time and some tediousness.

The published product begins with a cover page that includes the title ("The African Adventure: A Choose-your-own-adventure Book") and the authors' names ("by Shelley and Sarah"). Next is a dedication and publisher's imprint: "Dedicated to Mrs. Crowell, our favorite teacher. Borton Primary Magnet School, The Sunshine Room, May 1990." The third page gives the reader specific instructions:

> READ THIS FIRST!
> Do not read this book from front to back. These pages contain many different adventures. From time to time as you read along, you will be asked to make a choice. Your choice may lead to success or disaster. The adventures you take are a result of your choice. You are responsible because of your choice. After you make your choice, follow the instructions to see what happens to you next. Think carefully before you make your move.
> GOOD LUCK!

And then the story begins:

> You and your friends are going to go to Africa tomorrow. Right now, you and your friends, Kim and Stef, are in your room planning your vacation. You all think you will have so much fun. You all want to go to the zoo and see all the African animals. You also want to go on an African tour. But you can't decide how to get there.
> If you go on a boat, turn to page 3.
> If you go on an airplane, turn to page 2.

The story continues as the reader makes decisions in the African jungle that sometimes save her from terrible tragedies (like a charging rhinoceros) and sometimes lead to excruciating death (like being eaten by a tiger). The story is complex, it follows the pattern of other published CYOA books, and it is long—fifty typewritten pages. As the reader makes choices and alters the story, the plot proceeds not only forward but backward, just as typical CYOA adventures do. The multiple endings written by Sarah and Shelley, twenty-two in all, vary considerably in their outcomes. Here are two extreme examples, one happy, one not:

> You think you want to try and get home, so you start walking toward the African village. When you're almost to the African village, you see a triangle that has African writing inside it. You all step in it and all of a sudden, you're flying home. THE END

> You stay on the back of the elephant. The elephant goes on through the clearing. After the clearing, you go into the trees. All of a sudden, you fall off the elephant. Then the elephant gets attacked

by a leopard. The elephant falls on you. He squishes you and you die. THE END

These descriptions of processes and products only touch on the variety of literacy events that I observe taking place with enthusiasm and energy each day during writing workshop. Many students have more than one writing project going at a time; their writing includes a variety of genres, languages, styles, topics, and collaborative relationships with other children and with adults. Authentic whole texts are the norm for reading and writing; basals, textbooks, or workbooks are virtually nonexistent, and talking constantly surrounds, accentuates, and evokes all written language. In these ways, language is kept whole.

Most days during writing workshop, the children work on pieces of their own choosing. Even though I do not tell them what they should write, I will usually offer "invitations" to become engaged in particular types of writing. Journals and letters are almost always on this list of suggestions, but other genres are added based on what we have been reading aloud or talking about during class discussions. When the children are fascinated with the format of a particular book, such as the die-cut pages of Eric Carle's books, I suggest they try something like that on their own. In a similar way, when we read the chapter in Roald Dahl's The BFG *in which the giant reveals his collection of dreams to Sophie, almost everyone in the class wants to share their dreams. I put out some baby-food jars and invite the children to write up one of their dreams, put it in one of the jars, label the jar with a category from the book, and place it on a shelf. Children who are involved with ongoing writing projects do not take this particular invitation, but others who are having a hard time deciding what to write begin a "dream rack" of real and imagined nightmares.*

While children work on their own pieces of writing, I like to move around the room like Kathy does, stopping briefly to chat with as many students as I can. In this way, I get a sense of what each child is working on and where they are in their writing process. By spending time at the beginning of the year helping children learn how to listen and to comment on another person's writing, I earn myself the time I need later on for periods of observation and individual revision and editing conferences.

When children are ready to confer with an adult— at a revision or final editing point—Halie and I make appointments to listen to them read their writing. During the conferences, we focus first on the meaning and discuss with them how their stories make sense. We usually ask the children what help they would like in the way of editing. In this way, we encourage the children to take control over this final stage of the writing process. Some of our students want to have all of their spelling edited, others may ask for only a few words. When we see that children are experimenting with some convention (attempting to punctuate dialogue, for example), we offer suggestions and examples on using quotation marks and speaker designations. This enables us to meet each child's individual needs at the most teachable moments. Vygotskians might suggest that as we mediate in these ways, with individual students and small groups, we are teaching within children's zones of proximal development.

At other times, we focus as a whole class on one particular type of writing or on a convention of writing that is being explored by a majority of the class. For example, in the middle of the second year of the study, I observe that despite being exposed to a wide variety of reading material, most of the children are beginning every story they write with "One day" or "Once upon a time," even if the story is not a fairy tale. I give everyone a three-by-five note card and ask them to record the first sentence of whatever book they were reading during DEAR time earlier that day. We put all the sentences on big pieces of butcher paper and post them for analysis.

We discover that all the sentences establish some sort of mood and usually leave a question in the reader's mind. We spend a couple of days reading opening lines and discussing what the author's purpose is in writing them, settling on the idea that they encourage the reader to continue reading. Subsequently, a number of children in the class begin their next stories in exciting and interesting ways. "It was dark when my friend came in the door," Travis's mystery begins. Paul's story about the new patio his family is building starts, "It was a very hot and smelly morning and my dad was sweating heavily." Angélica introduces a fantasy story with, "I had not gone into the rose garden since last time."

This description gives a sense of the routines within which the critical events in our story occur. DEAR time, literature studies of various types, and writing workshop are regular parts of the Sunshine Room. Although they vary widely, depending on who's participating, what's happening in the classroom and in the children's outside lives, and what's interesting to individual community members at a particular time, they are predictable each day and week and immerse the children in language and literacy for many hours each day. Additional language and literacy experiences occur during other parts of the day, of course—during math centers and theme studies, for example. But this literacy block guarantees that the children will be soaked in real reading and writing events each and every day, regardless of what the rest of the day's activities involve.

The next three chapters describe additional language and literacy events in connection with our discussion of the three remaining critical events. Chapter 5 discusses a literature study about fairy tales that is part of a thematic study of the Middle Ages. Chapter 6 explores a literature study about a text set of books organized around the issues of war and peace. And Chapter 7 describes both oral and written language events two girls engage in as part of their bicultural friendship.

OUTGOING MAIL

5

Inventing Curriculum
From Cinderella to the Middle Ages

ONE DAY in the middle of October when I visit the Sunshine Room, I'm greeted with evidence of change. The room is empty (the children, Caryl, and Halie are at lunch), so I can meander around without disturbing anyone, trying to make sense of the artifacts.

I notice the materials remaining from the last curriculum theme, about the human body. A bulletin board on one wall contains depictions of body movements. A newspaper the class wrote to present the findings from their study of the body waits on a round table for collating and distribution. Large models of internal body organs sit on a counter and big books related to body topics rest on the easel.

There are also indications that a new topic is beginning. "Castles" is written on the schedule at 9:45 A.M. A chart comparing several different versions of *Cinderella* hangs in the group meeting area, a new list of questions about the Middle Ages is posted, and new books crowd into bins on the window sill. Another clue is a sign by the books that tells me: STOP! DO NOT TAKE BOOKS FROM THIS SHELF YET. And in Spanish, the same message: ALTO! NO SAQUEN LIBROS DE ESTE ESTANTE HASTA QUE YO LES DIGA. Each message is signed *Caryl*. Finally, an art print of a misty castle scene painted in watercolors is perched on the piano.

This chapter describes curriculum organized around the theme of the Middle Ages. The theme is a critical event in that it explains how curriculum is regularly invented in this bilingual classroom. It illustrates how literacy development flourishes during content-learning experiences and how the children and their teacher constantly invent themselves as learners. The chapter details a large-group comparison study of *Cinderella*, Middle Ages–related activities conducted in the group work centers, and supporting writing workshop and lit study experiences. Examples from other theme studies are also included as appropriate.

Thematically organized curriculum is referred to in professional education literature and in instructional settings by varied terminology—*thematic units* (K. Goodman 1986), *theme cycles* (Edelsky, Altwerger & Flores 1991), *inquiry circles* (Short & Burke 1991) and *theme studies* (Gamberg et al. 1988). The more generic label *themes* accurately reflects the language used by Caryl and the students in the Sunshine Room. The process they use during classroom themes reflects the characteristics of theme cycles, although that specific label is rarely used as they work together. Themes are developed from children's questions about the world, for the instructional purpose of integrating subject areas into more cohesive, realistic, and functional units of curriculum.

As I finish observing the classroom changes, the students, Caryl, and Halie return. I watch as they gather on the floor in the group meeting area.

"The story we'll be reading today will be in Spanish," Caryl says, holding up a copy of *Cenicienta*. "You'll be able to understand it, though, even if you don't speak Spanish, because you are so familiar with the story. Before I begin to read it, let's talk about some ways you can get ready to understand." Caryl pauses, then adds, "You know, this is what it's like for Marisela when we read stories in English. I want to read stories that Marisela can understand easily, too."

Caryl suggests that the children can look for comparisons with other versions of the same story they've read before as a class. She introduces some of the Spanish vocabulary within that context—like how the name Cenicienta comes from the word *cenizas,* or *ashes.*

Next, Caryl asks for predictions from the children about the story. The conversation is in English, the primary language of most of the children, but Caryl writes the children's ideas in Spanish on the chalkboard while they talk. This process allows her to work with the children's vocabulary, including the names of the prince, the father, and the stepmother, as they prepare to listen to the story.

"What do you think you'll need to know to understand the story?"

"We can look at the pictures."

"We can listen for Cinderella's name."

"Those are good ideas," Caryl responds, in English. "Since you already know the story, you can watch the illustrations to understand. You can also listen for the words we wrote on the board. When you know there are doves, you can listen for *palomas.*"

Caryl talks through the vocabulary list they've generated, code-switching between languages, and reminds them, in context, about their previous understanding of Spanish.

"*Zapato* is the word for shoe that you probably already know. But since Cinderella had such a tiny foot, it's called a *zapatito* in this story."

Then Caryl reads the story. The children listen quietly. Marisela particularly seems to enjoy it, from her seat in front of the book and at Caryl's feet. Following the reading of the story in Spanish, the children and Caryl complete a template of categories about this version of *Cinderella* that enables it to be compared and contrasted with other versions they've shared previously. The children are familiar with the routine and they answer in both Spanish and English as Caryl moves down the list of items:

"Grimm or Perault?"

"Perault," the group responds.

"How about the setting?" asks Caryl, "Remember, it's the place where the story takes place."

The class lists the author, illustrator, setting, characters, and plot. Each of these is listed in Spanish, as well.

"Coming tomorrow, the Chinese version of the story," concludes Caryl, and the class moves on to their next activity.

Genre plays a significant role in the fairy tale portion of the Middle Ages theme. The genre structures of fairy tales provide a firm foundation for comprehending new fairy tales or familiar fairy tales encountered in new versions or new languages. Materials from predictable genres give second language learners (in the case of reading *Cinderella,* English speakers learning Spanish) texts that build on their previous knowledge, simultaneously supporting success while introducing a challenge.

During a written interview, I ask Seaaira what types of materials she selects to read in her second language (Spanish). She writes, "I read fairy tales in Spanish because I know the fairy tales in English that I read in Spanish." Seaaira's comments, stated in the intuitive language common to eight-year-olds, reveal her conscious strategy for writing and reading in a less-controlled language. She realizes there is a greater predictability of meaning in familiar genres because of the structural expectations.

Seaaira's hypothesis about prediction in second language reading is put to the test when she and a girlfriend, Elliott, another English reader, follow along as Lolita reads *Las Tres Melliza y Cenicienta* out loud. Elliott says, "It was a good book and I could sort of tell what it was about." Although the girls didn't receive any direct translation of the book, they convey a general understanding and can provide ideas about specific language—that *bruja* (witch) has to do with magic, for instance. "I read with my eyes as Lolita read," Seaaira says. "I could understand the words."

The inclusion of a study of fairy tales early in the year is a very deliberate choice on my part. Children are supported as readers, in their first or second language, by knowing the schema of stories. Fairy tales have very specific features and language styles that remain consistent across languages. In either English or Spanish, they include a good character, an evil character, some kind of search or wandering, magic, and a happy ending.

Brooke is a child who, like Seaaira, has set a goal for herself to learn Spanish. When she chooses to read a Spanish version of Sleeping Beauty, *I remind her that the Spanish readers in her group can help her with her self-appointed task, but she says she doesn't think she'll need any help. She spends all of one day's literature study time and part of the next day's reading the Spanish text, then makes the entry shown in Figure 5-1 into her literature log. She explains it is a list of words she has figured out all by herself.*

Not only is Brooke's list an accurate interpretation based on contextual clues, but she reveals the extent to which her understanding of story schema has influenced her understanding. She selects cottage *as a meaning for* casucha, *a tumbledown hut, rather than the more common word* house, *knowing that fairy tales are more likely to contain cottages than houses. Brooke's knowledge of story structure in English has mediated her learning of Spanish.*

The Middle Ages

Each morning, the children are involved in work organized around the thematic content that they negotiated at the beginning of the year (as described in Chapter 3). The class moves into "centers," or group work stations, where they complete small-group activities with or without the assistance of an adult. During most themes, the class also works on individual or small-group research projects. The cur-

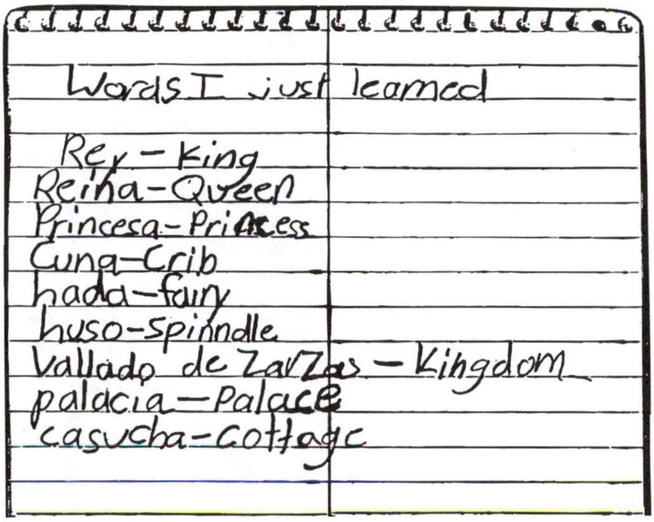

Figure 5-1. Brooke's list of Spanish words learned by reading a Spanish version of *Sleeping Beauty.*

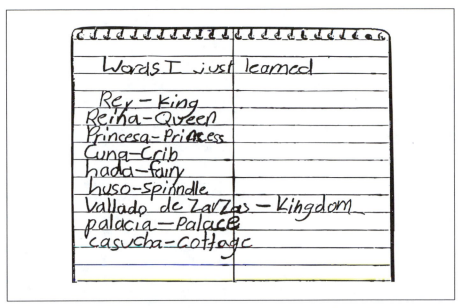

rent theme for all the activities during this period of the day is the Middle Ages. Supplemented by an accompanying fairy tale literature study, a writing workshop component, and individual and group projects, the theme involves the children in an integrated study from mid-October until the winter holiday break. Figure 5-2 is an annotated calendar for several weeks of the theme. Notice the normal elementary school disruptions of testing, conferences, and holidays that the class adjusts to and works around. These weeks demonstrate just one of the values of a theme cycle approach to curriculum—flexibility.

The topic of the Middle Ages is number six on the list of theme topic choices voted on by the children at the beginning of the year. It provides an opportunity to merge several expressed goals of this group of children's and of Caryl's. Many of the children want to know more about subjects related to the Middles Ages, like knights and kings and castles. They also want to learn to write using calligraphy. Caryl, in her planning, realizes that the text set of fairy tales she hopes to include in this year's curriculum will blend beautifully with this topic.

In preparing for the study, Caryl collects wide and varied liter-

Mon	Tue	Wed	Thur	Fri
10/8 WHOLE GROUP↓ Begin Fairy Tale Study Cinderella-chart setting, charac., plot illumination & magic	10/9 Categorize ?s RE: Middle Ages WHOLE GROUP Grimm Bros version of Cinderella chart same elements as yesterday-compare	10/10 Finish categories for Middle Ages WHOLE GROUP Spanish version Cinderella →	10/11 WHOLE GROUP Chinese version Cinderella →	10/12
10/15 Book talk for Lit Study Groups on Fairy Tales Read-aloud from District Writing	10/16 Lit Study Groups meet to read-record story elements in Lit Logs Middle Ages books all week. Assessments	10/17 Lit Study Groups meet-(see yesterday) →	10/18 Lit Study Groups meet (see Tues.)	10/19 PLANNING DAY
10/22 Lit Study Groups begin working on comparison charts Read-aloud ← Begin writing own versions of Cinderella (started as a homework assignment)	10/23 Lit Study Groups Continue work on comparison charts from Middle Ages books all week → Early dismissal for conferences	10/24 Lit Study Groups-fairy tale maps	10/25 Lit Study Groups-self-evaluation	10/26 Meet with committees to prepare for next week's centers
10/29 Author's Circle to share Cinderella stories - suggestions for revisions & additions	10/30 Middle Ages Centers-1st Round 1st Rotation Movie-Medieval Manor Revise/edit Cinderella stories	10/31 Middle Ages Centers 1st Round 2nd Rotation	11/1 Middle Ages Centers 1st Round 3rd Rotation Revision/edit Cinderella stories	11/2 Middle Ages Centers 1st Round 4th Rotation
11/5 Final editing conferences for Fairy Tales (Begin a new lit study)	11/6 Middle Ages Centers 1st Round 5th Rotation	11/7 Finish-up centers & Illuminated Letters & Castle Painting Outside	11/8 Begin a "What Have We Learned Web" Castle Painting Illuminated Letters Meet w/ Paper Bag Princess Grp	11/9
11/12 Meet w/ Dragons and Knights Group	11/13 Middle Ages Centers 2nd Round 1st Rotation Paper Bag Princess-read for play	11/14 Middle Ages Centers 2nd Round 2nd Rotation Lit Study-Fun w/ Fairy Tales Gp. other groups meet on own	11/15 Middle Ages Centers 2nd Round 3rd Rotation Lit Study meet w/ Dragon & Knights others meet on own	11/16 Middle Ages Centers 2nd Round 4th Rotation Movie-"The Reluctant Dragon"
11/19 Students work on final publication of Cinderella versions (all week in Writer Workshop)	11/20 Middle Ages Centers 2nd Round 5th Rotation Lit Study-Caryl meet w/ Paper Bag Princess & Dragons & Knights	11/21 Finish-up centers-Illuminated Letters, Painting Castle Lit Study-meet w/Fun w/Fairy Tales	11/22 THANKSGIVING	11/23 BREAK
11/26 Lit Study Groups Read on own- Final publ. process of Cinderella stories (all week in writer's workshop)	11/27 Begin a class book on Middle Ages - Each category on web=1 page in book - kids divide into group	11/28 Work on class book webs & paragraphs →	11/29 → Rehearsal of Paper Bag Princess play	11/30

Figure 5-2. Caryl's planning for most of the Middle Ages theme.

acy materials, filling the classroom with information in both Spanish and English. She gathers over one hundred titles (which are listed in Appendix A) for the Middle Ages theme. Pieces of art, posters, and artifacts also find their way into the Sunshine Room, contributed by the teachers, the support staff, the parents, and the children. Caryl, for example, plays the medieval song "Parsley, Sage, Rosemary, and Thyme" on her guitar and brings an accompanying poster with the lyrics and examples of the spices. Filmstrips, magazines, and wall hangings provide information about the Middle Ages.

During a theme, the children work from a list of questions, sometimes visually organized as a web, that will increase their understanding of the concept. Together, the members of the community plan a group of centers to help them answer their questions. Figure 5-3 shows the questions about the Middle Ages the children have brainstormed and listed on butcher paper.

The students' questions serve many purposes. They provide Caryl with a rich baseline of the knowledge the children bring with them into the theme. They also provide her with some parameters for her planning. The two rounds of centers that she and the children participate in during the theme are clearly developed in response to these questions, so that both the content and method of the centers meet the needs of the students. Writing workshop and literature study groups further integrate the curriculum.

Center Experiences

Children rotate through centers involving a variety of related open-ended experiences. Most centers are completed by all the students during a rotation, but as usual negotiation is part of the process.

Upon examining a book on the history of games, the children discover that during the Middle Ages, King Alphonso X of Spain wrote a book describing the games of his time. In one center, they experience games of the past (and present, in some cases) as they play "Nine Men's Morris," "Alquerque," "Chess," and "Checkers." Through their active participation, they are able to judge the quality of "fun" available during the Middle Ages, an issue children wonder about early on. This experience is made more authentic because Caryl has reproduced the "Alquerque" game board from the book about historical games and toys.

Children's map skills are stretched as they play another game that requires them to visit five castles by moving around a playing

Domestic Animals
Did they have cats?
Why do they use dogs?
Did they have horses?

Make Believe
Are there really wizards?
Were there really dragons?

Royalty/Laws/Government
How did kings and queens get to live in castles?
Why did they live in castles?
How did princesses become princesses?
Was it fun being a princess?
Who was the president?
Did they have a king?
Do they have a queen?
How did people become kings and queens?
What is a baron?
Was there a president and mayor?
Did they have a government?

Castles
How were castles made?
How many castles were made?
How many rooms were there in the king's castle?
Where did they build the first castle?
How long did it take to make a castle?
Who built the castle?

Fun
Did they have toys?
What did they do for fun?
Was it fun? Was it boring?
Did they have swimming pools?

Language
Did they have the same voice?

Figure 5-3. Children's questions about the Middle Ages.

board. The children must measure the distance of each move according to scale and use information about cardinal directions and standard measurement in inches. The game is played on a real map of England and calculators are on hand as tools for thinking. Playing on a real map entails social studies experiences; moving around the map requires math thinking and action; and reading the directions (see Figure 5-4) exercises language skills. The children also develop their abilities to share, take turns, and work in a group.

At another center, the children are experimenting with the arts of the period. One is the art of calligraphy, using a variety of nibs and pen angles on various papers. Lolita and Seaaira approach this opportunity seriously but with enthusiasm. During their time at this center and some free-choice time, they create a book full of their developing talents. The cover of their book is reproduced in Figure 5-5. Inside there are poetry, descriptions, silliness, and nonsense, all of which provide Seaaira and Lolita with calligraphic practice.

Another table of children works on illuminating the first letters of their names. Angélica, Antonia, Colin, and Aaron have a number of books showing examples of illumination used in illustration and print. Each letter, in final form, will be ornamented on a designed background, colored with markers and gold paint.

David, Marco, Thomas, and Randy are scattered on the floor of the group meeting area. They share an interest in knights from the Middle Ages and have joined forces to investigate answers to the questions on the above class list that address the topic. The bins of books that were previously sealed are now open, and the boys use these materials to conduct their research. Caryl has told the boys, and the other small research groups, that they are to choose questions from the list to study, and use the resource books and theme cycle books to find answers. Then they are to write a mini-report, draw a sketch and label it, or find some other way to share what they learn with the class. In addition, each group has been asked to contribute illustrations and explanatory text to be used in a class big book on the Middle Ages. As part of this content-driven study, the children will use strategies involving indexes, tables of contents, and encyclopedias. This small-group research experience also prepares the children for a future opportunity to complete an individual research project. Surrounded by a circle of peers who share similar curiosities about an issue, the children are being gently initiated into the research process.

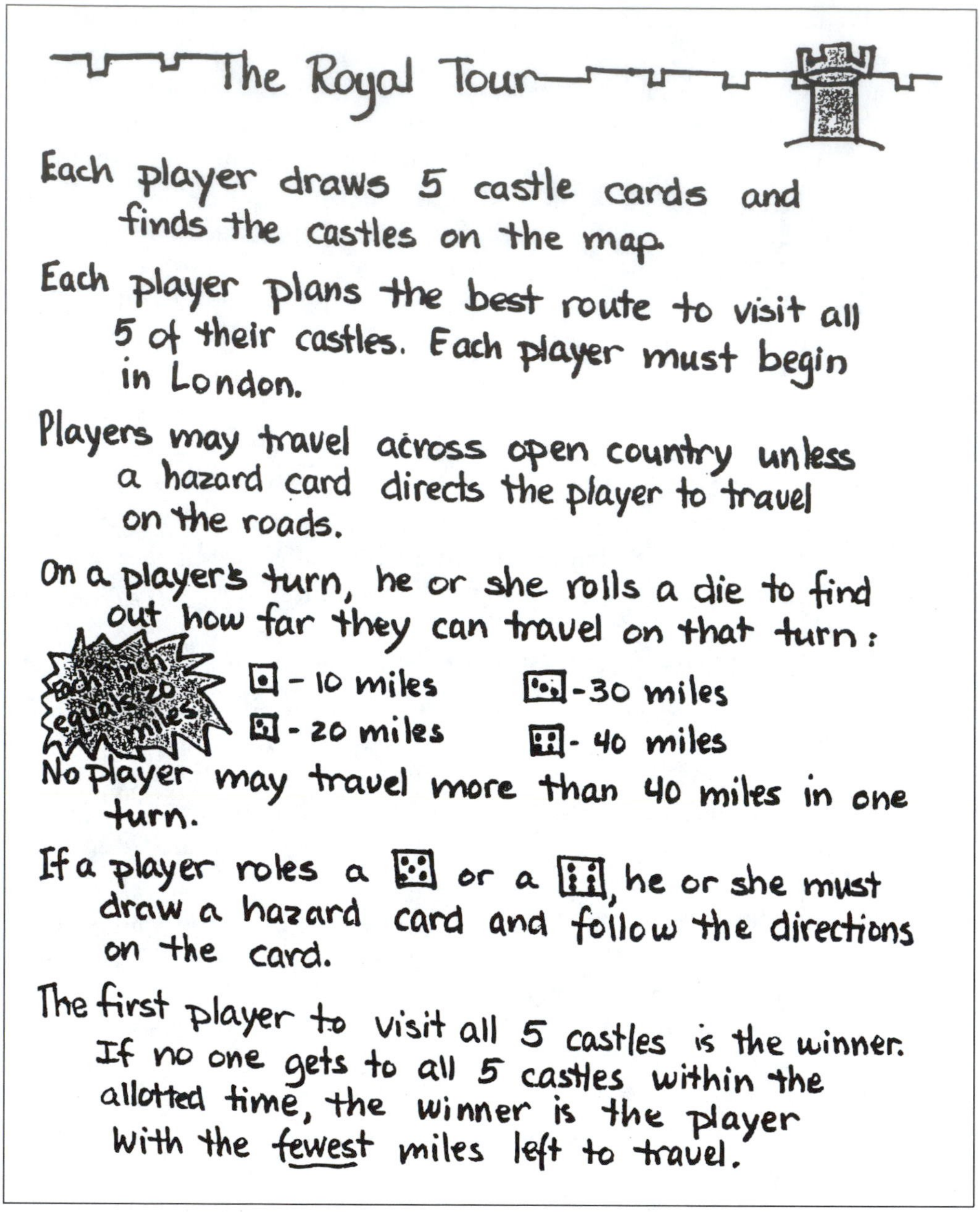

The Royal Tour

Each player draws 5 castle cards and finds the castles on the map.

Each player plans the best route to visit all 5 of their castles. Each player must begin in London.

Players may travel across open country unless a hazard card directs the player to travel on the roads.

On a player's turn, he or she rolls a die to find out how far they can travel on that turn:

⚀ - 10 miles ⚂ - 30 miles

⚁ - 20 miles ⚃ - 40 miles

No player may travel more than 40 miles in one turn.

If a player roles a ⚄ or a ⚅, he or she must draw a hazard card and follow the directions on the card.

The first player to visit all 5 castles is the winner. If no one gets to all 5 castles within the allotted time, the winner is the player with the fewest miles left to travel.

Figure 5-4. Directions to "The Royal Tour."

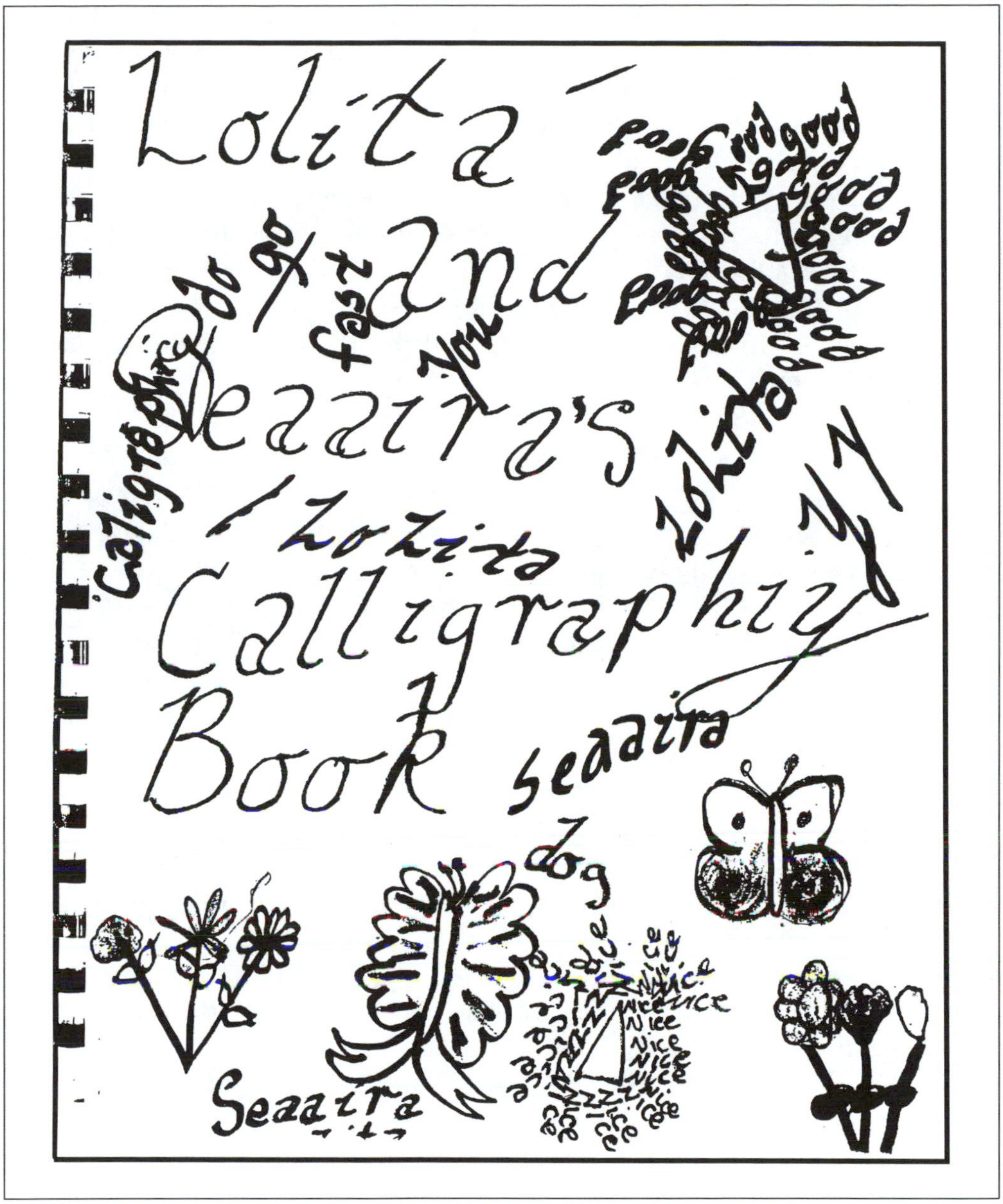

Figure 5-5. Cover of calligraphy book.

Another center provides children with scrap materials for creating castle replicas. They study detailed illustrations and diagrams in books to create accurate models with features like an outer curtain, a gatehouse, a portcullis, an inner curtain, a bailey, a keep, turrets, battlements, and towers.

In yet another center the children design a coat of arms that represents something about themselves. For example, Mark's depicts the meaning of his name, Cari's reveals her singing talent, and Aaron's reflects his artistic nature and his knowledge of geckos. The coats of arms are displayed around the room before they go home to the children's families.

Many of these learning experiences take a long time. Because they are process oriented, they are returned to time and again by the students before they are completed. Center time often expands into other periods of the day and the week's free-choice times. Frequently, children ask to stay in from recess or return to the classroom right after lunch to continue their work. As long as Caryl feels the children are receiving plenty of fresh air and exercise, she often grants their requests to add details to their castles, spend quiet time with the illustrations in a book, or finish inputting their stories on the word processor.

Writing Workshop

During the weeks of center experiences just described, writing workshop involves the children in personalizing the class' group study about the many versions of *Cinderella* in the world. They each compose a unique version of the fairy tale, building on the general components of the genre and the special characteristics of the Cinderella story as they write.

As you'll see in the examples below, Mark and Angélica bring their cultural and linguistic backgrounds into their more recent knowledge about the tale. Other children do the same as they write in Spanish or English or a biliterate format. Some name their characters after their friends at school; others bring family members and family stories into the plots of their stories. Although Angélica writes her story in English, she conveys her Mexican American heritage, too.

CYNDEE, BY MARK

Once upon a time there was a poor servant named Cyndee. She worked at a Circle K. She had to work full time. She worked from

1:00 in the morning to 12:00 in the night. Four robbers were making Cyndee work 23 hours or they would kill her.

One night Donald Trump was having a costume party. But the robbers made Cyndee stay at the Circle K because they are going to go and steal Donald Trump's money. Cyndee wanted to go but all she had was a dirty uniform.

All of a sudden a 3 Musketeers candy bar started talking. It said, "I will give you a lottery ticket and a beautiful costume if you don't give me away." Cyndee promised the candy bar that she would not give him away. "There is a limo waiting outside," said the candy bar. So Cyndee left to the party.

When Donald Trump saw Cyndee he went and sat with her. Cyndee told Donald Trump that somebody was going to steal his money. So Donald Trump called security. The security caught the robbers. When Donald Trump got back he did not see Cyndee but he did find Cyndee's credit card.

It said that Cyndee worked at a Circle K. Donald Trump said that he would go to every single Circle K in the state until I find this Cyndee. His search began. It took a couple of years to get to the Circle K that Cyndee worked at and find Cyndee.

Cyndee never had to work again.

Donald Trump turned on his TV to see if he won the lottery. Donald Trump got mad because he didn't win the lottery but Cyndee yelled, "I won! I won!" And they lived happily ever after.

The End.

Cenicienta, by Angélica

A very long time ago in a small city in Mexico lived a girl named Maria with her mother and father. One day her father left and never came back again. Years later her mother remarried. But her life wasn't as happy because her father wanted her to be his slave. He had a son who didn't have to do anything. She had to feed the cows and horses, she had to make tortillas, tamales and empanadas.

One day her mother and her stepfather and her step brother left out of town. She expected them back at 11:30. She was out in the field feeding the cows and horses when a young man approached and he asked if she would like to go dancing. "No, I can't go, I don't have anything nice to wear." He told her if you change your mind I'll be waiting.

The more she thought about it she thought she could wear

something of her moms. She borrowed her mom's favorite pearl necklace. She wore the most beautiful shoes she had ever seen in her life. They had white beads on them. She waited for the young man to show up at the dance and when he came she felt a little nervous. Then the clock struck 11:30. She ran out of the dance with out saying goodbye. But while she was running, her mom's pearl necklace fell off and on to the steps. The young man picked up the pearls and said: the lady who has such a little neck I shall marry her.

It was the mom's, but they didn't fit her. The next day the young man set off to find his new wife. When he finally came to Maria's house, she ran to the door in such a rush that she forgot about her father. But her mom beat her to it. "Hello," said the young man. "I would like to see all the ladies in the house." So the mom got Maria. She put on the pearls. It fit perfectly. And they got married and lived happily ever after.

As for her cruel stepfather and step brother they became kind and lived with Maria.

The End.

As the authors begin the publishing process, they make several decisions about the final format of their book. They decide whether or not to add the ornaments of illuminated first letters and calligraphy to their written texts. They also determine if they will illustrate the final version. They even choose the size of the paper they want to use and if they will use the word processor to produce the book. Mark decides he wants his story published on full-size white paper on the computer, using the Appleworks program. He also decides not to use illumination, but he does illustrate his final book. Angélica publishes her book with full-size paper, using calligraphy, illumination, and illustration. The books are taken home, but many are photocopied first and added to the classroom library.

Fairy Tale Study Groups

To extend the Middle Ages theme, the class participates in a literature study centered around fairy tales. The children regularly meet in groups for literature studies, having selected a group based on Caryl's book talks on each choice, as we describe in Chapters 4 and 6. The fairy tale literature study, like the others, illustrates how content can support reading development and literature response.

In this case, as small groups investigate multiple versions of new tales, they build on their large-group experiences where they've learned to compare different versions of *Cinderella.*

A few days into these literature study groups, Caryl tells the children, "Today, when you sit down in your group, pick a different version of the story. Tell each other about the version you read yesterday, talk about it with each other. You can use the same recording sheet as yesterday. The goal is to compare and contrast versions. Today, pay attention to what's the same and what's different and make notes. Buddy reading is okay, but both of you have to do some of the recording sheet."

The children scatter to tables covered with books. Each table has a set of books containing versions of the same fairy tale presented a variety of ways, in both English and Spanish. I sit with Lolita, Seaaira, and Marco, the *Little Red Riding Hood* group, and listen to their conversation. Marco reads *Caperucita Roja* aloud to himself in Spanish. He runs his finger under the words of the text. Seaaira also begins to read aloud in English, from *Little Red Riding Hood,* while Lolita looks on. This is these girls' favorite way to read together, taking turns page by page.

Marco finishes his book first. "I'm done," he announces to no one in particular. Caryl sends him off for a recording sheet when he can't remember what to do next. He works on the date for a long time, while he listens to Lolita read the familiar section, "Grandmother, what big eyes you have!" He is still listening as Seaaira finishes the last page of reading.

"The end. That was good," she declares.

The girls record their responses quickly. They negotiate their answers, but each writes on her own paper.

Marco takes longer. He observes the girls as they work and listens to their talk. Finally, as they rush off in a flurry to put their papers away and I leave the area, Marco is writing like crazy in Spanish on his recording sheet (see Figure 5-6).

The next day, the same characters gather around the same table. Today, Gabe is here (he was absent yesterday), and Marco wants to buddy-read with him but can't find him in the room. So he selects a book in English after rummaging through the choices. He begins to read in English aloud, with a noticeable Spanish pronunciation for unknown words. He reads about half a page, then

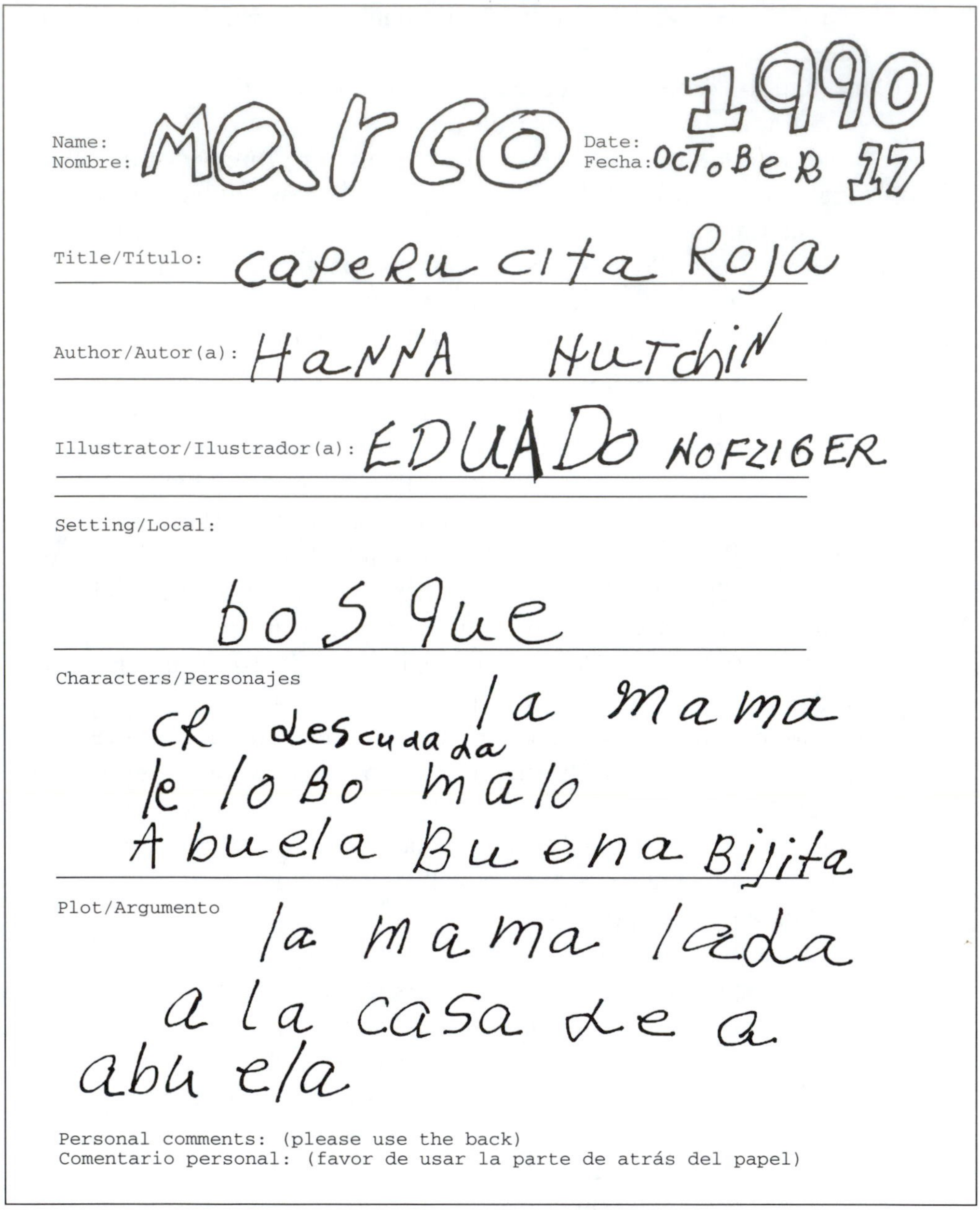

Name:/Nombre: Marco

Date:/Fecha: OCToBeR 17 1990

Title/Título: capeRucita Roja

Author/Autor(a): HaNNA HuTchiN

Illustrator/Ilustrador(a): EDUADo NOFZIGER

Setting/Local:

boSque

Characters/Personajes

CR descudada

la mama

le loBo malo

Abuela Buena Bijita

Plot/Argumento

la mama lada a la casa de a abu ela

Personal comments: (please use the back)
Comentario personal: (favor de usar la parte de atrás del papel)

Figure 5-6. Marco's recording sheet.

closes the book. He turns around and plays with the calendar and a pencil.

"Come on, Gabe," he mutters under his breath as he leaves the table in search of his friend.

Meanwhile, the girls are busily making comparisons as they read another book together.

"It's the same!" they pronounce together when the book is finished. They display lots of book knowledge about authors and illustrators, details of plot, and so on while they chat about their reading.

Marco returns to the table with Gabe in tow. They look at the English book that Marco had previously tried out, turning a few pages before closing the book. They are clearly looking for the book with the least written text. They pick up another, it's the one the girls read yesterday during literature study group. Marco reads first. He stumbles over the words, and Gabe can't help.

"Let's find a shorter one," suggests Gabe.

"I've already read the two shortest ones," Marco responds.

They examine many more books and finally return to the original one. Now the boys read chorally. They read slowly and they stop at times to look at the illustrations. Soon their conversation changes to the topic of birthdays, not reading at all. But they eventually return to the reading, looking at the illustrations and talking about the characters. When I leave the group they are still struggling.

The difficulties that Marco and Gabe experience in their fairy tale literature study group are a common occurrence. For both boys, school is the most consistent, dependable part of their lives. Marco has been witness to domestic violence and spends enough time worrying about his mother each day that he and I strike a deal—I will allow him to phone her whenever he wants if he will come to me when he feels angry or frustrated instead of striking out against another child. Gabe has moved around several times during his first years of school and moves out of Borton to return again within this one year. Even though his circle of friends at Borton is very small (perhaps to ease the pain of eventually having to leave them) we are sorry to see him go and grateful for his return. His report card from the two quarters he was at another school indicates failing marks in reading and writing. On the first day back in our community, he begins writing a new story, which he comes to call "Coming Back to Bor-

ton," in which he compares his two schools and states how happy he is to be back in the Sunshine Room.

In order for kids like Marco and Gabe to feel successful in school, they require a learning community that will respect them as learners, include them in the community when they choose to be included, and encourage them to participate when they do not. For Marco and Gabe, buddy reading provides encouragement to persist at a difficult text. Alone, Marco is not willing to take the risk. With Gabe as a buddy reader, the two boys are able to read more than either one can alone.

Marco also finds support as a learner by being included in small-group learning situations. While Seaaira and Lolita enthusiastically discuss the Little Red Riding Hood *version they have read and make their notes, Marco is quietly watching and listening. He is unsure of the task and learns what to do by observing the girls as they work together. The next day, he takes responsibility for reading and making notes, seeking out a friend to support him as a reader. Although Marco is inconsistent during the year in showing such initiative, he can count on the community in the classroom to provided the help he needs when he is ready to take risks as a learner.*

Another group of children is involved in reading humorous and critical versions of fairy tales. This set includes *The Paper Bag Princess,* for example, which pokes fun at the sexist portrayal of men and women in classic princess stories. The children in this group are participating in similar activities to the others, but they are also challenging stereotypic images of fairy tales and considering them in a present-day context. Their work evolves into a play that they perform for the rest of the class.

Still other groups read text sets with versions of different tales. Each group eventually shares their learning with the others, in a variety of ways. Although fairy tales are not literally from medieval times, they extend many of the issues the students are interested in. These studies strengthen children's concepts of comparison, which they will continue to use as the year progresses.

Presenting Learning

Theme studies move from the initial brainstorming into intermediate stages of planning and a wide range of center activities and research work. They conclude with presentations of various types, in which the children share their ideas and new knowledge with others in the classroom community and the school. The Middle Ages theme presentation emerges during the center experiences. The children are so fascinated by illuminated letters that they ask Caryl if they can make an entire alphabet frieze. Coincidentally, at this same time the class is responsible for filling a large bulletin board in the cafeteria.

So the class decides to display the information they've learned about the Middle Ages on an illuminated alphabet mounted on the cafeteria bulletin board. The result is a fanciful medieval alphabet, packed with information for everyone in the school to enjoy while they eat lunch, stand in the lunch line, and participate in other events in the room. The text below each illuminated letter is scripted in calligraphy, so the children's developing artistic knowledge is displayed too. All in all, the presentation is an ideal symbol for what the children have learned.

High Level of Intellectual Expectation

In Chapter 3, the research of theorists concerned about the politics of education, like Anyon (1980), McLaren (1994), Moll and Díaz (1987), and Oakes (1985), was presented in the context of negotiating curriculum in the Sunshine Room for the year. These researchers document the manner in which curriculum content and processes are determined according to the stratification of the greater society, with children at the lower end of the societal classes receiving instruction that is far less challenging, less interesting, and less controlled by the learners. Anyon, in particular, documents that for children from working-class and middle-class homes (homes similar to those of many of the children in the Sunshine Room), curriculum requires children to follow the "steps of the procedures" and "get the right answer." Curriculum that expects creative activity to be carried out independently by children or that pushes the development of learners' analytical and intellectual powers is typically reserved for children from affluent, professional backgrounds and executive elite communities (Anyon 1980, 1981).

Children in the Sunshine Room, however, are experiencing the type of curriculum advocated by critical theorists to push social and educational change (Banks 1992; McLaren 1994; Moll & Díaz 1987). These theorists suggest that if we resist the assumption that working-class and minority children's intellectual abilities are reduced, children will be empowered to demand challenging experiences and expectations, not only in the curriculum of schools, but in life.

> It is our contention that existing classroom practices not only underestimate and constrain what children display intellectually, but help distort explanations of school performance. It is also our contention that the strategic application of cultural resources in instruction is one important way of obtaining change in academic performance and of demonstrating that there is nothing about the children's language, culture, or intellectual capacities that should handicap their schooling. (Moll & Díaz 1987, p. 300)

The children in the Sunshine Room begin to learn how to ask their own questions early in the year. Not all children are familiar with being responsible for asking their own questions at school, in part because their previous school experiences have taught them to be passive. Some children need a great deal of help to think through their interests for the very first time and to recognize that they have interests and abilities that are relevant at school. Caryl builds on each child's funds of knowledge to support his or her thinking in these ways. Funds of knowledge are areas of expertise learned incidentally or directly in the community and shared through social networks (Moll et al. 1990; Moll et al. 1992; Moll, Tapia & Whitmore 1993). As the year progresses, children's interests and strengths resurface as they realize that the curriculum in third grade is inquiry centered. Through the repetition of the process of asking questions at the outset of each theme, the children become more comfortable with the conventions of the problem-solving process, use the process with more sophistication, and gain confidence in pursuing personal interests.

We regard all children's questions about a particular topic as legitimate, from the ones whose answer is obvious to some members of the class to the questions whose answers may not ever be discovered. Information about dragons is just as important to the child who asks, "Were there really dragons?" as knowledge about royalty and class systems is to the child who asks about government during the Middle Ages. Sometimes, the difficult questions are the more interesting ones, and when we gain only a partial understanding of an idea or topic we are left wondering, a healthy way to pass the time. I do not expect that the children will learn everything there is to know about the Middles Ages or that we will find answers to all of our questions. However, I do expect that each child will learn something that he or she wants to know.

As long as interest is maintained, we continue to work within a theme study area. Before we reach a point where our activity would no longer be fruitful, we move on to a new theme area, leaving ourselves with unanswered questions to ponder. Often, a few projects are still being finished while books for the next theme are being gathered and new questions being raised.

At a Whole Language Umbrella Conference, a colleague and I were listening to Ken Goodman speak when something he said (neither of us remembers exactly what) sparked a simultaneous reaction. We began writing furiously on our programs and laughed out loud when we looked at our nearly identical thoughts. After a bit of revising, we had a new slogan for whole language classrooms: We will never be quiet. We will never be still. We will never be finished.

As part of my interviews with the children during the first year, I ask Lupita and Brooke to respond to a broad request, "Tell me about your classroom." The request is easy for Lupita.

She says, "Well, we're studying Egypt. And we're gonna do a museum, we're gonna turn our classroom into a museum so other classes can come and see what we've done. And we're going to make a mummy out of paper mache and we're also going to make an imaginary Nile to go across the floor. . . . And we're going to make the loft into a pyramid. And we're also going to make a filmstrip. We're going to draw our own film. We're also gonna make brochures for the museum and brochures for Egypt. . . . It's a place that I like to learn."

Lupita's enthusiasm for her classroom is shared by her classmate Brooke. Brooke explains the Sunshine Room thus: "I think it's a neat classroom, 'cuz we do a lot of neat things—what we learn in centers. So far we've learned a lot about dinosaurs, Native Americans, and now we're studying Egypt. And when we studied Native Americans we had to write a report and we put them all in a book."

The girls' comments indicate a value of process over product in the curriculum. In the Middle Ages theme (as well as during literature studies and writing workshop), the children are not only learning about rich content, they are also learning processes, such as "how to research." The children are responsible for conceiving their own questions, guiding their own learning with biliterate materials and experiences, and following a sophisticated research procedure.

By the end of theme studies like the Middle Ages, they are expected to display developing skills in using reference materials and are able to articulate their awareness of the reasons for keeping records of reference materials. The research process often culminates in aesthetic presentations in which children learn to write in specific genres. At the same time, the presentations provide the school community with real, researched, and referenced information. In this way, the children are following the process Lois Bird (1991) recommends for achieving classroom research that helps "students experience the joy of learning" (p. 296). A learning process that includes inventing products that grow out of inquiry is a pleasure for children and teachers.

The materials in the classroom extend the amount and type of learning possible for any child. Many of the books are at an adult level. The children read these books selectively, and glean information pertaining to their self-selected topics and specific questions. This may mean reading the captions under illustrations or photographs or finding brief paragraphs that answer fine-tuned questions. Although the books are sometimes very difficult, Caryl assumes that they can be read and used by all of the children and sees to it that those who need assistance receive it.

I want the children to recognize that there are many different sources of information and many ways of obtaining knowledge. Most of the children are not intimidated by materials they are not able to use independently. I also want to be sure that language never becomes an obstacle to learning, so the adults in the room do whatever is necessary, reading aloud, interpreting and discussing in the child's native language, to ensure that children have access to information that will help them answer their questions.

This is illustrated by an interaction between Veronica and Caryl during another theme about Native Americans. One afternoon, Veronica is studying the Yaqui. Caryl sits with her, reading to her from an adult-level book written in English, about the Yaqui tribe. After she reads a passage, Caryl translates the ideas into Spanish and discusses the text with Veronica in terms of her personal research question. Veronica incorporates a second source of information in her research project when she interviews Mrs. E., a Yaqui teacher assistant at Borton, who speaks Spanish.

In this example, Caryl helps Veronica by translating a difficult text from English into Spanish instead of assuming that Veronica, as a Spanish-dominant reader, cannot handle the information or that she needs an easier task. She intuitively engages in a strategy Moll and Díaz (1987) call bilingual communicative support, wherein participants who share a literacy event, especially in a second language, "switch to Spanish as needed, to clarify the meaning of the text" (p. 306). Children are not expected to understand, participate, or excel in these highly intellectual processes without guidance and support from Caryl. She demonstrates all parts of the process, especially supporting children who are experiencing such events for the first time. In order to answer their personal research questions, for instance, the children need to learn how to manipulate the conventions of indexes and tables of contents in reference materials. Rather than being assigned activities that isolate reference skills for instructional purposes, the children in this third-grade classroom *need* to use reference procedures to find answers to their real questions. This creates an intellectually challenging inquiry process.

It is critical that all of the children are offered the same opportunities to engage in the theme activities, regardless of their level of experience as learners. Children who are just barely emerging as readers participate alongside highly proficient literacy users and make important contributions to class activities. An example is Judith, a Spanish-dominant child from the school neighborhood. She is thoroughly captivated with the calligraphy work we are doing in this theme. Although she usually chooses only highly predictable books in Spanish for her own reading and avoids most theme-related reading and writing tasks, she spends a great deal of time poring over the carefully crafted alphabets in the calligraphy manuals. At the back of one book she finds directions for making quill pens. The following day, she comes to class with a bag of pigeon feathers she has gathered from the alley behind her house. With Halie's help reading directions, Judith diligently cuts a writing nib on each feather so we can all practice our pen strokes with authentically medieval writing tools. Her gift to her classmates is a fondly remembered contribution to the Middle Ages theme.

Although Kathy and I have chosen to highlight children who are successful in assuming responsibility for their own learning, the classroom is also home to children like Judith who struggle as learners. Within the socially organized environment of the classroom there are many support systems to encourage them to try again. These children who have less experience with literacy, who speak little English, or who must push aside family problems before they can learn are not subjected to a reduced curriculum under the misguided assumption that they cannot learn. Instead, they are immersed in an educational experience typically reserved for students who are labeled as gifted or exceptional.

Symmetric Power and Trust Relationships

Research across disciplines finds that in most classrooms, as in other institutional settings, power is in the hands of the teacher because knowledge is thought to be possessed by the teacher (Board 1982; Freire & Macedo 1987; McLaren 1994; Wells 1989). This means the teacher controls the children's behavior, their opportunities to speak, and their positions in the physical environment, as well as the subject matter to be learned, the manner in which learning will occur, and the evaluation of learning. Children typically need to request permission for nearly every activity at school, including asking questions or moving about the classroom.

The children in the Sunshine Room have considerable and uncharacteristic control over curriculum building. They select groups, reading materials, writing topics, and theme topics. They generate their research questions and negotiate their learning tasks with their teacher. Caryl allows and promotes this sharing of power, based on her trust of them as learners.

While Caryl invents her role as a teacher, she operates within the conventions of her whole language philosophy of teaching. Her trust in her students' abilities enables her to set high expectations for them; their trust in her allows them to take risks, to experiment, and collaborate with her in learning. Learning in this classroom is not just an individual achievement but a joint accomplishment between adults and children.

Caryl frequently negotiates the specifics of curriculum management with the children, either as a whole class or individually. During a theme about Egypt, the whole class has negotiated that if children are ahead on their required center activities they can have free time, but if not, they need to continue their work. During a work period, Jaime requests free time during a private conversation with Caryl. As Jaime and Caryl look over a record of his progress, she answers, "Let's negotiate. If you work for fifteen minutes on language arts, religion, or vocabulary (specific center areas), you can have free time. What do you think?" Jaime agrees and hurries off to work. Azucena follows, with a similar request in Spanish. The conversation is repeated, and Azucena feels she has control in the process of meeting her teacher's and her classmates' goals for learning while still receiving her immediate goal of free time.

Through negotiating sessions like these, Caryl is able to exert her professional knowledge about her students. She can help each student set goals that are appropriately based on their previous experiences. This is not to say that Caryl develops curriculum that lowers expectations for certain students, but rather that Caryl can use her knowledge about how learning and development occur to make sure each child succeeds.

Caryl's role in the negotiating process is professional and theoretically informed. Not only does she seek opportunities to guide children toward appropriate behavior, but she captures moments that encourage children to assert their intellectual capabilities. For example, Caryl might suggest that specific children work with one another on projects, thus providing an opportunity for a typically quiet child to assert her knowledge or creating an opportunity for children with different Spanish-language abilities to work together.

This effectively sets the stage for a collaborative relationship that will build a natural zone of proximal development (Vygotsky 1978). As Moll and Díaz (1987) describe, Vygotskian theory stresses how instruction, to be effective, must lead students and be aimed at the strengths children display in collaborative activities. Thus, children look to Caryl for advice, assistance, and support. They expect their teacher to be interested, and they realize that although she won't complete their learning for them or permit them to be passive, neither will she allow them to slip through the cracks of institutionalized learning. Children and teachers are equally responsible for the success of the active whole language curriculum.

Trusting children as learners makes it easier to share control of the classroom and the curriculum with them. Our lives are necessarily messier. It takes longer to start theme cycles because the children are included in the planning and gathering of materials, and it's difficult to plan more than a few days in advance. Many days run smoothly, but sometimes the activities we try don't work out as we had anticipated. However, we don't dwell long on these failures since there's always something else to do. In the Middle Ages theme, the group research projects never get off the ground in the way I hope. But as you can see, the children are very actively engaged in a lot of other experiences. Some of these evolve into the final presentation of our learning at the end of the theme.

I am reminded one day that not all teachers are prepared to share power with their students. I need a substitute teacher while I attend an inservice in my building, and I've planned a day full of activities that require very little adult direction. The children will continue ongoing theme centers and literature study groups that have planned their own assignments. During writers workshop, the children can work on their individual writing projects. I talk briefly with the children at Pledge before my meeting begins. Later, walking past my classroom, I see the substitute walking in the opposite direction. When I go in to investigate, I find a note on my plan book that says she was afraid to stay in a room where the children have so much control. The children tell me to go on to the inservice, assuring me they can take care of themselves. It doesn't work out quite that way, of course, but I am rewarded by my students' willingness to take responsibility for their own learning and behavior.

When children participate in creating the curriculum, the norms of behavior, and the physical environment of the classroom, they own their learning. Most of the children respond to this invitation in the way that Seaaira and Lolita do, by unleashing their imaginations and demonstrating their learning in creative and powerful ways. I'm convinced that the children who are disruptive or are not fully and regularly engaged in our activity would be in even more trouble in a typical teacher-controlled classroom. By making negotiation the convention in our classroom, I am able to support all children as individuals, with very few complaints about any one child's being given preferential treatment. Occasionally, I need to explain how my negotiation with a particular student will allow that child's special needs to be met, but these straightforward explanations are accepted and honored.

The children have returned my trust in them by coming to trust themselves as learners. When the children work on math investigations, I usually ask them how they know their answers make sense. Juan doesn't think it's fair that I "just ask another question instead of telling the right answer." However, when he is asked to write about why he felt his solution to a problem is reasonable, he writes, "I know my answer makes sense because I trust myself as a math thinker."

Authenticity

Ken Goodman says that "experiences in school must have *all* the characteristics of authentic experiences outside of school and additional characteristics that are authentic within the social-educational context of the school" (1991, p. 281). The third graders in the Sunshine Room explore personal avenues of learning through their questioning. They represent their learning in ways that are logical according to the specific topics of the themes and responsive to the children's intellectual development.

The children are involved in a natural learning process that can be interpreted through E. Brooks Smith's concept of "coming to know" (K. S. Goodman *et al.* 1987). Coming to know helps us understand how learning happens when symbols are transformed and experiences are cognitively represented. This includes three components: perceiving, ideating, and presenting.

The Middle Ages theme provides numerous and varied opportunities for children to perceive and ideate. For example, as children manipulate calligraphy pens and ink and act out innovative versions of fairy tales, their sensory systems are exposed to new feelings, sights, and sounds. This is perceiving. When learning occurs outside of school, information is taken in by sensory perceptions of the world. Perceiving involves all semiotic systems and happens constantly, as new data is encountered and attended to selectively in the environment.

As children analyze stereotypic portrayals of women in literature through fairy tales and consider life from another period of history, their previous schemata about groups of people in the world are challenged and perhaps changed. This is ideating, when the learner's perceptions interact with existing knowledge from previous experiences. Ideating includes conceptualizing and generalizing, as the perceptions of experience are accommodated into one's own symbol system.

As children share information about knights and castles, create and display an illuminated alphabet frieze, and write poetry and essays dealing with fairy tale variations, their personal learning is shared with others. During these events, children are presenting. This third component of coming to know involves the process of sharing conceptualizations with others through a form that enables the personal to become social. Presenting occurs through all symbol systems, including language but not limited to language. It needs to occur through all modes of communication and symbolic representation in school. The presentation phase of coming to know opens opportunities for children to express their learning and represent their personal and collective meanings through mediums like drawing, acting, singing, painting, and building, as well as through speaking and writing. The theme as a whole provides enough quality time and enough encounters with new ideas for children to think about the new information being assimilated. As in all themes in this classroom, presentation grows out of the perceiving and ideating components of the process.

Over the course of these two years, the themes result in forms of presentation that are formidable for third graders. When Ancient Egypt is the focus, for instance, the classroom is transformed into the museum that Lupita and Brooke describe: exhibits, filmstrips created by children, a papier-maché replica of a mummy. Invitations to the entire school and extended community result in tours by visitors to whom tour guides from the Sunshine Room explain exhibits and Ancient Egyptian history in either English or Spanish, as necessary.

Another time, wrapping up a human body theme, the class publishes a bilingual newspaper on the topic, which is then distributed to families and other classrooms. This study involves the newspaper publishing process as well as learning and presenting the biologically oriented content.

During a theme about world geography, small-group presentations made to the class vary with the learning children experience at a personal level; Seaaira and Lolita read poetry and sing songs they've written in English, while Marisela and Carolina read a report in Spanish. Several groups present their research on different countries. Others develop filmstrips, write travel brochures, or share cultural foods and music with their classmates. The children's "passports" are stamped in and out as the class "travels" all over the country and the world.

The class contributes a published collection of reports about tribes of Native Americans to the library at the conclusion of another study. In addition to the written reports and illustrations, the volume includes a conventionally formed bibliography of reference materials used by the authors.

In each of these cases, the form of presentation is generated during the course of the thematic study— at the beginning of a new theme no one, not even Caryl, knows how the learning will be presented at the end. Forms of presentation cannot be planned ahead of time because the children, as active members of a learning community, must invent the forms for presenting their learning in the authentic context of the experience.

During the Middle Ages theme, all of the questions listed in Figure 5-3 become part of centers. The questions about literacy, language, and writing are grouped into one category and become the content of our calligraphy center. As we explore ancient styles of writing with sticks, quills, and nibbed pens, we learn how books were produced by hand on parchment and then illuminated with paint and gold leaf. We pore over examples in resource books and contemporary literature that emulate the style of medieval scribes. That learning is reinforced through actual practice with similar materials and tools as we work on illuminated alphabet panels that share our new knowledge.

We never know when we begin how we will present what we have learned. Sometimes, our presentations will make direct use of some process inherent in the theme, as happened with our calligraphy work. At other times, we may try some other format that interests us. The newspaper on the human body was such a project. Either way, the time spent preparing our sharing involves more learning as we organize, write, read, rehearse, draw, paint, or whatever else might be required.

Caryl typically assumes a low profile in the classroom. She is often difficult to find, as she is most likely at the physical level of the children and is as absorbed in the content and the process of their learning as they are. Although the students are able to find materials, complete activities, and make decisions with very little adult assistance, Caryl is keenly aware of the interests of each child and is actively involved. Her value of the children's learning is evident in the authentic questions she asks, probing questions that require elaboration, explanation, and thoughtfulness.

As a learner, I bring my university coursework to school and read articles and professional books during DEAR, and I share the trials and tribulations of writing papers with the children. Halie also works as an interpreter, so the children have opportunities to watch her search bilingual dictionaries and glossaries, looking for the best way to translate a text. The children are very aware that the adults in the classroom are learning for themselves as well as learning new ideas with the children. I feel that if I ever reach a point when I have nothing left to learn, I will need to leave the teaching profession.

As our class moves through the process of inventing our own curriculum, I pose my own questions about the theme topic. My questions are listed alongside the children's on our webs and charts. If other children share my particular interests, then a center may be planned where we can pursue those questions together. If not, I take advantage of the opportunity to demonstrate my own learning processes in front of the class.

For instance, when we study Native Americans, I want to know more about tribal mythology and legends associated with the sky. Stargazing is a favorite and frequent pastime under our clear, desert skies in Arizona. I have many star stories among my collection of children's literature. Because I am the only person in the class who asks questions about this aspect of Native American history and contemporary life, I choose to search for answers by publicly writing a research paper. From listing my questions to using resource and reference books to look for information, I do my work in front of the class, explaining my research process as I proceed. I read and take notes, discussing with the children how I choose what to write down on my note cards. I construct an outline for my paper on the chalkboard, and write my first draft on the overhead projector. Then, when the children begin their own research projects, they use the same procedures they have seen me demonstrate. It is important that these are not just directions, but an authentic research project of my own.

Additive Bilingualism and Biliteracy

The social exchange of knowledge that occurs naturally in communities and networks of friends and families, referred to as an exchange of funds of knowledge (Moll et al. 1990), is a social resource for curriculum and cognitive challenge at school. Knowledge of two or more languages and how to manipulate them for survival in the realities of social contexts translates into effective classroom instruction.

> Activity based, meaning-centered lessons allow students and teachers to take advantage of all of their [bilingual] resources, whether inside or outside the classroom, and create circumstances for the children's use of literacy in ways that far exceed what is currently offered in classrooms. (Moll et al. 1990, p. 8)

Society's view of language affects how language is dealt with in school. Within the existing framework of bilingual education curriculum, the societal view of language is frequently reduced to the extremes of being a "problem" or being "right" (Flores 1982; Ruiz 1984). However, when the societal view becomes one of language as "resource," schools transform into facilitators of language learning that appreciate minority language speakers as experts in their own knowledge and value children's contributions to the language and literacy curriculum. Bilingualism rather than monolingualism becomes the goal of the instructional program. Assessment is no longer measured according to an impossible "complete" competency guide but is based on growth and development in both languages.

In the study centers and groups, Spanish is used interchangeably with English so that the children learning English can both understand the content in their dominant language and expand their vocabulary and comprehension in their second language. In contrast, children learning Spanish have multiple experiences with their second language in use, also in an additive manner, although at an enrichment level rather than a survival level. Information is recorded in the appropriate language, the decision being made by the children and adults depending on the activity and the materials.

Caryl provides the children with materials in English and Spanish because they extend the children's perception and involvement in multiple linguistic and literate systems of knowing. She encourages her students to use their bilingualism to create interesting, advanced conditions for literacy use and language learning. But in general the students' and adults' bilingualism is used as a resource to expand opportunities to obtain, create, and communicate knowledge and to develop the social relationships so essential to this classroom's work. Bilingualism in this classroom meets Moll et al.'s (1990) recommendation that teachers, "treat bilingualism as a resource to expand the students' literate and social worlds, which in turn creates new contexts for their thinking" (p. 42).

Lupita's work during a Native American theme captures the value of bilingualism and especially biliteracy during theme studies in this classroom. All of Lupita's early work during an individual research project about the Sioux is written in Spanish. She webs her questions and ideas in Spanish, she writes personal research questions in Spanish, and she answers her questions on note cards in Spanish. At the end of the inquiry process, Lupita also presents her learning in Spanish, by writing a report for publication.

The intriguing component of Lupita's work, however, is the bibliography, shown in Figure 5-7. It records all of the resources Lupita examines in her search for answers to her questions. Those that she finds helpful are marked on the right side of the form so that they will

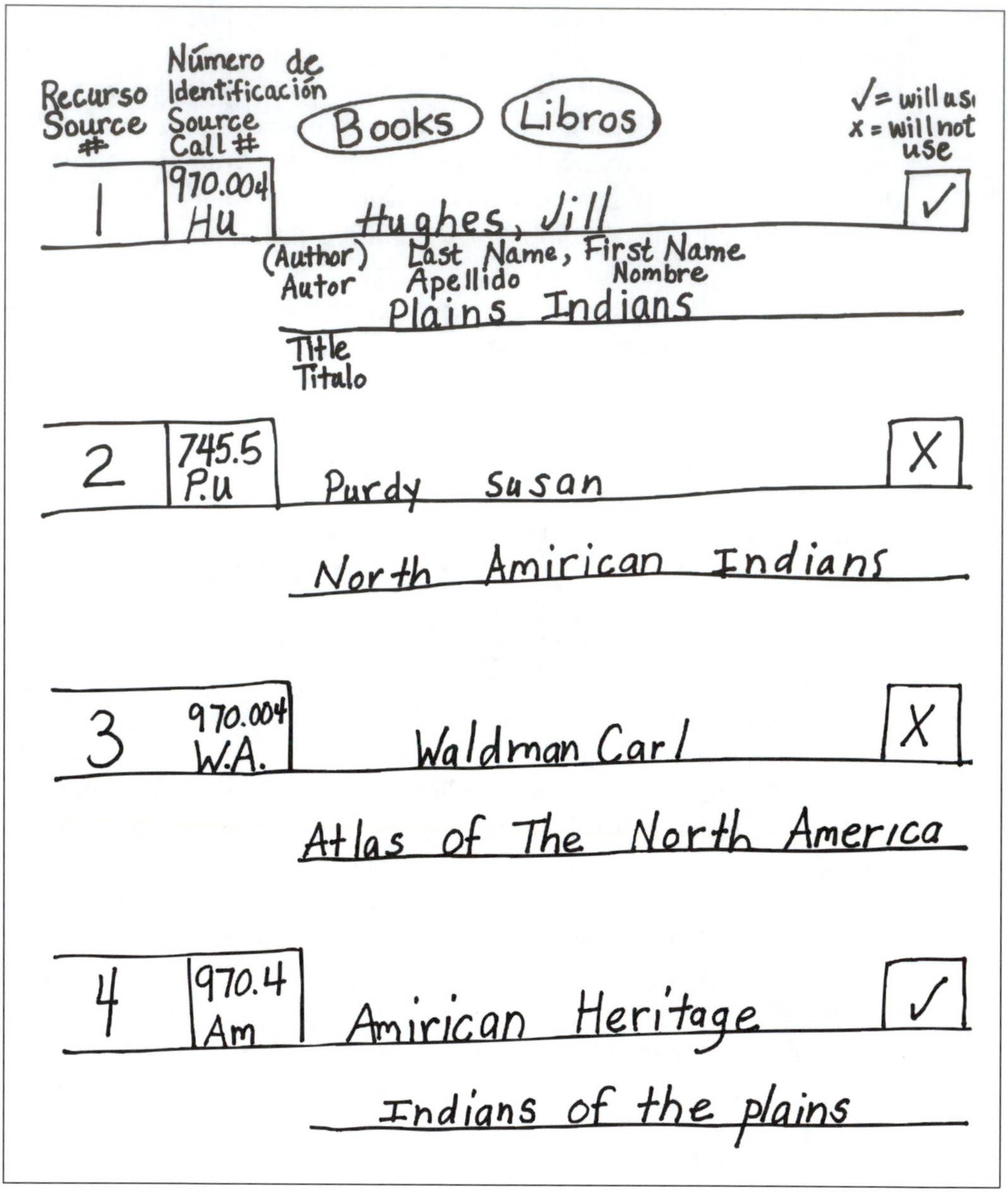

Recurso Source #
Número de Identificación Source Call #
Books
Libros
√= will use
x = will not use

1 | 970.004 Hu | Hughes, Jill | √
(Author) Autor — Last Name, First Name — Apellido Nombre
Plains Indians
Title Titalo

2 | 745.5 P.u | Purdy susan | X
North Amirican Indians

3 | 970.004 W.A. | Waldman Carl | X
Atlas of The North America

4 | 970.4 Am | Amirican Heritage | √
Indians of the plains

Figure 5-7. One page of Lupita's resources for her Native American Research.

easily transfer onto her reference list. Each item on this list, which in actuality is several pages long, is published in English. Lupita has posed questions in Spanish, read reference materials in English, and written her answers and their summation in Spanish, demonstrating the strength of bilingualism and biliteracy as resources in classrooms. The potential for literate thinking (Wells 1989) for all children is increased by valuing multiple linguistic systems in school. Lupita's work illustrates a naturally occurring bilingual zone of proximal development (Moll & Díaz 1987).

Children's personal goals for second language learning are built into Borton's goals for bilingualism and biculturalism. Several students each year in Caryl's room set personal goals to become adept at their second language, whether English or Spanish. One year Brooke challenges herself to write a report about the sea in Spanish at the end of a theme study. Another time, Seaaira selects a Spanish-only literature group to push her own linguistic development.

Caryl consciously moves children toward bilingualism and biliteracy, but often in quiet, gentle ways. For example, in addition to the expectation that materials and experiences will always be provided in Spanish and English, she occasionally suggests a specific language for a child to use during a literacy event. Based on her knowledge of her students and her ability to mediate their movement through individual and collective zones of proximal development (Moll & Whitmore 1993), she knows when to urge children to stretch their language abilities into a new genre or try a new author who writes more complicated plots.

On the other hand, when the content of reading material is new to a child, she might suggest he read in the language in which he is more comfortable and confident, once again making sure that the child is successful in gaining meaning from the experience. In these situations, Caryl is aware of how the children's individual zones of proximal development are influenced by changes in the context surrounding language use.

For instance, as part of the theme about the sea, Lolita and a number of other students are waiting to receive materials from Caryl to complete a strategy lesson on note taking. Each child receives a copy of an article about a sea animal, which he or she then takes to a seat in the classroom to read and use for sketching notes. As the children approach Caryl one by one, they tell her in which language they want to read.

Typically, Caryl responds by handing the child the materials in the language she's requested. When Lolita arrives for her turn, however,

Caryl says, "Lolita, why don't you try this in Spanish today." When Lolita agrees without hesitation, Caryl provides her with an article written in Spanish. Caryl later explains that she's noticed that Lolita hasn't been reading as much in Spanish lately. She knows that Lolita is equally comfortable in either language in school and she wants to encourage her to practice this new note-taking procedure while simultaneously ensuring that Lolita maintains and extends her facility with Spanish reading.

Bilingual individuals in the community outside of our school make choices about the language to use in any given situation based on who they are talking to, what materials they are using, the message they have to communicate, and the context in which they find themselves. I want the children in my classroom to make language choices based on the same conditions. When Lupita uses Spanish for all the writing she does in connection with her report on Native Americans, it's because she controls that language best, and because she recognizes the need for Spanish-language materials about the Sioux tribes she is studying. Her reading for information is done in English because that is the language of all the useful resource books we have in the room. The materials have controlled her choice of English in this instance.

For Lupita, these decisions are easy to make because she controls both languages very well in both their written and oral forms. Other children, who are still acquiring their second language, oftentimes must still make the choices that Lupita has made but need support to do so. When this happens, adults or other children help by reading and discussing in the native language as I did with Veronica. In this way, language never becomes an obstacle to learning. Children always have access to the information they need, either through their own bilingualism and biliteracy or through an intermediary.

Whenever possible, the children are expected to act as interpreters for each other. Many times during the year, children help Marisela in a variety of social and academic situations by translating comments for her and by supporting her attempts to communicate in her second language. When her mother visits the class during "Love of Reading" week to share her favorite childhood story, Marisela helps her classmates write thank-you notes in Spanish. These naturally occurring situations create opportunities for students' bil-

ingualism and biliteracy to function as important resources for learning and communication.

Inventing Whole Language Curriculum

Curriculum is a word that is bandied about in all types of educational circles—between parents as they compare experiences outside their children's classrooms, between teachers in staff meetings and the teachers' lounge, and in professional journals of educational research—and it has a wide range of sometimes ambiguous definitions. When I use the term, I refer to the actual learning engagements in the classroom, what Kathy Short and Carolyn Burke (1991) call "enacted curriculum."

Ken Goodman and colleagues (1987) propose a double agenda for schools: to create whole language curriculum that is thought and language centered and provides opportunities for learning to occur through language and thinking. They explain:

> The basic responsibility of school is to cultivate language and thinking and the knowledge which is acquired through their use. We see language and thinking as developing through the content of the curriculum and we see the development of knowledge in every area of the curriculum as always necessarily involving language and thinking. (p. 2)

The dual curriculum is a manifestation of the whole language philosophy that seeks to ensure that learners are provided with real, whole, purposeful, and language-centered school experiences. It is more likely that all learners will reach their potential as thinkers and intellectual language users through a whole language curriculum. Theme cycles are a natural organization for achieving the principles of whole language theory (Whitmore & Y. Goodman, in press).

Whole language puts integrated problem solving, as exemplified by the Middle Ages theme, at the center of curriculum development. It provides what Short and Burke call "uninterrupted engagements with meaning, [where] the focus is on classroom structures and activities that are open and allow learners at all levels of knowledge and proficiency to connect, in their own way, with those engagements" (1991, p. 36).

Whole language ideals for curriculum are not new, but are reinvented forms of progressive education curriculum, with deep historical roots in educational philosophy (Y. Goodman 1989; Miller 1990; Whitmore 1990a, 1990b). The ideas of progressive educators in recent history, like John Dewey and Hilda Taba, continue to influence present-day thinking. Taba and Elkins (1966), for example, call for an increase in the level of intellectual expectation for what they then termed "culturally disadvantaged" children. Although our more enlightened understanding of the role of culture in curriculum was in its infancy at the time of their writing, their ideas about curriculum implementation are valuable today. They say, "A serious attempt to change the educational program and to bring it into line with the life realities of these students produces some fairly radical changes in their functioning and in their capacity to learn" (p. 254).

They suggest that when children from parallel cultures are the learners it is especially important to

> allow each student to find his [or her] own way to the concept. . . . Both the gaining of command and contributing are of utmost importance, because involvement in what is being learned is absolutely necessary to keep the class going. Participation and contribution are part and parcel of that involvement. (p. 276)

Taba's emphasis on personal experience and involvement in active learning echoes the philosophy of John Dewey, for whom problem solving is the essential element of real learning.

> Dewey stressed that the school was a *community*. . . . [He] wanted schools to engage students in meaningful activities where they had to work with others on problems. Purposeful activity in social settings was the key to genuine learning in Dewey's view. (Phillips & Soltis 1991, p. 52–53)

The Middle Ages theme is typical of the content and processes that children experience in this classroom. Other themes, centered around different concepts or topics, evolve into different activities, experiences, and forms of presentation, but each follows the same basic process. Each provides a place, time, and necessary resources for children to invent curriculum through inquiry while they experience the conventions of the real world.

BOYS
SEASON
25

6

Inventing Classroom Discourse

Children's Questions About War

IN JANUARY 1991, the Sunshine Room's early morning classroom routine of reading picture books and recounting personal narratives changes dramatically. Half a world away, war breaks out in the Persian Gulf. Questions, comments, hopes, and fears take the place of the children's personal stories, and the daily newspaper replaces the picture books. For thirty or more minutes each morning, over several weeks, the class discusses the events of the world surrounding them and their country.

This chapter narrates how the Sunshine Room deals with the issue of war through literature study. By now you'll recognize some of the characters in this story, the children who have chosen to belong to this small group. Since Lolita is the only bilingual and biliterate child who chooses this literature study group, there is much less focus on second languages in this chapter than in others. In the Additive Bilingualism and Biliteracy section, however, we discuss biliteracy development based on other instances in the Sunshine Room.

Each day as the issues facing our country and the world become more heated and dangerous, the children ask questions related to the war: Where is the Persian Gulf? Why are we at war with them? How do gas masks work? Are Americans dying? Children and teachers worry for their family members and search for information about what is happening and why.

The newspaper provides limited information, both through articles and the captions of photographs. Each day, Caryl reads aloud from the paper that is delivered to the classroom. But the news focuses mostly on the technological nature of the war and does not adequately address the human issues that concern some of the children. Caryl responds to a clear need revealed by some children's questions for more information on the complex subject. She feels a responsibility to provide more accurate information to children who are witnessing a glossed-over, glorified view of war by the media.

To my dismay, most of the articles in the local paper concern the technological nature of the Persian Gulf war—the weapons, planes, communications systems—and the superiority of American and allied forces. There is little to give my students a picture of the harsh realities that accompany war, the devastation and death on both sides of the battle lines. The text set of picture books that I develop provides children with a humane, historically accurate look at war over time, particularly related to U.S. history, to help them answer their questions and to counter the distorted view of war they are receiving from mass media.

Caryl's uses of text sets in the classroom are described in Chapter 4. Jerry Harste, Kathy Short, and Carolyn Burke (1988) describe text sets as

> two or more texts that are related in some way, [to encourage children] to share and extend their comprehension of each text differently than if only one text had been read and discussed. (p. 358)

Books that are organized into text sets encourage discussion and comparison. They highlight connections between reading experiences and life experiences for children, and they help them understanding related texts. As a result of Caryl's thinking about the questions the children have about the issue of the United States at war in the Middle East, she puts together a text set of materials that come to be known as "the war and peace books." This text set provides the reading material for a literature study group.

The whole class is presented with the war and peace books along with several other choices of text sets and single titles offered for the next literature study groups. In book talks, Caryl describes each book or group of books, shares illustrations, background information about the authors and/or illustrators, and makes connections between the texts and other shared experiences of the group. The choices enable Caryl to provide a range of possible experiences for the children to select. At this time, two of the choices available to the children for literature study are related to the ongoing curriculum theme of the ocean:

- Barbara Cooney books (*Miss Rumphius, Island Boy*). This set provides an opportunity for children to extend their current ocean theme by reading two books by the same author.
- Ocean books (a collection of fiction, nonfiction, and poetry related to the ocean). This set also extends the learning from the ocean theme, but provides an opportunity to read related books in either Spanish or English or both.

The three additional choices relate to the issue of war and peace:

- *La guerra de los hermanos* (*The War of the Brothers*). This selection of a single text helps children develop an understanding of the Aztec heritage of some children in the class in conjunction with war events.
- *Number the Stars,* by Lois Lowry. This selection, a longer award-winning novel written for children, pushes some readers into a more complex text about war.
- War and peace books (a collection of fiction, nonfiction, and poetry about U.S. involvements in war). This selection of picture books provides a forum for extended discussion about the war in Iraq. (These books are listed in Appendix B.)

I've chosen the books for this set very carefully. As a Jew, my own upbringing included vivid stories and photographs of the Holocaust. I realize these are not suitable for children who are about to come to grips for the first time with the suffering and atrocities committed by some human beings against others. Many of the books are included because they present characters of about the same age as my students. Rose Blanche, My Hiroshima, Thunder at Gettysburg, The Wall, *and* Number the Stars *all revolve around school-age children who become caught up in events beyond their control, characters who display courage and hope in the face of despair. A few nonfiction books contain information and photographs of war victims and devastated towns and cities, others are the true stories of survivors. The children page through these books, but choose to obtain most of the historical information they need in the context of our discussions.*

Five boys and three girls—Mark, Aaron, Travis, Trevor, and Colin, Seaaira, Lolita, and Elizabeth— select the war and peace text set as their first or second choice. The group meets with Caryl at the beginning of the literature study and mutually determines that they will first explore the collection of books informally and reconvene another day to negotiate their future operation. Many of the children pair off with a buddy to read; a few children make individual selections and settle in around the room to read alone.

A few days later, the children meet with Caryl to negotiate the process they want to follow during their group meetings. Caryl's intention is for the children to spend a week or two reading the different books in the set and then discuss the commonalities about war they discover in the books while connecting them to current events. Although she knows that not every child will read every book, at least not at the same time, she anticipates that the children will discuss across the set.

The children do compare books as Caryl expects and as is implied by a text set organization. However, they elect to discuss several of the books intensely, one at a time, more like a series of shared book groups (Harste, Short & Burke 1988). They decide they want to treat each book separately and make sure that everyone has read the book they are discussing when the time comes. So, at the close of each discussion, the children negotiate the next book they will focus on. The book they choose for the focus of the next discussion is selected by group consensus and passed around systematically before the next meeting to ensure that each child can read it and prepare for the discussion. The children take responsibility for this process. I also try to read each book before it is discussed.

Figure 6-1 summarizes the overall literature study by topic, time spent on each topic, and participants involved in the discussions. Audiotaping, transcribing, and analyzing have been of key importance in our understanding of how and why this group (and others) operates as it does. In the remainder of this chapter, Caryl and I use the terms *discussion* and *conversation* separately. We've captured the group's talk on ten audiotapes, each of which we refer to as a discussion. Within these discussions, multiple smaller conversations occur.

Caryl and I analyzed the structure and content of seven of the ten discussions in detail. The process by which we accomplished this analysis has been essential to our understanding of how this literature study group operates, but also of how a variety of types of interactions occur in the Sunshine Room. Indeed, intertwining the structure and content analyses in this chapter brought us together as a research team and led us to our joint understanding of what enables the Sunshine Room in general to invent itself as it does over the course of a year. The structural analysis, wherein we count turns and qualitatively describe turns participants take, is essential. The complexities of the structures in these discussions are summarized in the Power and Trust Relationships section of this chapter. The content analysis is reflected in the narrative of the critical event and elsewhere.

In the summary in Figure 6-1, the seven discussions we analyzed in detail are marked with an asterisk. They show a total time for each discussion, noted in minutes and seconds (min.sec). We find the length of time the children are captivated by their discussions unusual and remarkable when we remember these are eight- and nine-year-old children. Three discussions (1, 7, 9a) occur without an adult present; the children audiotape themselves, or Caryl or I place the recorder in the middle of the circle without becoming a participating member of the group. Discussion 9 occurs in two parts, one right after the other: after the children discuss *My Hiroshima* at length on their own (9a), Caryl and I join the discussion to clarify misconceptions about historical events and answer questions related to the text (9b).

The literature study really begins on February 20, when the children gather around several bins of war and peace books at an art table. No adult is present; although a substitute teacher is in the room, she is busy with other children. I am watching with great interest, but I stay outside the boundaries of the group, deemphasizing the children's awareness of me as much as I am able.

I've placed a running tape recorder in the center of the table, however, and this becomes the first recorded discussion in the literature study. Although individual children have done some limited reading at this point, this is also the children's first shared exploration of the text set. I am fascinated by what happens, although none of us (Caryl and the children included) quite realize at the time the value of what is occurring.

The startling realities of World War II and Hitler's involvement in the lives of Jews is the most harsh and captivating topic of the first day's discussion. Aaron, who is the only Jewish child in the group (Caryl is also Jewish but she is absent today), quickly becomes the expert, answering queries posed by other less-experienced members of the group to the best of his ability. Seaaira, the most openly innocent of the children in this regard, quickly takes the role of overt

Disc.(time)	Date	Topic	Participants
1* (24.48)	2/20/91	Text set	Children/no adult
2	2/25/91	*Rose Blanche*	Children/Caryl
3* (20.10)	2/27/91	*Rose Blanche*	Children/Caryl
4	3/05/91	Organizational	Children/Caryl
5* (18.00)	3/06/91	*Rose Blanche*	Children/Caryl
6	3/11/91	*The Wall*	Children/Caryl
7* (8.15)	3/20/91	*Faithful Elephants*	Children/no adult
8* (18.22)	3/21/91	*Butter Battle*	Children/Kathy
9a* (45.30)	4/02/91	*My Hiroshima*	Children/no adult
9b*		*My Hiroshima*	With Caryl/Kathy
10* (28.20)	4/05/91	Text set summary	Children/Caryl

Figure 6-1. Description of war and peace literature study by discussion session.

questioner. This is Seaaira's initiation into the concept of the Holocaust. She has large gaps in her background knowledge about war and U.S. history, as most eight-year-olds do, and is horrified, while fascinated, by the illustrations and written texts of the books she explores. The books expose Seaaira to concentration camps, children's deaths during World War II, and blatant discrimination against Jews, and she is impressed by the seemingly knowledgeable comments of her peers. Aaron and Seaaira's roles are obvious even to them.

At one point, Aaron asks Seaaira, "How come you're asking me all these questions?"

Seaaira responds, "'Cause you know more about the war than I do. 'Cuz you're Jewish and I'm not Jewish."

As the children browse through the collection, they read captions, study illustrations, and skip through entire volumes instead of concentrating on reading any one text.

Aaron is speaking when the tape begins. "I know. They're taking him to the uh, concentration camps."

Seaaira begins, "'Cause he's—"

"Jewish," interrupts Travis.

"Jewish?" she asks.

"They want to capture everybody who's different."

"Yeah," agrees Aaron. "Everybody who's different."

Seaaira naively asks, "What do they do at the concentration camps?"

"Well unfortunately they kill 'em," Aaron gently confides. "'Cause they go into like these showers and gas comes out."

"And it's poison."

"Poison gas comes out and then they die."

Travis adds, "They either get killed, they either get killed in the furnace or starvation."

"*Huge* furnace," says Colin.

Aaron continues, "Either starvation 'cause they know the fence is electrocute, will electrocute you."

All the children are involved in the discussion by this time.

"Or they—"

But Colin summarizes bluntly for his friends, "Seaaira, they stuff 'em in huge furnaces. Aaron, they stuff 'em in huge furnaces."

"Yeah, I know," murmurs Aaron.

Colin finishes his statement. "And turned on the gas."

"That's sad," says Seaaira, her eyes wide with new understanding.

Aaron comments soberly, "They thought it was showers."

The children's conversation shows their confrontation with the reality of these historical facts as they sink in, particularly the understanding that Aaron could have been involved in such an event as a Jew. Seaaira asks directly, "Like if you were alive back then you would be getting tooken to a concentration camp?" and Aaron's friends vow that they would have protected him from the Nazis.

The group establishes an initial definition of what it meant to be "different" during the Holocaust. Their comments show their childhood naïveté and their shared lack of knowledge at the outset of the study. Aaron's comment as the conversation continues conveys the strong link (be it accurate or not) between historical and current events that repeatedly enters the children's talk.

Seaaira, looking at a photograph in one book, says, "That's the concentration camps. And they put stars on them all?"

"Yeah," explains Aaron, "To show if they're Jewish. Those are the Jewish people and the people who don't have stars are just plain people who are different from 'em."

"Retarded?" she asks.

"Well, some of them are," he responds.

Travis joins in, "Yep, anyone who's retarded, anyone different."

"Anyone who has AIDS, any sickness," states Aaron.

The books involving the Holocaust and World War II capture the students' greatest attention for the remainder of this discussion. However, a nonfiction book titled *Why Do Wars Happen?* also stirs a lively discussion. In several of the book's photographs, African children are shown preparing for war. Many hold weapons of various types and this piques the children's curiosity, particularly Colin's.

Colin points at a black-and-white photograph. "This kid right here has, that's a real gun." He sounds amazed.

"I know."

Seaaira, the perpetual questioner, asks, "How come he's holding a real—that kid on the front's—"

"I think, he's in the ar—This kid?"

Aaron says, "Yeah, they're in the army."

"Because he's, I think he's got it so they can protect himself," suggests Colin.

"He's in the ar—But he's only little!" exclaims Seaaira.

"I know, but look at all these kids."

"But how come they have guns?"

Travis feels shut out of the conversation, "Can I see, can I see, Colin?"

As Colin gives Travis the book, he says, "Look at, this one isn't real, but look at this one," pointing to a rifle.

Trevor is now drawn into the conversation. "He's using a fake gun in war! Why is he using a fake gun in war?"

Colin answers, "I don't think they're in war. Lookit. I'm pretty sure this gun's real but I'm sure that this gun's real. Look at those bullets. Real bullets."

The children move on to other books, other photographs and illustrations, and other topics, including the attack on Pearl Harbor.

This general and informal discussion about the war and peace books initiates six weeks of lively discourse, authentic questions, and serious attempts to understand personally relevant social issues through the construction of a social meaning for literature texts. This initial meeting generates a set of patterns for the meetings to come. For example, a procedure for initiating conversation topics is established. New conversations often begin as a result of a child's attention to an illustration, as you'll see in the rest of the story.

Also, evaluation of the discussions is embedded in them, as is an assessment of the quality of the literature. The children will show you how they self-monitor their participation and the quality of their interactions while they talk. And—something very important—implicit rules for interaction as a speech community are established early on. It is clear that it is acceptable to interrupt one another, for example, and that conversations should be initiated by the children rather than Caryl. Toward the end of the literature study, Caryl and I realize that all of these patterns are established by way of posing and resolving questions, as the details of the discussions and conversations will show.

Questions About History

Through all of the discussions this group has, the children sort out historical fact from childlike innocence as they ask each other questions and search for solutions together. Caryl is only one resource for information, and only when she's a participant. Inquiries about how Jewish people were identified during the Holocaust initiate one conversation to which Caryl contributes her knowledge.

Trevor asks, "What does the star [on characters' clothing in an illustration from *Rose Blanche*] mean?"

"It means they are Jewish," answers Aaron.

"See this, Trevor. This symbol right here in my hand." Caryl shows Trevor the star of David that always hangs from a gold chain around her neck. The children examine the necklace and compare it with the picture in the book.

In another conversation, when America's role in World War II is questioned in the context of America's role in the Persian Gulf, Caryl shares her more advanced knowledge about these issues. Travis wonders how Americans responded to the nightmare of the Holocaust: "Did the Americans help the Jewish people?"

Caryl answers, "They tried. They tried. There's a lot of controversy."

Travis then makes a connection to the present war situation. "I've been hearing a lot about the Americans helping Israel, the Israelis." He's referring to the use of American SCUD missiles to protect Israel from Iraqi fire, something vividly detailed by the national media during the war he's experiencing at the time.

Similar connections between history and the current war are made frequently as the study progresses. The children are quick to condemn the United States for dropping an atomic bomb in Japan, as is depicted in the picture book *My Hiroshima*, by Junko Morimoto.

The book includes graphic illustrations that move the children emotionally and intellectually.

Travis says, "But there's some really sad pictures in here."

"She thought the plane was really far away," comments Aaron. "It shows the baby kind of flying away from the mother."

"And all the hands reaching up," notes Trevor.

Travis says, "It's sad, because it shows all these pictures of people with hardly any clothes on, ripped and torn and bombed and bloody."

"It looks like their skin's peeling off," notes Aaron.

"I'm sure it is," says Colin.

Aaron, who brings funds of knowledge about art to school with him, comments on the quality of the illustration as well as the content. "The author really made the illustrations with a lot of expression." He pauses. "That author was really expressional."

As the talk continues, the children are horrified when they realize that innocent people, including young children, were intentionally bombed by the United States. The children associate the historical bombing in Japan with the recent bombing of Israel.

Travis states his opinion. "They could've bombed at least on an air force base, not where people were innocent. That would be just like Iraq coming over here and bombing us, and we're innocent. Or like we going over there and bombing innocent people, which did happen. And Iraq bombing Israel." The intonation of Travis's voice reflects his awakening understanding.

"They were bombing innocent people that weren't even in the war," confirms Trevor.

"I know," agrees Aaron. "They were bombing Israel."

During another conversation the children associate significant personalities from two periods of history, Adolf Hitler and Saddam Hussein.

Travis remarks, "And some of [Hitler's] men hated him, didn't like what he was doing."

"Well," Seaaira interjects with emphasis, "well, same about Saddam Hussein."

Seaaira's comment hits Travis like lightening. "Ah!" he exclaims, "Hitler's like Saddam Hussein."

"Exactly," says Trevor. His voice smacks with newfound authority.

One day, I share a television news report with the children about the plight of the animals in the Kuwaiti zoo during the Persian Gulf conflict. Later, the children discuss the tragic story *Faithful*

Elephants, by Yukio Tsuchiya. It describes how zoo keepers in Tokyo had to euthanize the potentially dangerous zoo animals when the Allies began bombing the city.

Seaaira recalls my earlier comments when she says, "But you know, in the Gulf War, they had to do this too."

"Yeah."

She continues, "They had to kill them in Kuwait 'cause what if the animals got loose and ran away and started knocking down the people's houses just before the bomb."

"And killing people," adds Colin.

"But that's mean that they had to kill them and then the Gulf War ended. They killed the animals and then the war ended."

Slowly, over weeks of confronting the historical facts that underlie wars and hypothesizing about their causes and the fates of those most intimately involved, the children begin to put the current war into a new perspective. One day, they explore their beliefs about the Persian Gulf war.

Colin proposes his view of how wars can begin. "Yeah, because, like one kind of people don't like the way that the other people do things, and so they decide that they want to stop those people. So, they get into a war trying to change the other people's ways."

Seaaira reveals an awareness of her own growth in knowledge about war, something evidenced repeatedly in her comments throughout the discussions. "I thought in wars everybody got killed. But in the Iraqi war, when they were fighting the air war, I didn't believe there was such a thing as a air war. I thought there was only a ground war. And then how only twenty people got killed in the air war."

"There weren't many Americans, right," confirms Caryl.

"Only about twenty-five," answers Colin.

Caryl prompts some more thinking. "I just wonder about the Iraqis."

"That's what I mean," says Seaaira.

Colin voices a realization for the group. "Only twenty-five [Americans] got killed, but we killed hundreds, maybe thousands."

Questions About a Character

Roberto Innocenti's *Rose Blanche* is a captivating story about a small girl who accidently discovers a concentration camp and returns repeatedly to feed the prisoners. One illustration prompts several days of discussion about Rose Blanche's motivation for helping the prisoners and the circumstances surrounding her eventual death. It shows Rose Blanche, with a Nazi flag in her hand, patriotically waving at a procession of soldiers through her town.

Seaaira opens the conversation about this book with one of her typical questions. "How come she's waving a Nazi flag?"

"That's what Travis's question was," says Aaron, who had been Travis's buddy when they read this book the day before.

"'Cause right there she is waving a Nazi flag," Seaaira points to the illustration.

"What do some of you think about that?" asks Caryl.

"Well, I couldn't, I kind of tried to answer some of his questions about that but I didn't really know it either," admits Aaron.

Travis suggests one explanation. "I thought that since she was German and she was waving a Nazi flag, I didn't know what was wrong, 'cause she may have pretended to be a Nazi so she wouldn't get captured that's what I thought."

"Well," begins Aaron, "I think, I don't think she—"

"Maybe they were forcing her," ponders Seaaira.

"Yeah, but why would she be smiling?" asks Trevor.

Aaron argues, "If they were forcing her, they would take her—"

"To the concentration camp?" worries Seaaria.

"But, why would she be smiling then if she was, ya know, if she was being forced?" Trevor asks.

This conversation continues for over twenty minutes. The depth of the children's unresolved questions urges them to continue the *Rose Blanche* discussion the next day. Finally, three discussion days later, Colin offers a new hypothesis for the group's consideration. "Ms. Crowell, I think one of the reasons that when she was waving that is because a lot of the people didn't know that the Nazis were so mean to the, to the Ger, um to all those people."

Travis agrees. "Yeah."

Aaron also agrees calmly. "Yeah."

But Trevor reacts strongly to this idea, suddenly exclaiming, "Wow! I never thought of that."

"You hadn't thought of that before?" Caryl asks him.

"No, I think that might be right."

"Why do you think so, Trevor, why does that make sense to you now?"

"I just didn't know. I just didn't know about that. I thought everybody in the world knew that Nazis were mean."

Trevor's statements magnify his new understanding about the text he's read and about the world. They illustrate two important things that occur several times in these discussions. First, Trevor demonstrates the children's willingness to pursue responses to their questions over time without requiring immediate correct answers. Second, he highlights the social nature of the children's learning. Reading the text set and making meaning from the experience is a social transaction mediated by oral language. Trevor couldn't have reached this "aha" conclusion if he had been reading alone. He needs the group's mutual construction of meaning to make his own personal sense of the text.

Travis, the originator of the central question about Rose Blanche's intent in carrying the Nazi flag, also becomes aware of the learning he is accomplishing through others. One day he states, "'Cause it says somewhere in there that the little girl is German."

"It does?" asks Aaron with surprise.

"Uh-huh."

"Then how come you're asking me why she was waving a Nazi flag?"

"I know." Travis admits the incongruity of his earlier question and the statement he just made. "Well, I didn't know the first time I saw it but I just went over it a little."

In actuality, Travis has experienced the benefits of the group's concentrated effort to come to an understanding about a shared question. Important questions generated by the group take time, extended conversations, and the suggestion of multiple hypotheses before they are resolved to the children's satisfaction.

Questions About Questions

According to our count, almost one-fourth of all the turns (24 percent) that the children take over the course of the entire literature study are phrased as questions. We think this is a marker of the inquiry-like nature of the discussion. Sometimes the children talk about questions and how they use them as a strategy for discussing and evaluating literature. They pose difficult questions of themselves and are determined to continue searching until they find acceptable answers.

The children are very aware of how their questioning impacts their talking and learning about the books. One day, during the extended discussions about *Rose Blanche,* Aaron comments, "This book gives you a lot of questions."

"Doesn't it," Caryl agrees. "I have a lot of questions too when I read that book."

"Every time I read it, I usually have questions about it."

"How many times have you read that book, Aaron?"

"About three times."

"And do you have different questions each time that you read it?"

"Yeah."

Travis says, "Because this book has a lot of questions . . . I might write a book about all the questions I have in here."

The children display a metalinguistic awareness, or the ability to talk about language, in terms of their discussion process. They recognize that the time spent raising difficult questions is important to their group's process. Questions become indicators of successful talks, of quality literature, and of completed topics for the children.

Resolution of questions, for example, indicates that the group can finish a discussion of one book and move on to a new topic. Following a pause of twelve seconds at the end of their conversation about *Faithful Elephants,* Lolita negotiates a plan for the group's next meeting:

"Do you guys want to talk about this book again?"

"Nah," the group choruses.

"I solved all my questions," Travis states matter-of-factly, apparently equating "solving questions" with the purpose of the discussions about each book.

The number and level of complexity of the questions raised also indicates the quality of literature and conversation for the children. The group realizes that some authors intentionally leave room for readers to develop their own responses to texts and that understanding this writing strategy provides content for their discussions.

Caryl says, "It's hard when the author doesn't directly say it. You have to kind of figure it out on your own, don't you?"

"Yeah."

"I don't like when they leave questions and they never answer them," Seaaira says.

"Do you think the author did that on purpose?" asks Caryl.

"Yes," says Travis.

"Why do you think the author did that?"

"So you could decide your own answers," he replies.

The Butter Battle Book is a pivotal text relative to the children's growing value of questions as a literary technique. In *The Butter*

Battle Book, Dr. Seuss's allegory of the arms race, the characters on two opposing sides develop continuously more sophisticated weapons until, at the end of the book, both sides are poised at a wall holding their ultimate weapons of destruction. When the children describe this unresolved ending as boring, I'm surprised.

"What do you think?" I ask the children. "You guys usually have so many ideas. You're so quiet today."

Travis tells me, "'Cause this book isn't the best book."

"It's not the best book?"

"No."

"What makes you say that?"

"It's boring," Travis says. "Well, it's not boring, it's just—there's nothing. There's no questions, nothing to talk about."

"The only question is what happens," suggests Colin.

"And that's a dumb question," Travis thinks. "In all the other books, it tells you what happens, but there's more questions. Like in *Rose Blanche,* there's more questions. That means they're more interesting."

Elizabeth, so often quiet and seated on the perimeter of the group, eloquently defines "good questions" during this conversation. "What makes a question good," she asserts, "is, if, because if the question is real hard to answer it, and you don't really know it, and it takes a long time to find out, that's what makes it interesting."

We all agree.

Trevor restates the group's critique of *The Butter Battle Book* at the study group's final meeting, when Caryl is present and leading the discussion.

"There was *The Butter Battle Book,*" offers Aaron.

"I wasn't here the day you talked about *The Butter Battle Book,* tell me about that. I missed that."

Trevor tries to summarize. "We didn't really. It wasn't a question book except for what happened at the end."

"What do you mean it wasn't a question book?" asks Caryl.

"It didn't have any questions hardly except for at the back."

"So you didn't like that one?"

Aaron says, "Well, we liked it but it wasn't that—"

"It didn't make you think," states Trevor.

Using their own criterion of asking good questions in response to illustrations and stories that evoke personal, emotional reactions, the children unanimously choose *Rose Blanche* and *My Hiroshima* as their favorite books. Aaron and Trevor articulate the group's mutual agreement.

Aaron says, "But these two books are the best."

"Yeah, the sadder they are, the gooder they get," adds Trevor.

"I liked *Rose Blanche* and *My Hiroshima* because they make you kind of really feel it. The author does."

"Me, too. Those were my two favorites. I think we like talked about them the most."

"The authors made you think. They really made you feel it," says Aaron.

"And wonder what it was like," finishes Trevor.

Understanding War Through Books

The children in the war and peace literature study group, through their conversations, clarify their questions about the human element of war. They grow in their understanding about why wars happen, about what constitutes a war, and about how its impact is felt on both sides. On the final day they meet as a literature study group, the children all share with Caryl how much they have learned about the historical contexts depicted in the books and how their thinking on those subjects has changed.

Caryl begins with a request. "Think about whether or not the books that we've read have had any kind of impact on your thinking, if they've helped you understand a little better about what's going on [in the Middle East] or changed your thinking in any way."

She and I, as well as another teacher who is visiting that day, sit in awe as we listen to the children's responses.

"I've changed my thoughts about war," Trevor begins without a moment's hesitation. "I used to, like, play war, but now it makes me sick."

Travis builds on his idea. "Now I think about it a lot more . . . what's going on, what was going on in Iraq and about other stuff."

"I felt the same way as Trevor did," says Colin. "Now I just don't play that way any more because I think it's so gross, after I read the books."

Aaron agrees. "I did both [played with war toys and acted out roles in war games]. But then, when I was reading the books, I didn't play with them that much."

The girls jump into the conversation less quickly. But when there is a pause, Lolita quietly contributes, "I don't fight as much with my brother any more." Her comment, perhaps less dramatic on the surface, articulates how strongly the children have been changed personally, in their real lives, by this reading experience. She articulates in a small and inexuberant way that she has internalized the concept of "conflict" and how it plays out in her life, not just the lives of those involved in war on a larger scale.

The children's innocence early in the literature study is revealed during that first day of interaction, when the children gather around the books and voice their knowledge about war. By the conclusion of the study, this group of eight- and nine-year-old children has acquired a comparatively mature understanding about the realities of war. This maturity can be interpreted through the issues salient to all events in the Sunshine Room: high level of intellectual expectation, symmetric power and trust relationships, authenticity, and additive bilingualism and biliteracy.

High Level of Intellectual Expectation

The result of these children's collaborative attempt, through literature, to understand their world and what is happening in it is learning and thinking of a high academic quality. It is also learning of a very serious and mature nature, given its subject matter. Much of the children's conceptual learning occurs as they ask questions together, voice their questions to one another and to Caryl and me, and resolve their questions over time through collaboration. During a large portion of the war and peace literature study discussions, the children are trying to resolve their questions about the historical settings and events depicted in the literature and about why the war in the Persian Gulf has occurred. The literature study is inquiry centered, opening the potential for intellectual challenge to the children's needs and interests.

Although the questions the children ask—their questions about history, for example—are of instructional value, they go much further than the types asked at the ends of chapters in social studies textbooks or basal readers. The literature group's questions are driven by a heartfelt quest for knowledge and understanding. When Travis ponders, "I wonder what it was like in the war," and Aaron explains how the best books are those that make you "really feel it," the children are tying their real questions about the world to their academic learning experience. In the Sunshine Room, this natural connection meets Dewey's goal for curriculum: "to start where the learner is in time, place, culture, and development" (K. Goodman 1992, p. 40). It also connects children's emotional response in the real world to their emotional and aesthetic response to quality literature.

Gordon Wells' work (1989) helps me value the content of the children's discussions. He says that language researchers and educators should be asking how it is that any language event in the classroom enhances the development of children's literate thinking. Literate thinking, in his words, "refers to all those uses of language in which its symbolic potential is deliberately exploited as a tool for thinking" (p. 253). Wells argues the inappropriateness of the dichotomy between speech and written language, explaining that the *quality* of oral language in the classroom needs to improve, not the *quantity* of talk increase. He continues, "From the point of view of intellectual development, therefore, what is important about reading and writing is not so much the communication of information, as the possibility of developing ways of using language as an intentionally controlled tool for thinking and feeling" (p. 254).

Wells' ideas about literate thinking are helpful in interpreting the war and peace literature study because his transcripts of third- and fourth-grade children's talk are similar to Caryl's and my transcripts of her students' talk. Wells listened to children talk while they planned a theme-centered experience. From his transcripts of what he calls "collaborative talk," we see how children's interests extend their knowledge and challenge them to develop their thinking. In a classroom that is a "community of collaborative enquirers" (p. 269), the children Wells studied, "from lower class, ethnic communities in which a language other than English is the main medium of communication" (p. 271), have the opportunity and the support to discover interests and abilities of a high intellectual level of expectation.

The war and peace literature study group is a similar collaborative group, created in response to children's questions about the world. Wells suggests that children's asking their own questions has the political effect of empowering them as learners. Courtney Cazden (1989), though, claims that ways of speaking in English-speaking classrooms impose implicit evaluation criteria that must be made explicit by teachers if children from "non-dominant speech communities—working-class students, those from linguistic and cultural minorities, and any who are learning varieties of English as a second language" (p. 116) are to be protected from further disadvantages.

The children's conversations about war and peace books suggest to me that rather than explicitly teach children "English for academic purposes" (Cazden 1989), we need to guide children in the process of inquiry, challenge them to ask personal questions, and provide them with multiple opportunities to seek their own answers through socially mediated experiences in school.

As Wells (1989) concludes, "Where the aim of the teacher is to facilitate each individual's construction of knowledge through literate thinking and collaborative talk in the context of student-chosen topics of enquiry, all learners will be empowered, whatever the background from which they come" (p. 271).

Ultimately, the children in the war and peace literature study group come to understand the power of questioning and its role in their personal and social learning processes. Caryl promotes children's control of the content of discussions through questioning, based on her trust of them as learners. Her trust enables her to set high expectations for them; their trust in her allows them to take risks, to experiment, and to collaborate with her in exploring their world through language.

When I mention my decision to initiate this war and peace literature study group in presentations to other teachers and preservice education students, it is often questioned. "Don't you think these children are a little young for these books and the subject of these discussions?" "Do you think they really understand the historical importance of these wars?" Nonetheless, the askers of these questions are impressed with the obvious quality of our proceedings. This literature study group is started in response to my students' desire *to discuss what they see happening every single day in the newspapers and on television.*

Precisely because they lack historical knowledge, the children are fearful for their lives. The fact that innocent civilians in Israel are being shelled by the Iraqis is not lost on them. They don't know that the continental United States has never come under enemy attack. Seaaira admits that whenever she hears a siren, she wonders if it's an air raid warning like the ones she hears on the news broadcasts. The children are aware through local newscasts that Tucson has an Air Force base, and that detachments of A-10s with pilots and mechanics based here have been sent to Kuwait. Some children have parents who work for Hughes Missile Systems and know that Tucson was once surrounded by siloed missiles. They know that Borton students and staff have spouses, parents, brothers, sisters, and other family members among the U.S. troops engaged in the fighting.

These are all issues we talk about honestly. The children's fear is real, and so is their need to talk about it.

Symmetric Power and Trust Relationships

I recognize that children have power as language participants in the Sunshine Room during literature study groups. Their power is reflected in many ways: in the fact that they've chosen to belong to the group, in the manner in which they've organized their meetings against the expectations of their teacher, in the substance or content of their conversations, and in the structure of their discourse.

It is through our detailed analysis of the structure of these discussions, particularly the ways the participants take turns, that I realize that these children have unique power in their talk in school. As I listen to their talk, and later when I pore over the transcripts with Caryl and by myself, I come to realize that this discourse contains features that do not match the discourse described as taking place in typical classrooms. The children determine their own turns of talk on a predictable basis, they gaze at one another as they speak, and they choose what they will talk about. They compete with one another and the teacher for attention and the floor. They freely interrupt one another, and they ignore attempted initiations that don't meet the goals of the group, even if they are made by their teacher.

These features contrast strongly with the types of discourse behaviors children display in transmission-oriented classrooms. Susan Philips (1983) is an anthropologist who compared the communication systems of home and school on the Warm Springs Indian Reservation. She found that teachers control virtually every component of every speech act in what she calls the "official" structure of classrooms. They are the focus of attention while they talk, they allocate turns of talk, they interrupt without permitting interruptions of their own turns, and they determine how students will be organized and involved. Discourse structures in other classrooms are similarly described (see Board 1982 for specific references to reading instruction; Moll & Díaz 1987 for biliteracy development; and Rosebery, Warren & Conant 1992 for scientific discourse).

Part of a student's job in school is to learn the rules of the official structure of language. As Philips says,

> In traditional grade school classrooms, children are expected to master not only the content of curriculum material presented by the

teacher, but also the socially appropriate use of communicative resources through which such mastery is demonstrated. (p. 73)

Philips also identifies an "infrastructure" in the classroom, which is the communication that occurs between students and away from the teacher's control and instruction. This type of communication is controlled by the students. Topics are usually not related to instruction. In fact, teachers typically attempt to keep children from using the infrastructure because it calls students' attention away from the official structure, which they control.

Educational and anthropological research has described the rules of the official structure in school talk in great detail. I use three features of classroom discourse that are predictable in transmission settings—turn-taking patterns, number and type of turns teachers and students take, and the amount of time "on" or "off" task—to interpret the power structures in the war and peace group.

Turn-taking Patterns

In typical transmission classrooms, teachers are known to encourage a teacher—student—teacher turn-taking pattern (Board 1982; Cazden 1988; Mehan 1979; Philips 1983; Saville-Troike & Kleifgen 1989; Wells 1989). In *Classroom Discourse* (1988), Courtney Cazden outlines this common pattern in reference to a typical sharing, or show and tell, time. She says, "[They] all have the same basic structure: (1) The teacher initiates the sequence by calling on a child to share; (2) the nominated child responds by telling a narrative; and (3) the teacher comments on the narrative before calling on the next child" (p. 29). This three-part sequence is referred to as an initiation, response, and evaluation (IRE) pattern. It is used by Cazden and her colleague Hugh Mehan (1979) to describe the structure of all classroom discourse at all grade levels.

Since initiations are clearly described by Cazden and others as one of the turns routinely taken by teachers, Caryl and I are very interested in who initiates talk in the Sunshine Room. We agree on a definition of initiations as turns that (1) begin a new topic, (2) develop into an extended conversation, and (3) draw in other students. During the literature discussions, the children's questions, not Caryl's, drive the topics of conversation.

As described earlier, the children spend several days of discussion debating the reasons why Rose Blanche waves a Nazi flag in one illustration in the book by the same name. Seaaira initiates the opening conversation by voicing a question that is perplexing the whole group. She asks, "How come she's waving a Nazi flag?" This initiation is the first topic of the day, and is therefore new. It extends through much of the talk of the day and continues over the next two meetings. It is a question that captivates the attention of all the participants in the study over the three days, although only five children take turns in this segment.

Following Seaaira's initiation, the children offer individual responses. After a few turns, Caryl asks an open-ended question that prompts Travis to voice his early hypothesis. Trevor and Seaaira consider an additional complication in their turns and Caryl contributes an early explanation. In the total of seventeen turns during the conversation, Caryl speaks four times and Aaron is interrupted twice by Seaaira.

This example shows how Cazden's and Mehan's original IRE pattern does not appropriately describe discourse structure for this classroom. The discourse pattern in this conversation is not as easily predictable as their typical teacher—student—teacher lesson structure supposes. Rather, the turn-taking pattern is varied, many responses occur following an initiation (made by a child, not the teacher), and Caryl makes no evaluative responses. A detailed analysis of conversation after conversation in literature study groups over time suggests that the turn-taking patterns in whole language classrooms like Caryl's are more like conversations outside of school than typical school talk.

When I first began to organize literature studies, I was determined to have "grand conversations" with my students, discussions in which I would function as a "curator" and shoot the "literary arrows" that Maryann Eeds and Ralph Peterson (1990) and Eeds and Deborah Wells (1989) describe. I saw my responsibility as an adult participant in the literature studies as raising the level of discussion and helping children understand how authors work. Shooting literary arrows meant taking advantage of teachable moments to enrich discussions of elements, characters, and other literary characteristics.

The first year that Kathy and I analyzed turn taking in classroom discourse a group was studying the work of William Steig, author of Sylvester and the Magic Pebble, Solomon the Rusty Nail, *and many other delightful books. Steig's work uses many of the traditional archetypes that my students had encountered earlier in our study of fairy tales. I was anxious for them to recognize those characteristics in Steig's stories. During a discussion of* Sylvester and the Magic Pebble, *I tried repeatedly to make the group aware of the seasonal cycle that Steig uses. Sylvester's plight as a rock continues as he sleeps through the fall and winter, a period of dormancy in nature. His subsequent awakening in the spring represents a period of birth and renewal. I wasn't very subtle in my effort; I opened four copies of the book, each one to a page showing the meadow where Sylvester meets his demise as it looked in a different season of the year. The children did humor me by talking about the seasons for several minutes. However, they never did recognize the same theme in the other books we read, and at the end of the study when we listed the characteristics of Steig's work, they did not include my suggestion, seasonal cycles. I brought it up again and they put it last on the list.*

In my analysis of those transcripts, I realize that even though the group did not appear to benefit from my literary arrow, perhaps because they did not truly own the idea, they did discuss several other traditional archetypes, including journeys, magic, and transformations, and in addition analyzed the roles played by major and minor characters. Unwittingly, their talk reminds me to trust my students and follow their lead. It also reminds me of the value of listening to children's responses to literature rather than pushing my own agenda. This is one of the benefits I receive in the tedious process of transcribing and analyzing classroom talk.

A year later, as I meet with the war and peace group, I am careful to raise my own questions only in the context of sharing personal reactions to what we are reading, usually in the initial discussions about any one book. For example, Rose Blanche *contains an interesting shift in the author's voice. It begins as a first-person narrative and suddenly changes to third person about halfway through the story. This interests me and I would like to discuss it with the group. I share my thoughts, but am never able to initiate any sustained conversation about this issue. The children have their own questions to pursue. Similarly, Eve Bunting's* The Wall *moves me to tears, perhaps because of my very strong personal connections to the book. The children understand my emotional reaction and ask a few questions about the war and that period of history. They even ask*

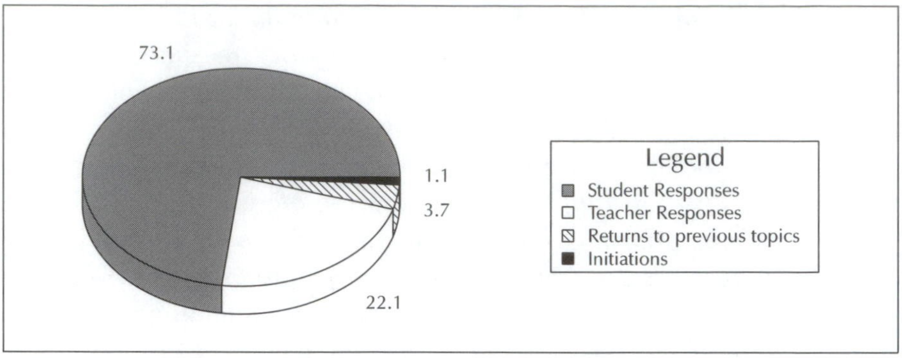

Figure 6-2. Total ratio of types of turns for the whole literature study.

to meet my husband, who served a tour of duty in Vietnam, but this book does not generate the lengthy discussions typical to Rose Blanche *and* My Hiroshima.

Amount and Type of Turns Teachers and Students Take

If the IRE pattern is not an expected one in this classroom, how do the turns taken by both children and adults compare with those in typical classrooms in terms of amount and type? In typical transmission classrooms, teachers talk at least two-thirds of the time, and their turns are expected to involve initiating and evaluating. Caryl and I are interested in counting our turns as teachers in relation to the children's turns. Our count shows that children take 1,427 of the total 1,831 turns (78 percent) throughout this literature study.

Figure 6-2 visually represents the ratio of turns of various types throughout the literature study. Here, *children* talk approximately three-fourths of the time when Caryl is present.

It is important to Caryl and me to separate the seven analyzed discussions of the literature study when describing our counting because the content of each shows a different purpose and includes different speakers. The number of student turns versus teacher turns within each of the seven discussions is depicted in the graph in Figure 6-3.

The variation across the discussions stems from the changing purpose of the literature study sessions over time. For example, the children sometimes meet without any adult participation, giving them 100 percent of the turns of talk. On other occasions, as in the fifth and tenth discussions, Caryl has a more focused goal for the group and is more involved in the talk. In the fifth discussion, she is determined to help the children resolve their questions about *Rose Blanche* so they can move on to other topics and books. This requires more direct involvement in guiding the children's conversations than she might otherwise take.

In the final discussion, Caryl is pursuing a research question of her own regarding what the children have learned and how they have changed. In this discussion, she spends a significantly larger amount of time asking questions and clarifying responses than she would in a more typical session. Caryl's purposes for the other discussions (third and ninth) are more open-ended. She sits back and listens, interested in the children's responses and intentionally giving them the floor. (The discussion of these varied roles for a teacher in literature study discussions is continued in the next section about authenticity.)

Conversation-like Discussions

In classrooms like the Sunshine Room, where curriculum is negotiated and participants strive for authentic learning experiences, topics are initiated and controlled by children and literature study discussions vary considerably over time and topic, depending on the roles and purposes of the participants. The speech involved in literature study discussions approximates what Charles Goodwin (1981) calls "the apparent disorderliness of natural speech" (p. 55). Face-to-face interactions like those in the Sunshine Room more closely resemble the genre

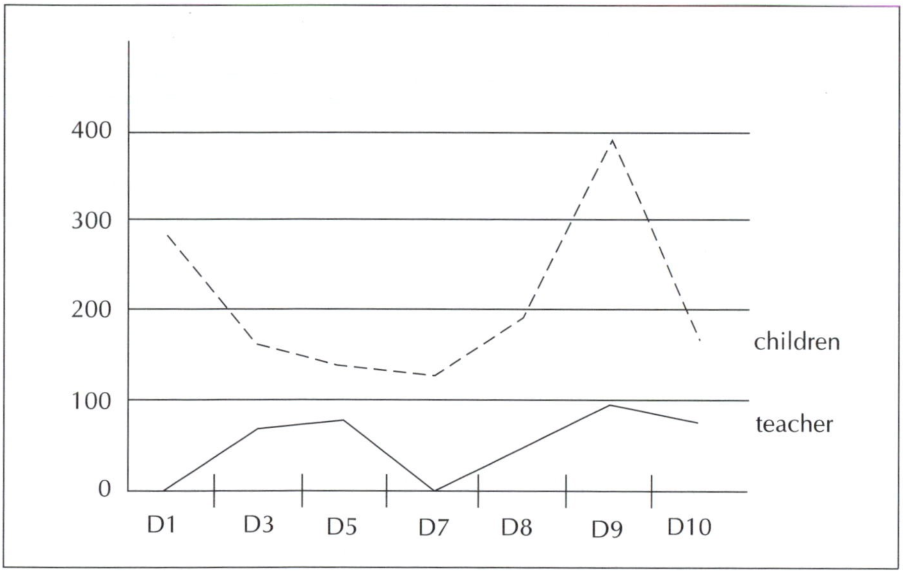

Figure 6-3. Numbers of turns of talk by participants across all discussions.

of conversation outside of school than they do the language of instruction that is frequently reported in classrooms.

During conversations outside of school, one person usually talks at a time, although there may be more than one conversation occurring simultaneously within one space, like a large table or an area of the floor. The speakers themselves determine turns of talk according to the regular constraints of the social structure, and the speech demonstrates shared knowledge.

Analyses of talk in whole language classrooms highlight the conversational nature of school talk when children are enabled to take charge of their learning. Thomas Newkirk (1992) reports on a full year of listening to first and second graders talk, especially about books, in a classroom that doesn't fit the pattern that sociolinguists describe. He frames his analyses as meetings of two oral cultures—that of the teacher and that of the children.

Newkirk proposes that being "on topic is socially defined instead of being a self-evident function of the texts under discussion" (p. 83). The conversations among first and second graders that he listened to suggest that a definition of "on topic" in discussions is culturally different for adults than for children, implying that returns to "topic" are less necessary for successful children's conversations than we have previously assumed.

Vivian Paley (1981, 1992) also listens carefully while young children talk. Her descriptions of kindergartners in the classroom lend an understanding of how language happens in school from the children's point of view. Like Newkirk, Paley calls attention to the invaluable method of understanding children by listening, audiotaping, and transcribing their talk. Such analyses encourage expanded sociolinguistic hypotheses about the "patterns of communicative behavior involved in the construction of events at the level of face-to-face interaction" (Bloome 1981, p. 7) in elementary school classrooms, particularly in whole language programs.

One difference between the discussions in the Sunshine Room and those in the classrooms Paley and Newkirk describe, and between the Sunshine Room discussions and the social conversation of everyday interaction, however, reflects the overarching purpose that creates the group. Topics of talk in whole language classrooms are usually connected to the instructional activity in which they occur, even though these topics are interwoven with the occasional intertextual layers of talk about friends, families, and special events. The overall topic and purpose of the discourse described in this chapter is to discuss the war and peace literature books as a way to understand a current war. As the examples in this section show, the purpose of the group is returned to by some member of the group, even when off-task talk occurs, until the decision is made to conclude the session. Like the collaborative talk that Wells (1989) describes, the purpose of this talk is "to enable progress to be made towards the achievement of a goal, and it is against this criterion that individual contributions are judged" (p. 259).

In our analysis of these discussions, turns that move the discussion back to a previously initiated conversation are labeled *returns.* They are necessary in focused discussions such as these because these are the turns that reflect the overall purpose that brings the individuals together as a group and distinguishes the discussions as learning centered rather than completely conversational. In these conversations, illustrations from picture books are likely to provoke a redirection to the topic. In fact, overall, twenty-five of eighty-eight initiations and returns are directly related to illustrations in picture books. The children in the war and peace discussions push their conversations back to their unanswered questions in a mature manner. Their determination to solve their own problems results in only seven brief conversations off topic, representing only 57 turns of the total 1,831 (3 percent).

During the group's first discussion, for example, two brief off-topic conversations are redirected by the children themselves after a very few seconds. Task-oriented topics of conversation resume, even following events that would be expected to call attention away from the task, like excessive misbehavior elsewhere in the classroom.

In one dramatic instance, a child leaps off the loft near the children's group area. The substitute teacher can be heard on the audiotape, summoning the principal to help with the misbehaving child. Noise from other children in the room makes the literature group's talk hard to follow at times. And yet, amid the apparent disarray, the children in the group pause only long enough to ask, "Hey, who jumped off the loft?" and predict a couple of suspects. Then a photograph of Hitler is found in a book and the children return immediately to their original, on-topic discussion.

In another example, the initiated topic of discussion is the tragedy of innocent lives lost during *My Hiroshima.* Travis has a "watery eye" that is noticed by the other children in the group, particularly his friend Aaron.

"Travis, how come that, this left eye is kind of watery?" Aaron asks.

"This is my left eye, Aaron," Travis responds, pointing to the eye that isn't watery.

"I know, that's what I said."

"Then how come you pointed to this one?"

"'Cause he's opposite from you," analyzes Seaaira.

"Yeah," says Aaron. "And I had to kind of turn my head."

"Because I poked it," explains Travis.

"With a pencil?"

"No, with my hand."

"Well, do you think we should end it?" asks Aaron, referring to the conversation they are having about *My Hiroshima.*

"No," Travis answers. "It's just sad how all the people, innocent people and their burning skin."

"There's one thing that I know about this book, that it's better than *The Butter Battle,*" claims Aaron, and the group is back to their discussion.

Aaron wonders if the detour from the topic of *My Hiroshima* means that it is time to end the discussion. Travis, however, is determined to talk through the issue he's most concerned about to his satisfaction. Aaron uses his turn to initiate a whole new conversation that brings in a new topic (a comparison of texts) and more speakers and extends the discussion at length.

At first appearance, the type of talk described in all of the passages from these war and peace literature discussions is similar, structurally, to Philip's notion of infrastructure. It is marked by the characteristics common to communication in the Sunshine Room. But the children's attention to the instructional purpose of this literature study group clearly distinguishes it. This type of communication is accepted and encouraged as the *official* structure in the Sunshine Room, it is not a hidden or underground type of talk. Also, literature study discussions are more likely to focus on instructional or academic issues with similar purposes, rather than on the nonattentive talk and behaviors characteristic of infrastructure, which vary considerably in terms of content.

The content of the talk, in addition to the structure, is crucial in the invention of communicative competence. In their work, neither Cazden nor Philips addresses the content of classroom discourse in as much depth as the structure. In the Sunshine Room, the structure and the content of discourse are dependent on one another. First, the structure enables the children to develop content that is authentic and is of high academic quality. Without the amount of personal control over turns of talk and initiations, among other structural variables, the content could not emerge as dramatically as it does. Second, however, the richness of the content, the fact that children have something important to talk about, necessitates and pushes the natural, conversational structure that results. When children have real questions about their real worlds, they push for helpful responses and interactions. And, as Wells states, as children participate in collaborative talk in response to their own inquiry-driven language event, they become empowered.

Kathy and I are impressed with the responsibility the children show in taking control of their literature study group. We have demonstrated how they control the topics of conversations and turn taking within their discussions, with and without my being present. A list of the critical decisions affecting the group that are made by the children and by me, shown in Figure 6-4, further delineates the balance of power within this group.

This list clearly indicates my trust in the children as learners and my willingness to turn over decision making to them. Because our classroom operates all the time in an atmosphere of mutual consideration and negotiation, the children respond by willingly accepting the challenge, expecting me to respect and abide by their choices.

Cazden (1988), quoting Michael Stubbs, alludes to classrooms like the Sunshine Room as compared to transmission classrooms. "What is special is that talking in these ways is 'radically asymmetrical. . . . [It is] almost never used by pupils and, when it is, it is a sign that an atypical teaching situation has arisen'" (p. 161). It is clear that the Sunshine Room is one of these "atypical teaching situations" in which requests for learning are capitalized on.

Authenticity

The war and peace literature study group epitomizes the authentic nature of language use in this setting. The classroom discourse it exemplifies is conversational, for the real purpose of answering important questions. It is completely owned by the children in the group. They have elected to belong to the group and participate in the event, they have selected the materials and the topics they wish to discuss, and they use all language-cueing systems in an interactive manner as they work with written and oral texts.

WHO MAKES WHAT DECISIONS?	
CHILDREN	**CARYL**
*Initiate conversation about war during sharing time	*Chooses to develop a literature study based on children's need to discuss war issues
*Choose which books to read and discuss	*Chooses books for literature set
*Choose to read with a partner or alone	*Chooses to tape and transcribe, creating a research setting in an instructional setting
*Choose to organize the group as a shared book experience rather than as a text set	*Invites children to participate in her learning as informants
*Choose topics of conversation	*Chooses to join the group as a participant
*Raise questions related to books, historical and current events	*Chooses to allow some discussions to take place among just the children
*Control turn-taking	*Places responsibility for evaluation on the children as individuals and as a group
*Choose which books are the most valuable to group and to themselves as individuals	*Asks for children's opinions on the value of such a literature study group and whether or not it should be replicated for others
*Evaluate their individual participation and their group's process	*Shares the conclusions of her research with the children
*Support their teacher as a learner	

Figure 6-4. Decisions made in war and peace literature study.

A real audience is one component of authentic speech. The teacher is the primary audience for children's language in many classrooms. The teacher also directs successive turns of talk to other children or to the next activity. In this manner, the teacher has an enormous amount of control over the language of the children, including narratives that would be controlled by the speaker in other, more natural settings.

In the Sunshine Room there are as many audiences for speaking, reading, and writing as there are authentic purposes for them. Children direct their language to whoever is appropriate: the teacher, their peers, their parents, other members of the school community (the principal, other teachers, other students), and themselves. The teacher is but one of many authentic audiences for speech and literacy events.

During the war and peace literature study group, the most frequent audience for children's statements and questions are the other children. The children are accustomed to talking to each other; they direct questions and statements to each other by name, or to the group in general. For example, during the fourth discussion about the meanings conveyed in *Rose Blanche,* Seaaira disagrees with Elizabeth's explanation for how Rose Blanche loses her life at the end of the story. Rather than directing her argument to Caryl, who is a participant in the conversation and would be the expected audience in a transmission classroom, Seaaira speaks directly to Elizabeth.

The conversation begins when Elizabeth states, "I think she got shot by a Nazi 'cause I don't think she'd be shot by another Jewish."

Caryl asks for clarification, "You said another Jewish. What do you mean by that?"

"She's Jewish," answers Elizabeth.

Caryl confirms, "You think she's Jewish."

"And I think she got shot by a Nazi because I don't think she'd be shot by another one of the Jewish," Elizabeth elaborates.

Caryl makes a procedural comment to Elizabeth, who continues to raise her hand to request a turn. "You don't have to raise hands, okay, but just wait for another person to stop before you speak."

"I've got something to say," says Seaaira.

"Go ahead, Seaaira."

Seaaira turns to Elizabeth and says, "Um, but Elizabeth, they didn't, how can they tell that she's, she might not, um if it was a person that shot her, but they might have been Jewish 'cause you think they're Jewish, they might have been Jewish 'cause how can they tell if she's Jewish or not?"

"'Cause when she was holding the um Nazi flag," Elizabeth responds, "They were um, taking all the Jewishes to that one cage and then—"

"But they didn't take her," counters Seaaira.

"I know but that's why she holds the Nazi flag because she probably held it because she didn't want them to know that she was Jewish."

Seaaira and Elizabeth's exchange is a small conversation within a discussion, after which Seaaira proceeds to state her own opinion to the group. Conversations like this one are frequent, when children direct their talk to each other without acknowledging or involving the teacher between turns.

The questions posed by Caryl in the context of the literature study discussions highlight the authentic nature of her participation as a teacher in the group. During the first year of the study, Caryl is always a member of the literature groups, although she tries to maintain a role of "more experienced reader" as she participates (Moll & Whitmore 1993). In the war and peace literature study, Caryl no longer feels her presence is required for successful discussions, but her contributions when she participates are those of an authentic, more experienced member of the group, not only an instructional leader.

My careful analysis of literature study discussion transcripts during the first year of the study leads me to pose my own research question for the war and peace study during the second year. I describe my research question to the children toward the end of the literature study:

> *I'm taping you and taking lots of notes and listening because I've never done a literature study group before where we did it because kids wanted to discuss that topic. . . . When I realized that you really wanted to talk about [the war in the Middle East], I decided to put the set of books together for you to read. And I'm wondering now if the opportunity to read those books and to talk to each other about war has changed the way you think about it, if it's made you think differently, or helped you to understand anything about war that you didn't understand before.*

Early in my work with Caryl, she would usually ask the children a question to prompt new literature study discussions. What did you guys think about this story? was a common opening. As discussions progressed she would ask, What made you think that when you read the story? How did you think differently about it this time?

Caryl's questions later in the study, especially during the war and peace group, continue to extend open-ended invitations, but they are intended to push children to think more critically about books (Sloan 1984): What do you mean by that? Why do you think the author did that? Would that change the way she feels about them, do you think? Other questions urge children to negotiate: Do you want to come back and talk some more about this story, or do you want to talk about another story next time? Still others request clarification: What is it about that picture? I don't understand.

All of these are real questions (Searle 1969), asked for genuine purposes, to elevate the quality of the discussion and to build authentic communication. They differ from the types of turns teachers reportedly take in other, more typical classrooms. For instance, virtually none of Caryl's turns request known answers (Searle 1969; Heath 1986) or are evaluative (Cazden 1988).

At one point, for example, Caryl responds to an earlier turn by Seaaira with an evaluative statement that she quickly softens, thereby reopening the negotiative nature of the conversation.

"Seaaira's right that—," Caryl begins, but quickly continues, "Maybe she's right. You kind of have to decide for yourself. The author leaves a lot of questions."

Frequently, the children assume more of the traditional teacher role than Caryl does. They initiate new conversations, they enter into the talk whenever they have something to contribute and can get a turn, and they freely disagree, ask questions, and invite each other to participate.

Children even make evaluative statements apart from Caryl or to her. In one interesting interchange where the children are reflecting on their experience with these books, Aaron asks Caryl, "Have *you* learned something?" Caryl responds, "Have *I* learned something? I hope so. I sometimes wonder if the world has."

In this example, Aaron illustrates the manner in which discourse patterns are invented by the group. Aaron feels comfortable taking a turn that requests a student's evaluation of the teacher, although both Aaron's and Caryl's intonation patterns express their awareness of the atypicality of their interaction.

According to Cazden (1988), a teacher "register" is similar to that used for caregiver baby talk (Ferguson 1978); the teacher also dominates two-thirds of all classroom discourse, initiates almost all interactions, and has permission to interrupt but not be interrupted. The transcripts in this study, however, show that Caryl's talk in the classroom does not fit these limiting criteria. Rather, the children use most of the time allotted to talk, they determine the topics of talk, and they initiate conversations. We record children interrupting Caryl and each other.

The role of the whole language teacher in classroom discourse suggests a new register of teacher talk. Caryl refuses to take the typical instructional register of many classroom teachers, but she also contributes to discourse in a manner that is different from the children, given her more mature and informed expertise. As she guides and supports, Caryl helps children take risks, focus their questions and ideas, and translate them into manageable conversations, ensuring that each child participates and finds academic success. As she actively participates in the learning, she researches along with the children, combining her own literary questions with demonstrations of the research process. As she evaluates the children's individual and collective development, she examines transcripts from literature study groups. As she facilitates, she consciously plans the environment, curriculum, and materials to provide functional and purposeful uses for language, literacy, and learning processes. All of these teacher roles constitute mediation (Moll & Whitmore 1993).

Pat McLure, the teacher in Newkirk's study of discussions about books, describes her lack of a predetermined strategy for participation in groups:

> That's almost an instinctive sort of thing. It's usually either because something really interesting has come up and I want to take part in the discussion. Sometimes because I think that maybe by coming in I can instigate a little more discussion from others—but I'd rather hold back and see what they're doing first. If you don't start with your own agenda, and let the groups take over, then you can react to it rather than being the one who controls it. (Newkirk 1992, p. 116)

Pat McLure's goal, like Caryl's, is to mediate the students' learning without intervening (K. Goodman 1992), thus supporting the authentic nature of the language events.

Additive Bilingualism and Biliteracy

Bilingualism and biliteracy are not highlighted as strongly in this literature study group as they are during other groups throughout the year. Part of the reason is the complexity of transcribing, translating, and reporting a large amount of speech in a language other than English for a predominantly English-only audience. It is also a result of the uncontrollable selection process children use in choosing literature groups. In this case, Lolita is the only Spanish reader who selects this literature study group.

For each new set of literature studies, however, Caryl consciously provides a minimum of one text set for Spanish-dominant readers. She seeks ways to include children's expanding Spanish-language abilities in each experience. In the war and peace set, Caryl encourages Lolita to read texts available in Spanish. Lolita's parents, who are monolingual Spanish speakers, describe Lolita's role during this period of time as a carrier of information home from school. Although Lolita is presented with primarily English texts during the war and peace text set, she takes the meanings and sometimes the books themselves home each night to share through translation with her family.

Bilingualism and biliteracy are important to Caryl during typical reading events. She wants the students to develop strong literacy skills in their first language; her efforts are evident in her constant endeavor to provide the class with whole, authentic, quality texts in Spanish. The children, however, make the choice about what language they use for reading and writing. Their desire to read and write in their second language (English or Spanish) is firmly supported and encouraged. Children intentionally choose to belong to certain literature study groups based on their goals to improve in their second language. Such efforts are strengthened by paired reading between students and between students and adults. The focus on meaning in all literacy activities smooths the transition from monolingual to bilingual competence; the result is a gradual movement toward a bilingual/biliterate community.

Caryl's efforts to provide children with biliteracy are frequently commented on by the children in the class. In October, when asked to reflect on her reading development, Lolita writes: "A mí me gustó porque trabajé con una niña que habla puro inglés y me gusta traducir lo que dice en inglés. También me gustó trabajar con ella porque pude concentrar." She says she likes to work with a girl who only speaks English and she likes to translate what the reading material says in English. She also likes to work with her because she can concentrate. In these and other examples, from both English-dominant and Spanish-dominant children, the addition of a second language into the reading or writing experience gives children a new insight into the world of language, and they welcome and enjoy it.

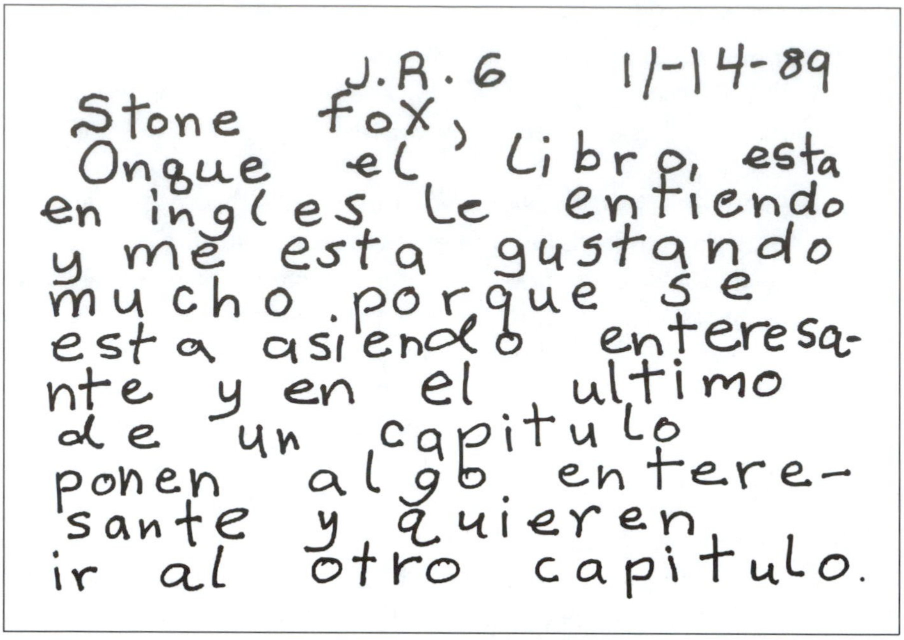

J.R. 6 1/-14-89
Stone fox,
Onque el Libro, esta
en ingles Le entiendo
y me esta gustando
mucho. porque se
esta asiendo enteresa-
nte y en el ultimo
de un capitulo
ponen algo entere-
sante y quieren
ir al otro capitulo.

Figure 6-5. Susana's log entry about *Stone Fox* (Translation: Although the book is in English, I understand it and I like it because it's becoming interesting and at the end of one chapter they put something interesting and you want to go on to another chapter.)

Spanish readers reading English as a second language often rely on knowledge of story structure to help build meaning as they read, as revealed in Susana's entry regarding her work in the Stone Fox *group (see Figure 6-5).*

Susana knows how chapter books work, having read such extended stories in her native language. It's an understanding that she is able to express and use as a resource in reading her second language. She also relies on her group's discussion of stories for support. She writes, "A mi me ayudó hablar con los otros miembros de mi grupo antes de ir a mi grupo porque si no entiendo algo me lo dicen. A mí no me gustó que unos no se prepararon antes de ir al grupo." (It helped me to talk with the other members of my group before going to the group [discussions] because if I don't understand something, they tell me. I don't like it when some [members] don't prepare before coming to the group.)

Like Virginia Allen (1989), I find that illustrations play a major role in supporting second language reading. Illustrations provide visual clues and often serve to extend the text, helping readers arrive at a deeper meaning. During the year, Susana also participates in an author study of the work of Chris Van Allsburg. She reads The Polar Express *in Spanish translation, but all the other books in the set are only available in English. Much of the discussion in the group focuses on the illustrations, especially in the book* The Mysteries of Harris Burdick, *which has almost no text at all. Still, we have extended discussions about the characteristics of Van Allsburg's work. The children come away with a number of insights.*

Susana characterizes the mysterious quality of this author's books in her comment on Jumanji, *her personal favorite: "También me gusta porque nos hace hacer preguntas y de allí puede salir historias." (I liked it because it makes us ask questions and from there can come stories.)*

Francisco, who is also in this group, comments more directly on the role of the illustrations in forming his understanding of Van Allsburg's work (see Figure 6-6).

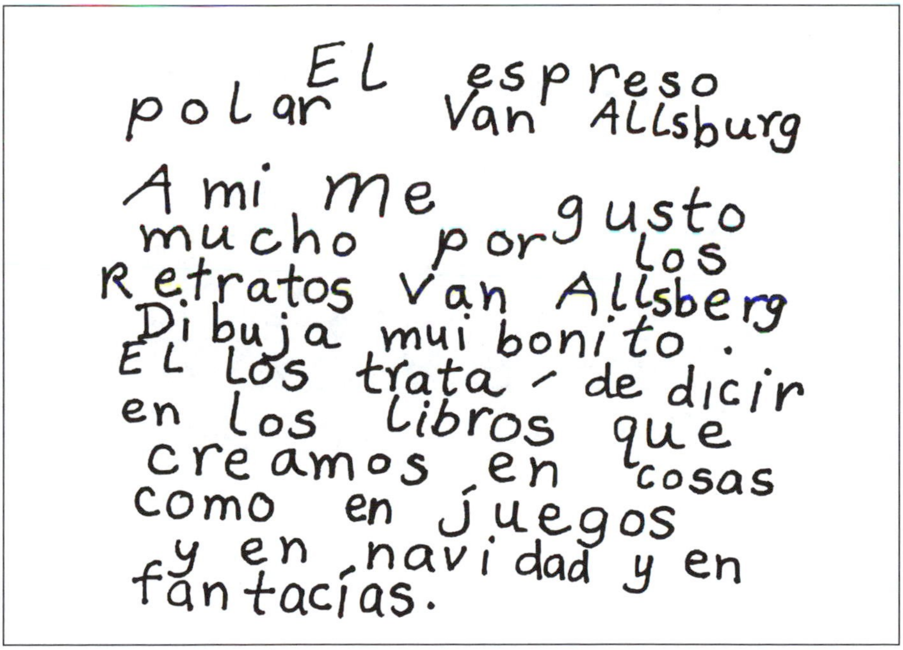
EL espreso polar Van Allsburg
A mi me gusto mucho por los Retratos Van Allsberg Dibuja mui bonito. EL los trata de dicir en los libros que creamos en cosas como en juegos y en navidad y en fantacías.

Figure 6-6. Francisco's literature log entry about *El Expreso Polar.* (Translation: *The Polar Express.* I liked the pictures a lot. Van Allsburg draws very pretty. He tries to tell us in the books that we should believe in things like games, Christmas, and fantasy.)

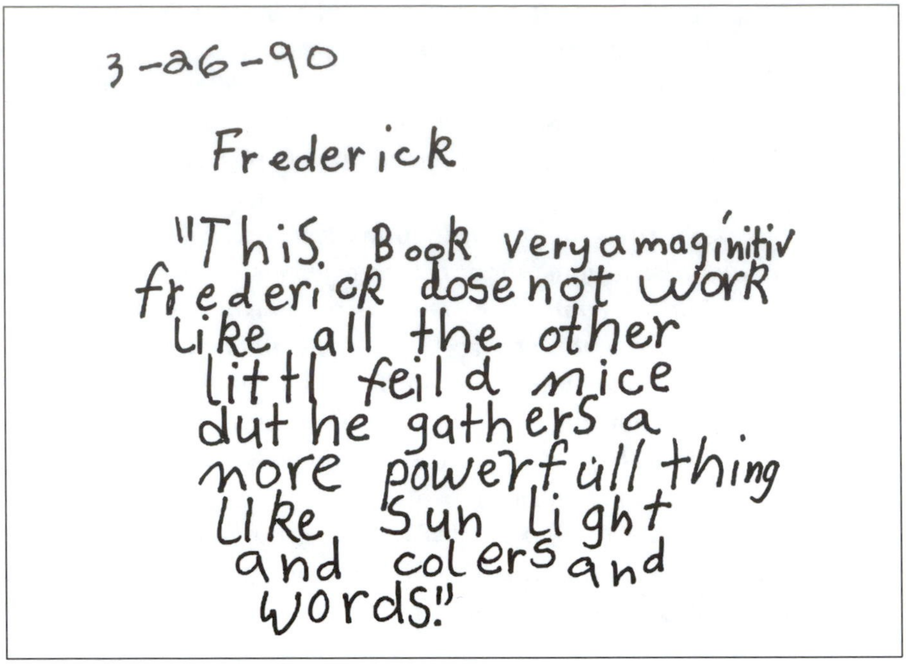

3-26-90

Frederick

"This Book veryamaginitiv
frederick dosenot work
Like all the other
littl feild mice
dut he gathers a
nore powerfull thing
Like Sun Light
and colers and
words!"

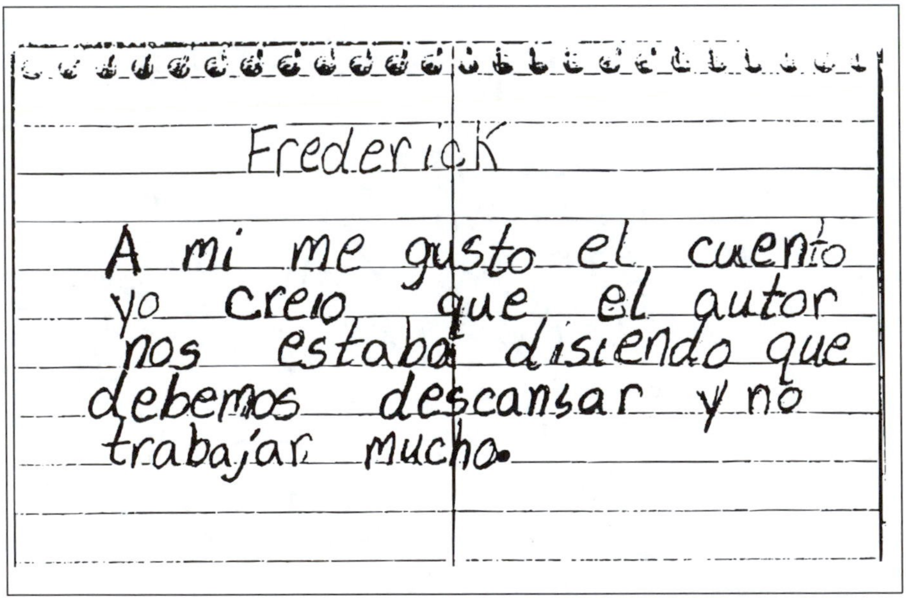

Frederick

A mi me gusto el cuento
yo creio que el autor
nos estaba disiendo que
debemos descansar y no
trabajar mucho.

Figure 6-7. Ethan's and Lupita's literature log entries. (Translation of Lupita's entry: I liked the story. I think the author was telling us we should rest and not work too much.)

Language differences do not impede lively discussion within bilingual literature study groups. In an author study group that considers the work of Leo Lionni, Ethan and Lupita clearly have differing opinions of Frederick, the little mouse that spends his time gathering warmth, colors, and words instead of grain. (Their literature log entries are shown in Figure 6-7.)

During group meetings, Ethan and Lupita engage in intense and often loud discussions that interrupt other proceedings in the classroom. Unable to come to any agreement, they finally poll other class members and outsiders in an attempt to settle their argument. In the end, they each hold to their own opinions, but they agree that without their disagreement, their discussions would not have been as interesting or fun.

It's important to note that even though these children are willing to take risks in their second language and are successful at making meaning and learning language through second language print, they choose to express their understanding in their native language. During the year, they become increasingly able to talk about their reading in their second language; however, they are never denied access to their native tongue. Sarah Hudelson (1987) states the importance of this most simply and eloquently. "For too long non-English-speaking children have been silenced because they could not use English to share their experiences, knowledge, and understandings. Allowing children access to their native language is one way of enabling those who have been silenced to speak" (p. 840).

Inventing Whole Language Discourse

Communicative competence in school means understanding the socially appropriate ways for participating in classroom discourse, both verbally and nonverbally. Much of children's success or failure in school depends on their ability to become communicatively competent, particularly if the "rules" for communicative competence vary greatly between home and school. Communicative competence, then, is an example of how personal inventions both are influenced by and influence social conventions.

To be communicatively competent in the Sunshine Room, a child needs to be an active participant, voice authentic questions about the real world, take turns as appropriate for the success of the conversation, initiate topics of interest, interrupt if necessary to get the floor, and direct utterances to the real audience during talk.

The discourse in the Sunshine Room is not merely an improvisation on the standard rules for lesson language. The inventions of discourse found in the Sunshine Room are goals from the beginning of the year, not exceptions to the rule. Cazden states that the rules of classroom discourse must be inferred because they are never explicitly stated. Philips, on the other hand, provides examples of teachers making clear statements like "Raise your hand if you want to talk" and "Don't interrupt when someone else is speaking." She says, "Teachers who wish to sustain a controlled and orderly classroom, rather than one which is relaxed and casual, endeavor to minimize the amount of interaction between students" (1983, p. 91).

Caryl is an example of a teacher who explicitly states language rules that encourage talking in the classroom in a positive, conversational manner. These rules give children power in authentic discourse. On one occasion, she tells the students, "Talking is the most important thing you can do in this classroom. You learn best when you talk while you work." Throughout the day, she provides clear and straightforward information about what she wants from children in terms of thinking, learning, and behavior. During one literature study, she tells a student, "I guess what I want is for kids to know *why* they think something is a good story." When she implements a cloze procedure (an instructional strategy whereby children predict meanings for hidden sections of text while they read), Caryl stresses that meaning is what counts. As the children read, she encourages them to guess at words and she accepts words that make sense. Comments and actions like these are overt guidelines for children's participation. They are followed through as all participants are awarded time to have the floor and discussion is encouraged. It is not necessary for children to raise their hand to obtain a turn during interactive periods like literature study discussions, nor is the teacher the only participant who may interrupt utterances or negotiate time.

An example from the children's discussion about *My Hiroshima* reveals their conscious understanding of the criteria for communicative competence. In this conversation, the children chastise two of the quieter members of the group and refuse to excuse their lack of participation and preparedness.

Caryl and I are seated outside the group when Aaron remarks, "Well, Mark you haven't said anything. Don't you want to say something?"

Travis says, "In any books you've hardly said anything."

"Mark, do you want to say something?" Aaron asks again.

"No," he answers abruptly.

"Okay."

"Anyone else?" Travis asks. "And Elizabeth hasn't."

Elizabeth murmurs under her breath, "I didn't read the book."

"Well, you're supposed to be reading it," Aaron exclaims.

Seaaira comes to Elizabeth's defense. "She was sick!" she reminds Aaron.

"Not all the time!" says Travis.

"You're supposed to be reading it—" begins Aaron.

"Whenever you get a chance," finishes Trevor.

"Whatever, you know how Ms. Crowell always gives us time to get ready," comments Aaron.

The group continues to consider the possibilities.

"She had lots of warnings."

"She had lots of time."

"DEAR time she could have read it."

"I know."

The lack of overt participation by these two children creates an opportunity for the others to define their invented conventions. Less visible in the critique of the children, but available to Caryl and me, are the other ways Mark and Elizabeth are learning with this group. Mark often writes responses in his literature log, for example. And it was Elizabeth who was able to articulate what makes questions "good" for the group in an earlier discussion.

In the Sunshine Room, requests for learning are capitalized on in discussion just as they are in broader curriculum planning. The children's questions about war illustrate the sophisticated inquiry that results when the power relationships in a classroom invite questions to be shared and acted on. The children's discussions shed light on how and why whole language discourse operates differently from typical talk in school, offering rich examples of inventions that other whole language teachers can adapt to their own settings and learners.

CLASSIC
Clifford's
KITTEN

7

Inventing Culture

Bicultural Best Friends

An unexpected and wonderful relationship develops between Seaaira and Lolita, two of the primary characters in this story, during the second year of my time in the Sunshine Room. The friendship that these two girls enjoy is as devout and thrilling as being "best friends" is for any pair of eight-year-old girls. The girls spend hours on the phone after school, they spend nights at each other's houses, they travel with each other's families, and they parade through their school lives in matching "best friend" T-shirts made by Lolita's mother. Seaaira and Lolita get acquainted early in the year and they quickly become inseparable for most academic activities as well as for extracurricular experiences. You may remember their involvement in the fairy tale and war and peace literature study groups in Chapters 5 and 6.

Seaaira and Lolita's relationship is a symbolic representation of the culture and community of the Sunshine Room. Since Seaaira is an Anglo English-speaking girl from the extended volunteer community, and Lolita is a bilingual and biliterate Latina from the barrio surrounding the school, their friendship represents the bicultural experience that is fostered in the Sunshine Room. The relationship of these girls to each other and to learning, evident in their homes and their classroom, is the critical event that characterizes how culture is invented in a classroom setting. This chapter is not intended to be a thorough explication of culture in school, but it provides a glimpse into the potential of multicultural education that supports and is supported by invention. Two instances in particular, when the girls spend the night in each other's homes and when they collaborate on the composition of a bilingual play script, highlight the impact of multicultural experiences for children in school.

Meet Seaaira

Seaaira is a lanky, blonde-headed girl with big, expressive blue eyes and a freckled face. Her long legs, which usually stick out of baggy

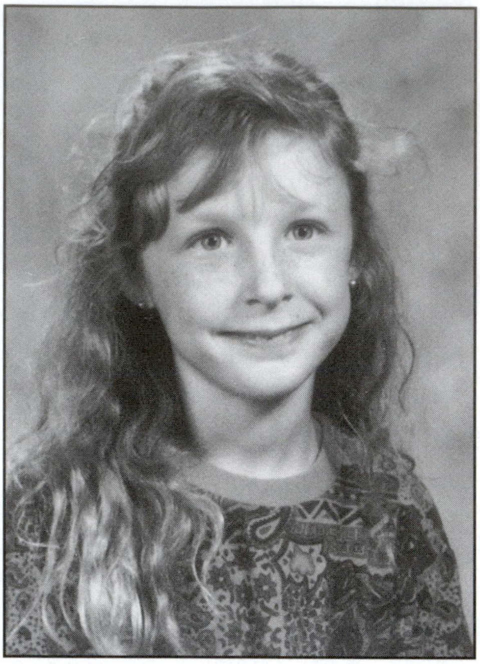

Seaaira

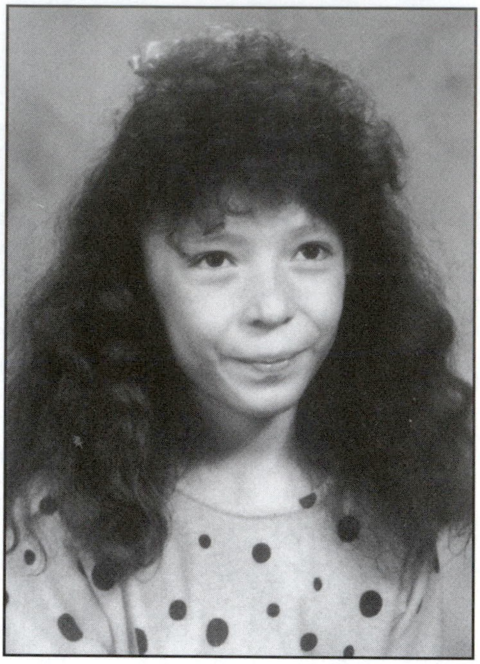

Lolita

shorts, are always rushing and her long hair is often in a tangle. Seaaira participates in the activities her girlfriends at school enjoy, but she seems more comfortable as she swims, plays soccer, reads, writes stories, or plays with her hamsters. To say that Seaaira is energetic is an understatement. She greets opportunities for new experiences with enthusiasm and a gusto for learning. I seldom see Seaaira in an uncooperative spirit; rather, her desire for learning keeps her from ever looking bored or refusing to participate in new things.

Seaaira at home

Caryl and I visit Seaaira's home in the spring, where we meet with Seaaira's family and get a glimpse of their life together. We arrive in the late afternoon and are greeted by her mom and her young brother. Jazz plays quietly in the background while we talk, there is a faint scent of incense in the air, and the atmosphere is comfortable and relaxed. Outside, a station wagon sits beside a large camper and a boat in the driveway. We chat with Seaaira's mother until her father arrives home from work; Seaaira's younger brother plays on the floor, enjoying a popsicle.

Seaaira's family is professional. Her mother is an elementary school teacher in a nearby border community and her father is a criminal investigator. Each has a college education and would like to go on to graduate degrees. Seaaira's younger brother, Ben, is a three-year-old who attends preschool and will eventually become a Borton kindergartner. Seaaira describes him from her position as older sister as a "troublemaker" because he gets into her hamsters. Seaaira's family lives in a comfortable home on the east side of Tucson. It is a three-bedroom house with a fireplace, a partially completed family-room addition, and two large dogs in the backyard. Seaaira and her family tell Caryl and me that they enjoy time with each other, their pets, reading, camping, and boating.

The members of Seaaira's family are monolingual English speakers. Although Seaaira's mother teaches in a bilingual community, her Spanish-language abilities are very limited. Both of Seaaira's parents see written Spanish "pass by" in their occupations, but neither interacts with Spanish print. They share Seaaira's goals for learning Spanish, although unlike their daughter, they have made no arrangements for formal instruction.

All the members of the family enjoy reading: Seaaira's dad likes mysteries and espionage novels for recreation, Seaaira's mom reads a great deal of professional literature related to education, Ben likes pictures books. They receive monthly publications like *National Geographic* and boating magazines and they use cookbooks. Examples of these forms of print are neatly placed on the end tables in the living room and several bookcases are full of novels, encyclopedias, and record albums. Although they don't receive a newspaper regularly, they buy them occasionally and Seaaira's dad tells us he reads the daily paper at work.

All of the family members are involved in writing in their daily lives, as well. Seaaira's mom writes notes and school-related texts like lesson plans. Her dad dictates reports at work for a secretary to transcribe. Easter cards the children recently made are displayed on the mantle; Seaaira has helped Ben sign his name, although the family predicts he'll be writing his name by himself soon.

Seaaira and her mom write notes back and forth to each other every day their conflicting schedules keep them from seeing each other. Seaaira has a note waiting when her mom gets home from her long work commute. Seaaira's mom makes sure to leave a response the next morning, because Seaaira gets up after her mom has already left for school.

Seaaira also writes at home for other reasons. She writes letters to two of her mom's fourth-grade bilingual students, usually about once a week, so the bilingual girls from the border town have an authentic English reader as an audience for their writing. Her dad says that he frequently notices Seaaira pick up a notebook and start a story on her own, without prompting. Seaaira has her own savings account and keeps track of her balance and accrued interest on the monthly bank statements.

Caryl and I visit Seaaira's bedroom with her after we talk with her parents. It is chock-full of literacy materials. Several tall bookcases are crammed with books, including two books in Spanish that her parents weren't even aware of until our visit. Seaaira explains that she bought the books at the book fair at school. A calendar hangs on the wall across from Seaaira's loft-style bed, and she has noted important dates: Lolita's birthday, her dad's birthday, the day her hamsters were born, etc. Three hamster cages, posters, and hanging shelves filled with dolls also occupy this lived-in space.

Writing materials and tools are at Seaaira's and her brother's disposal. I ask Seaaira if she visits the library very often and she tells me that for her family it's easier to buy books: their schedules make it difficult to get to the library.

Seaaira shares a lot of her experiences from school with her parents. Like many young families, however, the rigors of daily life complicate the ideal goals Seaaira's parents have for their time together. For example, Seaaira's mom confides that she would like to read absolutely every day with the children, but finds it difficult to work it in. She is also disappointed when she is not able to discuss daily school events with them. Interruptions and work-related needs frequently distract from those goals.

The literature study about war and peace at school, described in detail in Chapter 6, provokes deep discussions about war at home. Seaaira's constant questions, similar to those she asks at school, are sometimes too difficult for her mother to respond to. They reflect Seaaira's very real concerns about the war in the Middle East. Sometimes, for example, Seaaira wakes in the night convinced that a siren on the street means the beginning of an air raid. At such times her parents reassure Seaaira and soothe her back to sleep.

Seaaira at School

Seaaira's extroverted personality allows her to ask questions freely and openly, state opinions, interrupt activities and other speakers' turns, and set high goals for herself at school. In whole language terms, Seaaira is a risk taker. During the first week of school, for instance, Seaaira discovers that Caryl is not as concerned with spelling and punctuation as she is with meaning and ideas, and Seaaira's writing takes off at a furious pace. Eventually, Seaaira comes to understand the value of conventional spelling and punctuation for her readers, but she never permits those conventions to suppress her inventiveness, creativity, or expression.

Seaaira appreciates the invitation to invent in her classroom. During interviews, Seaaira tells me that she prefers Caryl's teaching style to previous teachers who emphasized spelling tests and worksheets. She describes the Sunshine Room as interesting and Caryl as her favorite teacher, because, as Seaaira says, "She's nice and she does things in an interesting way instead of sitting down and doing ditto copies." Seaaira views herself as a good reader because she's been reading chapter books since she was in first grade. She explains, "And they were kind of pretty hard so I think that kind of makes me a good reader but I don't know." Seaaira perceives herself as reading all day long, since she reads during DEAR time, literature study time, and free time at school and at home. She enjoys the Laura Ingles Wilder books, and likes to read the same books more than once. Seaaira says she owns most of her books and repeats that even though they live close to a public library, her family rarely has time to go.

Seaaira is a writer at school as well as at home. She describes the writing she does every day, exclaiming, "We write all the time. That's all I can say. We write at writing workshop, I write at home, I write our homework, we sometimes write at free time, we do stories and we write then. We write all the time." In fact, Seaaira is so enthusiastic about all the subjects at school that she doesn't know what she likes best—reading, writing, or math.

One of Seaaira's most important goals is to learn Spanish. She expresses her interest in a variety of ways, including asking good questions about how languages work. One day she and I discuss her interest in learning Spanish.

Seaaira tells me, "I'm interested in like how if other people when they speak different languages and if they like think that means 'the' or if they think it in a different way. . . . Like Lolita speaks Spanish, too, and like if she says 'the' if she says like the other people think in English or if they think like in a different way." In other words, Seaaira wonders if bilingual speakers think in one language or the other, and if the concept represented by the word *the* changes across languages.

Seaaira has a goal to learn Spanish and a plan to accomplish her goal. She says, "Well, I just listen to the other people speak it and I read books." And sometimes she asks her friend Lolita how to say things. Being in a bilingual classroom helps. "It's fun having the board up in two different languages and Ms. Crowell speaking two different languages and everything else." Repeatedly over the course of the school year, Seaaira intentionally works to improve her Spanish. She collaborates in biliterate pieces of writing, like the bilingual version of *Little Red Riding Hood* that she and Lolita write and perform with five classmates. She requests membership in literature study groups reading Spanish texts, like *Pepón* (see Figure 7-1), for the express reason that it's written in Spanish.

Late in the year, Seaaira asks Lolita to create Spanish homework for her and Lolita provides a list of vocabulary for Seaaira to memorize each night. Seaaira's plan includes an emphatic request to her parents to enroll her in another bilingual classroom and school next year when she advances to fourth grade.

It is Seaaira's nature to be bright, inquisitive, and energetic, and it is clear that in a whole language classroom like the Sunshine Room, children like Seaaira blossom. Her development over the course of her third-grade year is undeniable. Appendix C contains an example of the whole language checklist Caryl developed to assess her students' development (Crowell 1992). This document is a record of Seaaira's improvement in all expectations in the classroom over the year. Caryl's annotations describe Seaaira's active participation in and across the curriculum areas, her creativity, and her determination to solve problems and really understand her world through a variety of means. They also call attention to the strength of Seaaira's inventions and the gradual development of her attention to the conventions of the society and the semiotic systems around her.

For example, Seaaira is very unconcerned with conventional spelling or punctuation in her writing early in the year. Her enthusiasm and speed while she writes affects the legibility of her handwriting as well. As Seaaira explains, sometimes her ideas just go too fast for her writing to keep up with in a neat, orderly, or conventional way. Since conventions have an authentic purpose in the Sunshine Room, however, Seaaira's writing becomes more conventional over time without diminishing the creativity of her ideas or

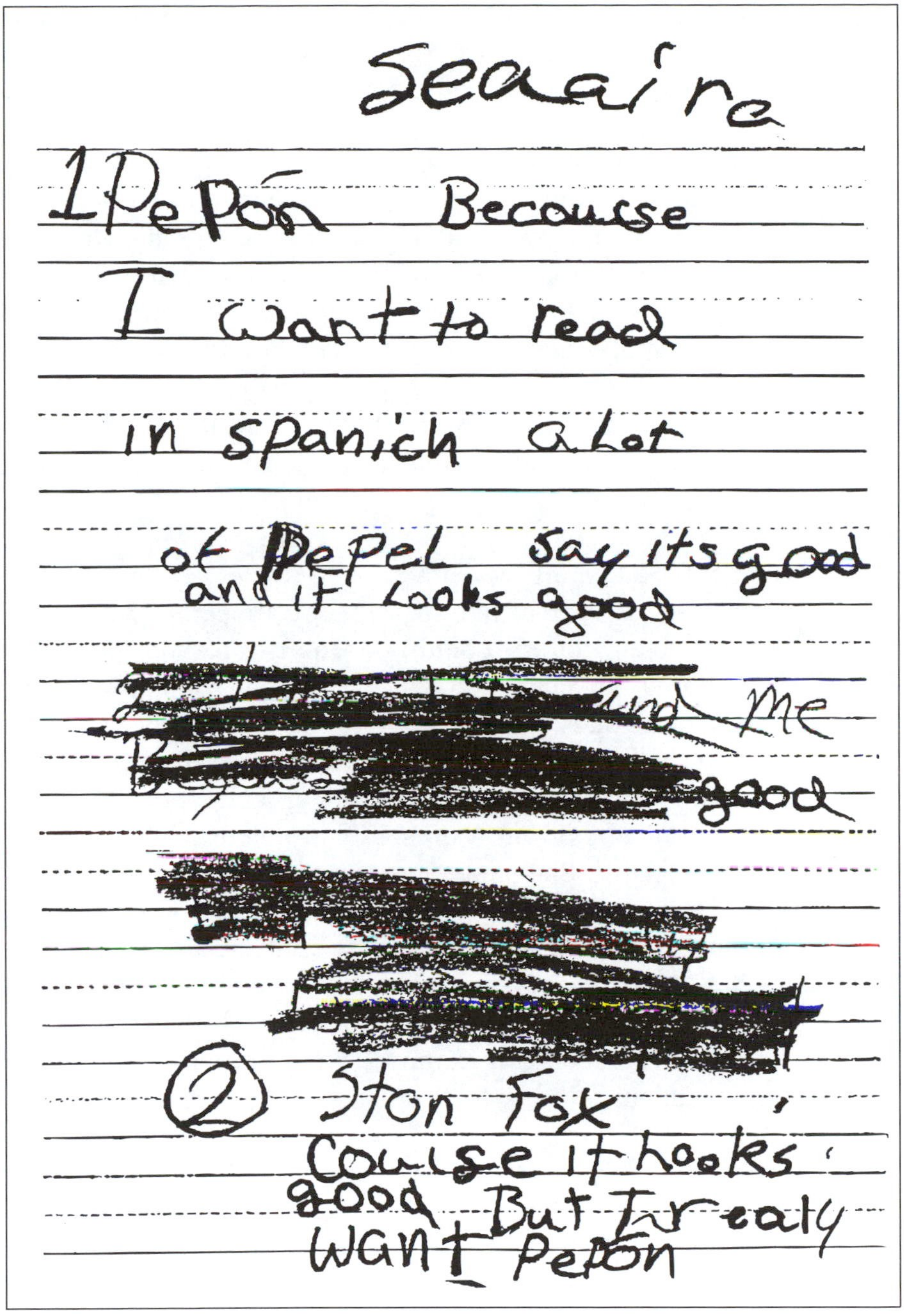

Seaaira

1 Pepon Becouse
I want to read
in spanich a lot
of Pepel say its good
and it looks good
[redacted] Me
[redacted] good
[redacted]
(2) Ston Fox
Couse it looks
good But I realy
want Pepon

Figure 7-1. Seaaira's request for membership in a literature group.

her enthusiastic inventions. Seaaira's awareness of conventions changes as she matures. She wants to include more conventional mechanics in her writing because the supportive environment of her classroom encourages her to do so without risking the loss of her personal ideas or goals.

Caryl's comments on Seaaira's evaluation demonstrate her value of Seaaira's strengths and her plan to provide learning activities for Seaaira that encourage growth without limiting Seaaira's natural curiosity or personal goals for learning. The comments returned by Seaaira's mother express her appreciation for Caryl's evaluation procedures and convey the interactive relationship that occurs between school and home in Borton school. There is a reciprocal sharing of knowledge about children and how learning occurs in this relationship.

Meet Lolita

Although Lolita and Seaaira are the dearest of friends, they are the antithesis of each other in outward appearance, personality, and cultural background. Lolita is a quiet, reserved girl who waits for invitations to participate. She has a heart-shaped face with a smattering of freckles across her nose; she usually wears her long brown hair in a ponytail or braid, her bangs raised high above her face thanks to a generous application of hair spray. Lolita is always dressed nicely, often in dresses and patent leather shoes with lacy socks or tights. She sits quietly in most group situations, like literature study sessions, although when asked to participate she does so without hesitation and she usually contributes insightful comments. Lolita has equal competencies in either Spanish or English regardless of difficulty of the material or task and across modes of communication. She feels, for example, that reading is the same process in either language.

Lolita at Home

Caryl and I visit Lolita's family—her parents, one older brother, and one younger sister—after school one day. Lolita's father comes home from work while we visit. He is a construction worker who, according to Lolita, works in various communities doing all types of construction, painting, and so on, depending on what is available. Lolita's mother stays at home with Lolita's sister, Casandra, who is physically and neurologically disabled from cerebral palsy and requires constant care. Casandra is referred to as a baby by the family although she is four years old. Lolita's brother, Francisco, is one year older than Lolita and was in Caryl's class the year before. Lolita occasionally receives recommendations from Francisco for good books to read, and her comments in school and during interviews imply they share a fond affection for the Sunshine Room.

Lolita's house is in the center of the barrio and protected by a chain link fence. It is an immaculate three-bedroom house; family portraits hang proudly in the living room and the family's bird chirps from the kitchen. There are very few books visible in Lolita's house. She has a few from school next to her bed in the bedroom she shares with her little sister, and there are several volumes of an encyclopedia on the living room shelves next to a Spanish-language anthology of children's stories.

Lolita's parents explain to us in Spanish that they don't use reading and writing much around their house. Lolita's dad reads plans and construction materials at work, but he says that if he brings them home he usually doesn't look at them. These materials typically involve more math-related print than alphabetic print. Lolita's mom insists that she doesn't keep lists or write letters to friends or families. A deeper search though, reveals that Lolita and her mother make regular journeys to the public library. There, her mother checks out novelas in Spanish to read for recreation and Lolita checks out books to read for fun and for school. Caryl and I find a note posted on the family's refrigerator, written by Lolita, that verifies the value of the library in this relationship. It lists the times the library is open each day and includes the phone number.

Lolita's dad volunteers another use of literacy in their home. He explains that Lolita and Francisco frequently tell about what they read at school during family discussions. For instance, during the literature study centered around the topic of war and peace, Lolita regularly brings home books from the text set to read, translate if necessary, and talk about with her parents.

My interest in Lolita's biliteracy development leads me to Lolita's second-grade teacher, Ms. Kathy Lohse. She confirms that Lolita's parents have "real strong Spanish" and that once Lolita began reading and writing in English during second grade, she was noticeably conscientious about making sure that "whenever things went home, there was something in Spanish" included.

Ms. Lohse reflects on the supportive nature of Lolita's family about school during our chat. She says, "What's always lovely about Lolita's family is the complete support from her parents. It's very, very important to them that their children get an education, and they both have a great deal of trust in the school. Lolita's dad, periodically last year, would check in for a verbal confirmation—'how is she doing?' They were very excited about what their kids were learning, and they showed it. Their kids knew that when they took their work home it was always looked at, even with the mom being busy." We share our sadness over Casandra's poor health. "Yeah, but they were always very, very supportive."

Ms. Lohse continues, "If you would say, 'You do this fifty times' to Lolita's parents, they would do it fifty times. That's the way they are."

Lolita's extended family includes relatives who live in the back of their house. She credits her cousin and her next-door neighbor for teaching her English. One day during an interview she explains to me, "Well, my brother learned English before me 'cause our next-door neighbor, he speaks English and Spanish, and he didn't like to play with us because we didn't speak English. But his mom, she knows my mom a lot, and she always gives us things and my next-door neighbor's mom she kept inviting us over there so we could do things and play over there and eat dinner and invite us on holidays and something and they would bring us things. They would give us Christmas presents, and we invite them over to our parties, and we got used to going over there and Josh and I, the next-door neighbor guy, used to let us go over there. They started teaching me and then my cousin she was teaching me a little bit and then I learned."

Languages in addition to Spanish and English are occasionally encountered in Lolita's home. Francisco has a new friend at school who is Chinese and who is teaching Francisco some Chinese vocabulary; he passes his knowledge on to Lolita. And one of the children's neighbors is African and is teaching Lolita a little bit of an African language. But English and Spanish are the main forms of communication, and Lolita's parents basically speak only Spanish.

Lolita was in kindergarten during her early experiences with English. She recalls Francisco teaching her the alphabet, "Then he showed me how it sounds, all the word sounds, and then he wrote some easy words, then he like made me, he told me to try to sound it out and then he wrote me words and then I learned."

Lolita at School

What will become my favorite image of Lolita at school develops early in the year. I'm busily involved in writing conferences with some of the boys in the class when Caryl calls me to the other side of the room.

"Kathy, you've got to see what Lolita just wrote," she says. "Go ask her to share it with you."

"Lolita, what are you working on?" I ask when I find Lolita and Seaaira at an art table. She hands me a rather hastily put-together book, the whole thing (not just the cover) written on construction paper. Her eyes are downcast and there is a slight blush creeping over her cheeks, but her sweet smile urges me to continue paying attention to her.

The book hasn't been created through the conventional writing-process sequence. Rather, it has been written on loose sheets of construction paper, straight through without revision or editing, illustrated (before or after the writing, I still don't know which), and hastily stapled three times down the left-hand binding. (The title and the first two pages are reproduced in Figures 7-2 and 7-3.)

Figure 7-2. The title page of Lolita's book.

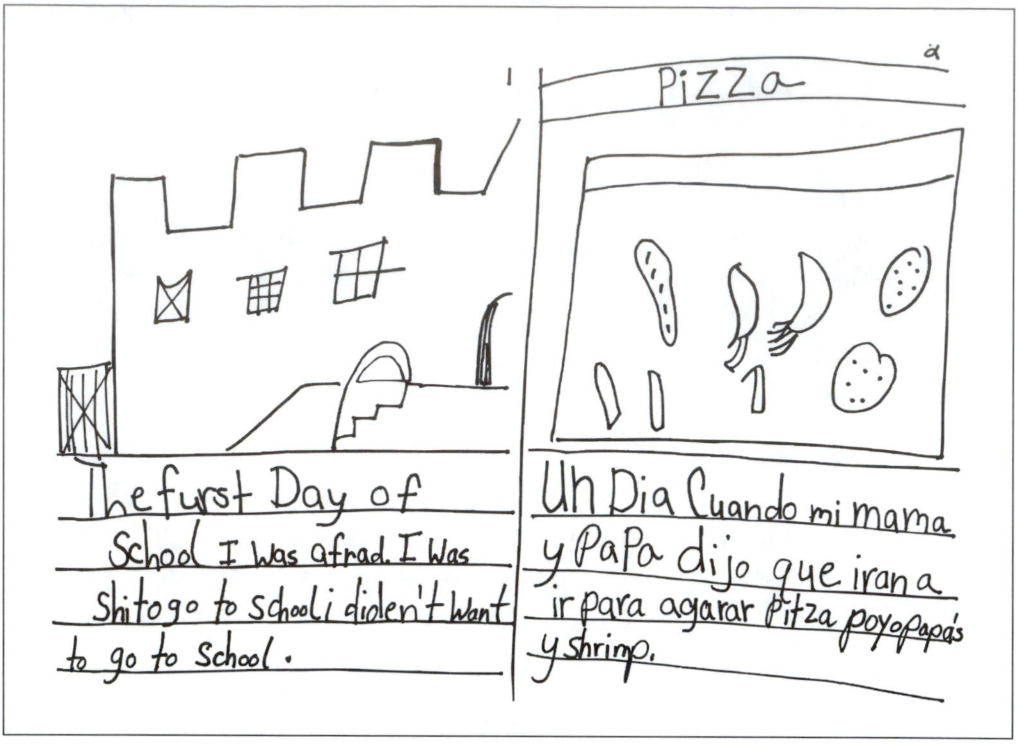

Figure 7-3. Pages one and two of Lolita's book.

Throughout the book, Lolita writes alternating pages in Spanish and English. As the languages alternate, so do the setting, the characters, and the plot. The English story reads:

> "In the Sunshine Room"
>
> The first day of school I was afraid. I was shy to go to school. I didn't want to go to school. When the second day of school I made a lot of friends. I liked the Sunshine Room. In school Halloween was coming up and we were studying the Middle Ages. And now it's today. Aren't you proud of that.

The Spanish narrative (with an English title) goes like this:

> "In the Romero's House"
>
> Un día cuando mi mamá y papá dijo que iban a ir para agarrar pizza, pollo, papas y shrimp. En la casa mi hermana estaba enferma. Y mi mamá y toda mi familia la cuida. Mi mamá llevó a mi hermana, nos quedamos en la casa. (One day when my mom and

dad said they were going to go get pizza, chicken, potatoes, and shrimp. At home, my sister was sick. And my mom and all my family take care of her. My mom took my sister and we stayed home.)

"Lolita, I love this book," I say when I finish reading. "I think the way you've created it is amazing. Will you tell me about why you made it like this?"

We talk about how she felt when school started at the beginning of the year and I sympathize with her sister's trip to the hospital.

"Lolita," I ask, "How did you get the idea to write a story in two languages, every other page?"

"I want my parents to be able to read my story because they'll like it. But I want Seaaira to read it, too."

Lolita poetically illustrates her proficiency as a biliterate writer. She accommodates two audiences: her monoliterate parents who speak, read, and write only in Spanish, and her monolingual English-speaking, -reading, and -writing friend at school. Her story(ies) demonstrate her strengths as a writer. Although her spelling, punctuation, and usage do not hold to adult standards in either language, she has the astute ability to maintain two story lines, two settings, and two sets of characters and events, all the while maintaining two linguistic conventions. Each writing decision Lolita makes is appropriate for her audiences and purposes.

Lolita's role as a bridge of knowledge between Spanish and English is significant at school and at home. Like Seaaira, Lolita has been a student at Borton since kindergarten, but she has been continuously involved in bilingual programs. Gradually, Lolita's strong Spanish abilities have been enhanced by her growing and now competent use of English.

Lolita's teachers from previous years remember Lolita fondly. They specifically remember Lolita's conscious attention to audience as she began to read and write in English. For example, Ms. Lohse recalls that in second grade she would ask other children in which language she should write things to them. This year, Lolita's attention to audience intensifies. She invents biliterate forms for her writing that allow both her parents and her English-reading friends to participate as her audience.

In bilingual classrooms, children like Lolita who are capable of all types of language events in either Spanish or English are important assets. Lolita is asked repeatedly over the course of the year to help out as a translator, a teacher of Spanish (especially for Seaaira), and a source of valuable language knowledge. Lolita transports news and information from school to home by switching languages, and carries information between classmates and between teachers and children in the classroom. She is called on by both adults and other children as a resource. I often ask her to assist me with translation, given my limited knowledge of Spanish and even more limited confidence in using it.

Marisela, a monolingual and monoliterate user of Spanish, often depends on Lolita to help her with both academic and social issues. When Marisela qualifies for the pull-out gifted education program at Borton, she finds herself in a challenging position. Although Marisela is a very capable student and can easily participate in the gifted program at a conceptual level, the teacher of the gifted class is a monolingual English speaker. Lolita, who is also in the gifted class, quickly becomes the bridge between the teacher and her instructions, stories, and lessons, and Marisela. She frequently acts as a direct translator. Thanks to Lolita, Marisela can continue to benefit from the challenges of a gifted program regardless of the limited linguistic abilities of the teacher.

In a similar way, Lolita helps Marisela and the other girls as they interact socially but don't understand each other linguistically, and as they write in their second languages (Spanish or English). Lolita is able to help other students with school work regardless of the language of instruction or participation.

Lolita is a strong, capable student and, like Seaaira, her strengths flourish in the Sunshine Room while she improves and continuously shows developmental growth. Lolita's end-of-the-year developmental record follows Seaaira's in Appendix C. It is written in Spanish for Lolita's parents. Caryl's comments about Lolita convey many of the observations I have described, that she is typically quiet in the classroom, that she codeswitches effortlessly depending on the social situation and her audience, and that her participation in learning experiences is always thoughtful.

Among the developments that Caryl observes over the year are Lolita's extensions into widely varied genres, including poetry during a social studies presentation; her new use of quotation marks and cursive; her improved use of the conventions of orthography in both languages (with some Spanish influence in her English usage); and her creativity, particularly in collaboration with Seaaira. Caryl concludes her comments by stating that Lolita is gaining confidence as she takes responsibility for her own learning. She is capable of reflecting on how she learns and successfully explains the processes she uses to others. Lolita seems to be particularly inventive and take risks more easily while working with her friend, Seaaira, but the confidence instilled in part by Seaaira is observable when Lolita works independently, too—during the gifted education class, for example.

Seaaira and Lolita Together

The year that Seaaira and Lolita share in third grade is their first year together in a classroom, since Lolita has always been placed in a bilingual classroom and Seaaira has never been in a bilingual classroom until this year. As mentioned earlier, two occurrences during their friendship characterize the bicultural nature of the Sunshine Room and its value in developing a learning community that invents its own culture. The first occurs outside of school, when opportunities to spend the night at each other's houses invite first-hand cross-cultural learning for the girls.

Following Seaaira's first overnight at Lolita's house a few blocks from Borton, she returns to school with her blue eyes literally widened from the experience. She remarks to me that things are different at Lolita's house, specifically describing a pile of beer cans in a neighbor's yard and the bums that Lolita cautions her to not look at and to stay away from. Seaaira is frightened by the sirens she hears at Lolita's house and by the homeless folks she observes each time she visits. Regardless, Seaaira says, "I like going there 'cuz she's my best friend." She is impressed that the video/candy store is so close to Lolita's home that the girls could walk there alone. Hearing so much real Spanish in a home is fascinating to her as well.

Lolita is also impressed by Seaaira's home. She comments on the proximity of her house to a shopping mall and the fun the girls have sleeping in Seaaira's parents' camper parked in the driveway. Lolita is invited to travel to Mexico with Seaaira's parents, but although the girls spend hours planning and discussing their trip, it doesn't happen during the school year. Seaaira tells me that Lolita wishes she lived in Seaaira's neighborhood, "because it isn't scary there."

Seaaira realizes there are some similarities between the girls' homes. She explains that each house has similar rooms, each has a brother and a mom and a dad, and each has some interesting businesses nearby. The girls wish they lived "right next door."

A second learning experience occurs in the classroom. The class is involved in the thematic study of the Middle Ages, augmented by a literature study of fairy tales, that is detailed in Chapter 5. Remember, Seaaira and Lolita selected membership in a literature study group that includes Marco, a Spanish-dominant speaker and nearly monoliterate Spanish reader and writer. Gabriel, another member, is bilingual. Their small group is involved in a study of multiple versions of the fairy tale *Little Red Riding Hood.*

Several days into the study, the group has completed its detailed and systematic reading and comparison work. It is time to invent a form for the learning they have done so they may present it to the class. Another group has read the feminist fairy tale *The Paper Bag Princess,* by Robert Munsch. To present their learning, this group acts out the book for the class. This demonstration piques Seaaira and Lolita's interest and they lead the Red Riding Hood group's decision to write a play as well.

Since the group has read a variety of versions of the fairy tale in both Spanish and English and the participants in the group represent both languages, the group decides that a bilingual play is most appropriate. Seaaira and Lolita take the initiative and act as recorders as their group invents a script for their own *Little Red Riding Hood* version; it involves two main characters—Little Red Jennifer and Little Blue Jenny—and stars Lolita and Seaaira, respectively. Several other classmates become characters at the group's request. Antonia, for example, is asked to narrate since she speaks both languages. A portion of the script is included in Appendix D.

The group spends a couple of weeks preparing for their presentation. Caryl and the children provide props like baskets for the two girls and a bathrobe for the grandmother, played by Angélica. Lolita's mother makes red and blue capes for the girls to wear. Rehearsing and practicing lines in both Spanish and English have the group absorbed during their regular language arts blocks as well as less-academic times like lunch and free choice.

Finally the preparations and practice are over and the children perform for their classmates and other Borton classes. I also arrange for them to present their play for another third-grade class in the district that is studying fairy tales at the same time. We go on a Thursday afternoon and the children are nervous. But they have fun and enjoy seeing another third-grade classroom. Following the pres-

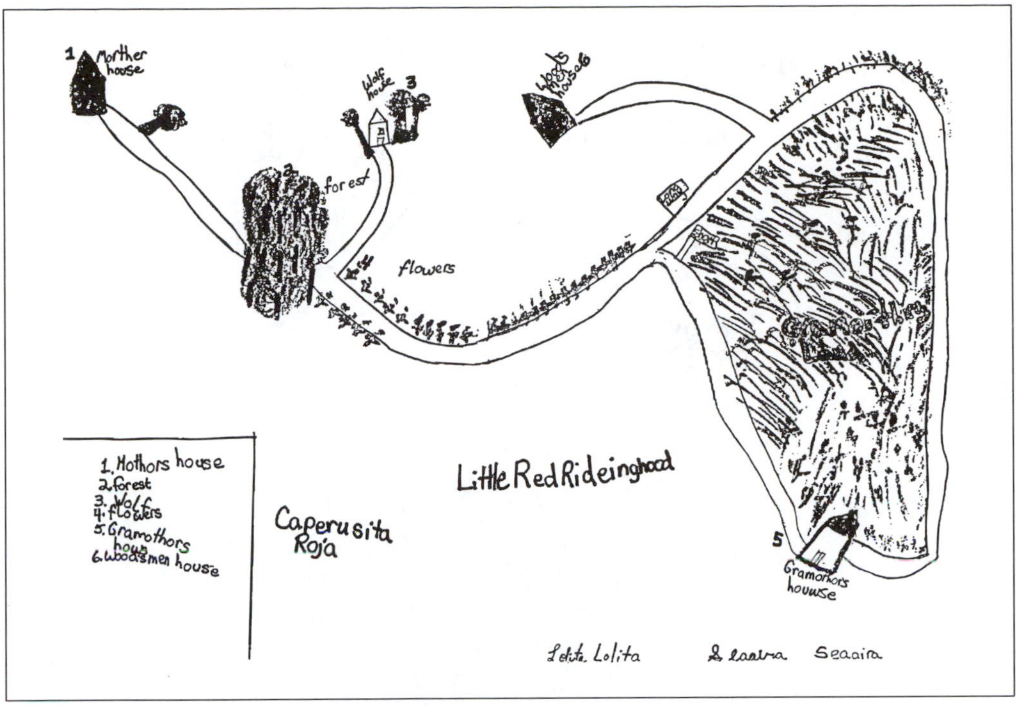

Figure 7-4. Lolita and Seaaira's *Little Red Riding Hood* map.

entation, the monolingual children in the audience raise questions about what it's like to be bilingual and to go to a bilingual school. The experience elevates the Sunshine Room students' images of themselves and their peers as bilingual and biliterate resources. It is a successful encounter for all the children.

Some of the other literature study groups during this period of time decide to present their versions of fairy tales by creating story maps for the classroom. Lolita and Seaaira observe the other children in this process, are attracted to it, and create two maps of their own, with an inventive twist. First, they draw the story of Red Riding Hood (Figure 7-4). Then they create a map of the lives of the Grimm brothers, well-known for their writing in the fairy tale genre. The map the girls invent (see Figure 7-5) carries the Grimm brothers through Germany and across time.

Throughout our study Seaaira and Lolita provide Caryl and me with much pleasure and enjoyment. We learn from them, we share their enthusiasm, and we're happy for the love they develop for one

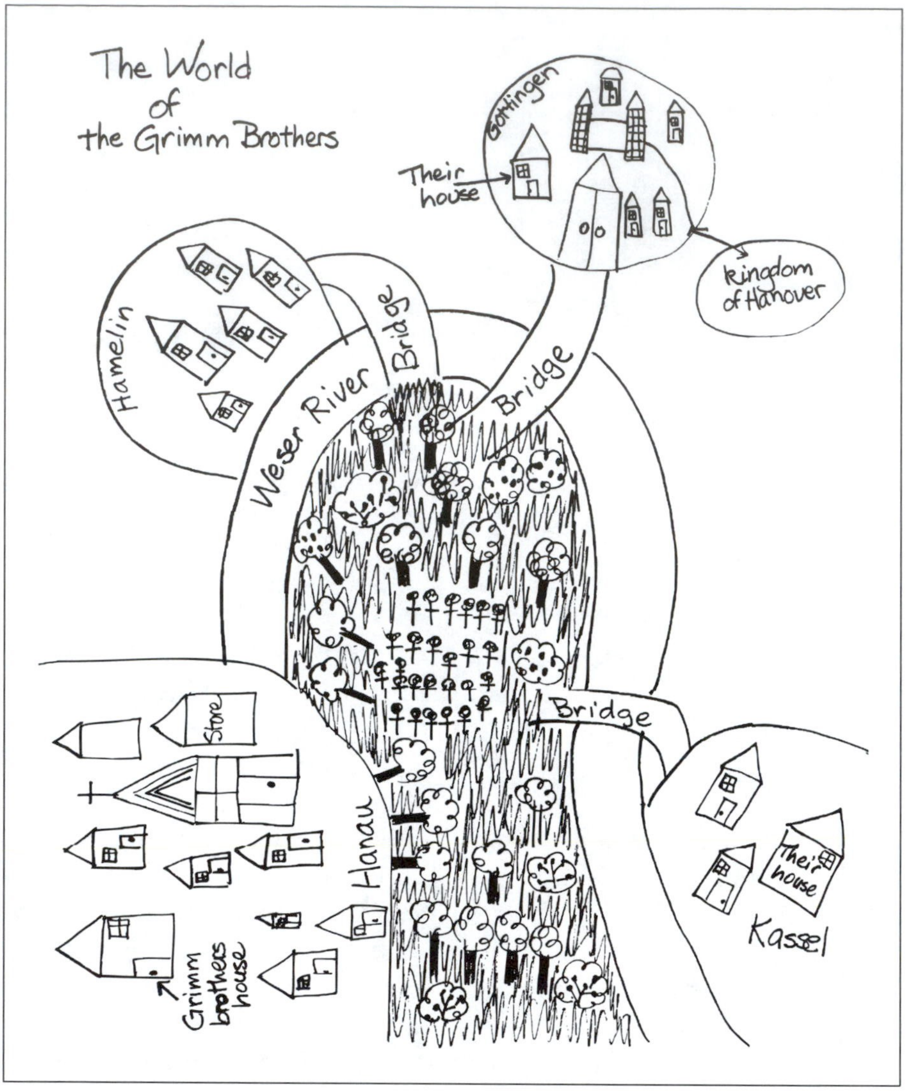

Figure 7-5. Seaaira and Lolita's Grimm brothers map. Caryl created this representation from their original poster.

another in school. We also appreciate their friendship as being representative of the value of culture in classrooms and regard their relationship as a critical event in our understanding of how culture can be invented in whole language settings.

High Level of Intellectual Expectation

The friendship between Seaaira and Lolita highlights the role of culture in their intellectual and social development because it provides each girl with the unique opportunity to confront their cultural assumptions. James Banks (1992) suggests that confronting cultural assumptions is an essential part of educating for freedom.

Banks, along with many other educators interested in diversity issues, asserts that children from nonmainstream cultures and ethnic backgrounds, poor homes, and homes where languages other than English are spoken have their cultural assumptions challenged when they enter school because there they confront a manner of behaving, speaking, interpreting, and valuing that is different from their home experiences. Lolita is a child in this situation. Children from mainstream cultures, on the other hand, like Seaaira, rarely confront opportunities that challenge their cultural assumptions, because these assumptions continue at school. As Banks says, "mainstream Americans often have an inability to function effectively within other American cultures, and lack the ability and motivation to experience and benefit from cross-cultural participation and relationships" (p. 35).

The effects of Seaaira and Lolita's cross-cultural experiences in each other's homes confirm Banks' ideas. Seaaira, although consistently a more vocal child in all contexts, is more obviously changed by her experiences in Lolita's neighborhood. Seaaira's eyes are opened to a new world where people interact differently than in her past experience. Lolita's experience, while also beneficial, is less dramatic. Although she is favorably impressed with the quality of the materialistic components of Seaaira's family's lifestyle and recognizes the social advantages of Seaaira's neighborhood, the experience appears to be less challenging in a conceptual sense than Seaaira's.

For each child, the exchange of cultural funds of knowledge, including their second languages, supports their intellectual growth. Herlinda Garza Flores (1992), an English teacher in Houston, describes the growing population of Hispanic students in Texas as most likely sitting "passively or shyly by in their classrooms. They don't ask questions. They don't challenge or even participate until they feel comfortable or until their shyness wears off" (p. 58). She implores teachers to "bother with" these typically quiet students. "We must believe, first, that these children do have the intelligence worthy of our extra efforts and, second, that we have the ability to make a difference" (p. 58). Flores asks teachers to respect their students' names, encourage them to reach out, end the exclusion of any groups, and appreciate family ties. She wants teachers to challenge Hispanic students academically as she criticizes the subtle discrimination that often cheats them from the best school experiences.

Seaaira helps Lolita challenge these cultural expectations for her behavior, perhaps more than Caryl does. She constantly pushes Lolita to take risks and to try new, sometimes fairly imposing activities. For example, she supports Lolita's early experiences with presentations of learning in front of their classmates. Although Lolita remains the more quiet and subdued member of the team, she increasingly opens herself up, and by the end of the year she is participating with enthusiasm in poetry, singing, drama, and speaking in front of the class. This is not simply a patronizing example of a majority child including a minority child in the ways of behaving and succeeding in school. Seaaira and Lolita *exchange* their cultures and intellects.

Seaaira is deeply intrigued by Lolita and her background. She is respectful of Lolita's abilities with two languages and enviously conscious of the range of opportunities available to her friend as a result of her bilingualism. Seaaira capitalizes on Lolita's bilingual capabilities in both formal and informal ways. There is a reciprocal respect between these girls that is grounded in their affection for each other. The funds of knowledge the girls share with each other contribute to the intellectual level of their cultural knowledge.

From their research about the funds of knowledge present in Lolita's community, Luis Moll and his colleagues (1990) conclude:

> The working-class Hispanic households in our study possess ample funds of knowledge that become manifest through household activities. Thinking of families in terms of funds of knowledge not only captures an essential aspect of household and community life, but helps define (and in many respects re-define) these families as important social and cognitive resources for education. We have every reason to believe that these findings are equally relevant to other populations. (p. 8)

Lolita and Seaaira exploit the potential for sharing funds of cultural knowledge through their friendship. Each child is enriched because of her intellectual and personal knowledge of the other.

The at-school friendship that Seaaira and Lolita nourish is not uncommon at Borton. In every classroom, children of different cultural backgrounds come together and establish relationships that last at least that year, if not all the way through their time at the school. What is unusual about Seaaira and Lolita is the extent to which their friendship is played out after school. The volunteer community of our school does not live close to Borton. Buses come from as many as twenty miles away to the inner city area where the school is located. Maintaining cross-cultural friendships is extremely difficult for students whose parents may be pressed for time or lack transportation. Lolita's and Seaaira's parents make a commitment to support their friendship and arrange for the girls to be together on weekends and during vacations.

In the Sunshine Room, we take advantage of every opportunity for all the children to share their home cultures in meaningful ways. Whenever possible, parents are encouraged to become part of our theme studies. They are always invited to become learners with us when they have time to spend in the classroom and they share their particular funds of knowledge whenever appropriate. When we study the ocean, Paul's stepfather, a marine biologist, brings jars of specimens and the tools of his work to school. Aaron's father, a surveyor, helps us learn how maps are made. Several fathers who work in construction provide able assistance when our class builds a playhouse for the patio. A study of the human body is enriched when José's father, who spends weekends with his son on a working ranch, sends in a cow's heart and hair from a horse's tail. While we groan about how gross the heart is, we stick our fingers into its chambers and compare human hair to horsehair under a microscope. Molly, a Spanish-speaking aide, teaches us how to needlepoint, and Marisela's mother helps organize and teach traditional Mexican folkdances for the Cinco de mayo party.

Other opportunities to bring individual families' funds of knowledge into the classroom are purposefully created through the study of themes that build on the variety of cultural expression in our community. During a study of toys and games, the children interview their parents and grandparents about the games they played as children. As the students share their interview notes, we learn traditional children's games in both English and Spanish, and contribute several Spanish jump-rope jingles to the collection that our P.E. teacher is assembling. Researching what people are afraid of on Halloween brings out a number of different versions of La Llorona.

La Llorona, or the wailing woman, is a traditional tale from Mexican folklore about a woman who drowned her own children in a moment of desperation. A common version of the story tells how she wanders the streets at night looking to replace the children she lost with (according to many barrio parents) children who disobey their parents.

Kathy and I have chosen to discuss the friendship of Seaaira and Lolita at length because they also represent the high level of academic potential available to speakers of different languages working together within the same classroom. When language and cultural differences are viewed as opportunities to enrich the curriculum rather than as obstacles to learning, children are able to expand their considerable intellectual and linguistic resources and see that both English and Spanish are legitimate languages of learning.

The map of the Grimm brothers' world is just one example of the kind of learning that can take place when the focus in the classroom is on academic pursuits. The map begins when the girls ask how long ago the Grimm brothers collected their fairy tales. The search for an answer leads us to an encyclopedia entry on the Grimms that Seaaira and Lolita read together, each one helping the other, with some assistance from me. When the town of Hamlin is mentioned as a place the Grimm brothers had visited, Seaaira creates a new question for investigation.

"Then Hamlin was a real place. Were there really that many rats in Hamlin?" she wonders.

"Let's look up Hamlin," Lolita replies.

So we do. We read together that Hamlin, like other medieval towns, had suffered many deaths from bubonic plague and that during the eleventh century many children left the town to join the Children's Crusade. Following a brief discussion of those two critical events in world history, I leave the girls with the encyclopedias to attend to other students. About fifteen minutes later, they are spread out on the floor with even more encyclopedias and an atlas, drawing on a large sheet of butcher paper. "Ms. Crowell, help us find Hamlin on a map," they plead. I notice they have already begun to work on their map, drawing in the town where the Grimms had been born and the Weser River.

When the Seaairas of the world enter public school classrooms, success is the usual expectation. She is eager, curious, and English-speaking, the daughter of successful professionals. In many places, though, Lolita might be viewed as a child at risk of failure. She is quiet and reserved, a demeanor that might lead some educators to assume she has language problems. Moreover, she is the daughter of working-class parents who do not speak English and whose literacy might be considered questionable by mainstream Americans who have a narrow view of what constitutes reading and writing. In many classrooms, such as the ones sampled by Anyon (1980) and Díaz, Moll, and Mehan (1986), Lolita might not be offered the opportunities to pursue the questions that she and Seaaira raise. Yet, we have seen that Lolita has unquestionable strengths as a bilingual, biliterate learner and that her parents are as supportive of her education as Seaaira's are. That students in the Sunshine Room are offered an unlimited curriculum and the opportunity to pursue their questions together, regardless of language and cultural differences, is inherent to their success (Moll & Whitmore 1993).

Symmetric Power and Trust Relationships

Seaaira and Lolita trust each other because they are best friends. Their behavior and interaction show me that they respect each other and value each other's knowledge. Sometimes their support is obvious, as they challenge the world literally hand in hand or arm in arm. They support each other's learning, even when the content is scary (when they read books together about the Holocaust) or when the language is new (when Seaaira joins a Spanish literature study group.)

These are examples of equal power and mutual trust. But power and trust are heated issues in the topic of multicultural education. What if typically marginalized groups of children become "empowered" and society's expectation for their lack of success no longer exists? What if bilingual learners become the privileged, and monolingual English speakers are recognized as truly limited? What if the Western traditional view of what it means to be an American is no longer the content of the canon that determines and values knowledge in school?

Banks (1992) places the culture of the classroom right within the area of tension between personal invention and social convention as he describes the purpose of multicultural education:

> Education within a pluralistic society should affirm and help students understand their home and community cultures. However, it should also help free them from their cultural boundaries. . . . [E]ducation in a democratic society should help students acquire the knowledge,

> attitudes, and skills they will need to participate in civic action to make society more equitable and just. (p. 32)

Banks presents multicultural education as a power struggle between what he terms multiculturalists and traditionalists, groups who attach very different values to how the roots of American civilization are characterized and therefore disagree about what (or whose) curriculum is best for our nation's students. The traditionalists, those who defend the typical Eurocentric content of classrooms, hold the balance of power over the multiculturalists, who challenge that content. Banks contends that no genuine discussion between the factions can occur until "power is placed on the table, negotiated, and shared" (p. 33). He continues:

> We should teach students that knowledge is a social construction, that it reflects the perspectives, experiences, and the values of the people and cultures that construct it, and that it is dynamic, changing, and debated among knowledge creators and users. (p. 34)

Ken Goodman (1990) contributes to the discussion in whole language terms. He urges whole language teachers to make these issues their own:

> Ultimately, whole language teachers seek to free the minds and creative energies of pupils for the greatest gains in their intellectual, physical, and social development. Whole language teachers know that their students can't become proactive participants in democratic societies without experiencing democratic classrooms. (p. 40)

Referring to children of all cultural and linguistic backgrounds, he adds, "A high academic quality comes from starting where learners are and liberating them to pursue learning. We are discovering we have underestimated children's possibilities because we seldom gave them the chance to show us" (p. 40).

I love Rudine Sims Bishop's expansion of Charlotte Huck's metaphor for multicultural children's literature as "mirrors" and "windows" (Bishop 1982; Huck, Hepler & Hickman 1987). She means that children should be able to see themselves represented culturally and linguistically in what they read, but that they should also be invited to experience other groups and ways of living through their reading material.

The Sunshine Room regularly provides children with mirrors and windows, although not always in ways as obvious as Seaaira and

Lolita's friendship. The children from the mainstream community who volunteer to attend Borton are provided with daily windows—opportunities to become acquainted with and understand another cultural group. Children who attend Borton from the barrio around the school share these windows, but they are also provided with mirrors that many minority children don't have at school. Their backgrounds are valued, appreciated, celebrated, and given academic attention.

It is also true, however, that Seaaira and Lolita's exploitation of the invitation to exchange cultural funds of knowledge is more unusual than Caryl or I would like. If children were involved in such intense friendships more often, this relationship would no longer appear unique. In the irregularity of their experience, these young girls provide Caryl and me with a learning experience. The symmetric power and trust relationship they share demonstrates to us the unrealized potential of the bicultural nature of the Sunshine Room as a place that truly, not superficially, values difference and makes it part of the daily curriculum for all of the children.

A drive through the Borton neighborhood would probably serve to strengthen the stereotypical beliefs that mainstream children and their families might bring with them to school. One cannot avoid the appearance of poverty presented by the project apartments, their barren common area glittering with broken glass, the gang graffiti on the walls. Yet, behind the walls are rose gardens, bird feeders, and survivors, enveloped by strong, loving families.

When our class leaves school on a field trip, the children from the Borton neighborhood always remark about the beautiful homes we pass as we drive through middle-class neighborhoods. Little do they know that the same problems that invade their neighborhood—drugs, gangs, divorce, and abuse—are also found within some of the neatly painted houses with trimmed hedges.

The classroom offers a more equal playing field where children from the dominant majority culture can come to know and trust the children from a parallel world and where children of color can also overcome their mistrust of mainstream, white America. Lolita and Seaaira offer proof that differences can be pushed aside and new understanding and respect created.

Not every child is successful in gaining the trust of his or her peers. There are several children in the Sunshine Room most every year, both from the neighborhood and the extended community, who have a very difficult time establishing respectful relationships with other children. I think about one boy who refused to talk in an instructional setting all year long, and a girl whose difficult behavior and personal problems prevented her from forming friendships with any of the others. Still, these outsiders are offered repeated invitations, from the children and the adults, to become members of the strongly knit community that is formed in the classroom. Sometimes we are successful at breaking down the walls that these children construct to keep us out. Sometimes we aren't. And all of us must struggle daily with the impact of drugs, divorce, violence, and neglect. Without one another's support throughout the school day, I believe we would not be successful as a learning community.

The trust the children have in each other supports them as they create and express their learning. They come to rely on each other, maintaining the expectation that they will live up to their commitments to each other. When Seaaira and Lolita are casting parts for their Red Riding Hood play, they naturally assume that everyone in their group will take part. They have decided that the wolf will speak Spanish and are able to convince Marco to take on the role. He learns his part with ease and practices willingly, but the day before the presentation, he gets cold feet and backs out. The girls are exceedingly annoyed with him. Fortunately, David, who has been watching the rehearsals with great interest, volunteers to take over at the last minute. Seaaira and Lolita wonder whether he can assume such a major part on such short notice, but David convinces them that he can and will take on this responsibility.

The day of the play arrives and Lolita and Seaaira admonish all the players not only to remember their lines, but also to be in the right place at the right time. They have planned for the wolf to chase the grandmother behind a panel that has been set up as a backdrop. Then the wolf will emerge alone, suggesting to the audience that the grandmother has been eaten. Once again, David assures the girls that he knows what to do. The play proceeds as rehearsed, to everyone's relief. David speaks every line as written and chases the grandmother behind the panel. When he comes out from the other side, he is patting a belly that has grown noticeably fatter with bags stuffed under his T-shirt, much to the surprise, delight, and howling laughter of the audience, the actors, and the authors, who have not planned this sight gag. Although he has not consulted them, Seaaira and Lolita recognize the value of his contribution and when the show goes on the road with Kathy, they remind David firmly, "And don't forget the bags!"

David's secretly planned addition to the play is admittedly the highlight of the performance. It is a moment that I'll never forget, especially the smile of complete and charming confidence on David's face and the unison laughter his action produces. It is a day when we are truly a community.

Authenticity

Seaaira and Lolita epitomize the social nature of authentic literacy and learning. They read together, write together, dream and play together. They show how social influences impact personal writing, reading, and learning. Each girl maintains her own personality, style, and cultural-linguistic knowledge while they grow together in their development of the conventions for their bicultural friendship. The girls' strengths complement one another: Seaaira is a more confident reader at the beginning of the year, for example, while Lolita is a more conventional speller in either English or Spanish.

Friendship can offer a strong purpose for a variety of activities, academic and otherwise, in school. A friendship is a real relationship, not contrived within the context of "school." The grouping practices in the Sunshine Room capitalize on the authentic nature of friendships that expands cultural and linguistic understanding. Children generally select their membership in academically focused groups, like research groups and literature study groups, based on the materials or topics involved and which other children will be a part of the future group.

Caryl's goal for all types of groups, whether self-selected by the children, selected at random, or determined by Caryl, is to help children learn to work with all types of people. She enters the group-making process only rarely—when monolingual students of opposite languages are working together, for example. When this happens, if it is helpful, she intercedes by placing a bilingual child in the group to mediate the communication between members.

"Authentic multicultural teachers realize that each child possesses different strengths, and that all people have weaknesses. . . . The combination of all strengths results in the best possible environment where each person can help someone else," say Gloria Boutte and Christine McCormick (1992, p. 144). With this philosophy in mind, Caryl rarely objects to Seaaira and Lolita's constant companionship in and out of school. The girls find multiple ways to use their friendship as an authen-

bring the hamster
books pleas
seaaira

Figure 7-6. Seaaira's note to Kathy.

tic link to literacy events. Many of these activities have been explicated in detail throughout this book: plays, projects, studies, and presentations are all created during the year. Poetry, calligraphy, artistic endeavors, and buddy reading tighten the link between the two girls through literacy. Reading and writing are nearly always a part of Seaaira and Lolita's play. They constantly create and revise authentic texts that document their friendship.

Seaaira and Lolita decide to learn about hamsters and gerbils when Seaaira's hamster has babies at home. In addition to searching the school library, they question the other members of the community for resources they might use. Seaaira hands me a note (see Figure 7-6) to remind me of one source I can contribute from my home. She is obviously aware of the purpose and the audience in her writing, something Lolita's double narrative (Figure 7-3) illustrates so strongly as well. The note is so personal and so related to a mutually acknowledged purpose that much of the typical language and structure of written communication is unnecessary. Seaaira doesn't even address the recipient (me) because she hands the note directly to me and we share an understanding about its meaning. However, Seaaira is aware of the additional context of the writing, that she is reminding me of her request of a favor, and she tags a "please" on her ending.

Just as the juxtaposition of "inauthentic" literacy events helps clarify the role of authentic literacy events, "pseudomulticulturalism" clarifies the authentic nature of multicultural education. Boutte and McCormick tell us, "An authentic multicultural approach is based on appreciation of differences in others" (p. 141) as opposed to the pseudomulticultural nature of isolated cultural activities prompted by a holiday or culturally centered attention focused toward only one ethnic minority in a class.

To change from pseudomulticultural education to authentic multicultural education, Boutte and McCormick say teachers must become thoughtful and critical in their avoidance of stereotypic attitudes that have "no place in the classroom or society," first on their own and next along with their students in classrooms. Caryl is actively attentive to understanding her students' unique backgrounds and funds of knowledge. Discovering the diversity of the inventive potential of the class adds substance to the development of a community.

Lolita and Seaaira have many opportunities each day to choose to work together. At other times, they are assigned to groups randomly. In this way, I can make sure that each of them will have opportunities to work with different children in the classroom. For example, we choose our committees for center activities by a random draw of cards. If you draw a two, you are in Committee 2 for the duration of any particular set of centers. This procedure separates me from any friendship disputes or power struggles that children might choose to engage in. However, it has its drawbacks, too. There have been times when Halie and I have had to live for two weeks with the "committee from hell" (an expression we share only with each other, of course). Such a committee is usually made up of all or most of the children who have difficulty getting along with others, who by the luck, or unluck, of the draw, have all ended up in the same committee. We never change the assignment or academic expectations for that group, but we do spend more time with them, mostly facilitating the social interactions and devising procedures for working together.

We understand that all of the children will not automatically get along well with all of the other children. We know there will be problems, but we also expect children to find ways of working together, with the support of adults and the more socially skillful children. It would be stressful to have to work with the "committee from hell" all day long, so throughout the day and year we have other ways of choosing groups and partners. I feel very strongly that children need to learn how to gain entrance to groups, how to find a partner, and how to be a group member. For this to happen, there must be times for them to choose for themselves what group they will join or form.

The children make these choices for a variety of reasons. Seaaira and Lolita often choose to be together because they are best friends. Their working groups change with activities because they invite different children to work with them. But they are usually at the center of each group's formation. Other children in the room work this way, too. Cari, Angélica, and Michelle are a similar team who are often together because they enjoy one another's company. Like Seaaira and Lolita, they support one another's creativity and risk taking. Angélica and Michelle are the more experienced readers and writers, but Cari drives the creation of many learning activities by her curiosity about everything. Together, they write a rap called "Cool Girls," which they sing to the class. It expresses their delight with their mutual friendship and their feelings of confidence in themselves as learners.

At other times, the children choose their working relationships based on the activity or the materials being used. Literature study groups are often selected in this way. The children are offered five or six different books or sets of books as the focus of the groups, and they choose which group to join based on what they want to read. Sometimes, different groups may be investigating different questions related to an ongoing theme study and the criteria for group membership will be the question that each child finds particularly interesting.

Collaboration takes place during writing activities, too, sometimes based on friendship, as with Lolita and Seaaira. Other times, a child who enjoys writing may invite a classmate who is a good artist to provide illustrations for a story. It's at these moments that the time spent declaring and celebrating individual strengths becomes especially fruitful.

I have noticed that children who want help with a particular task don't necessarily go to the child who is best at that skill. The child who needs help with spelling isn't likely to go to the very best speller in the class, but rather to someone who spells just a little bit better. In this way, children may establish their own zones of proximal development by working with peers who do something just enough more independently to be able to teach them, but not so much better that they are intimidated. Even two children who are not yet independent learners will be able to accomplish more together than either one of them will alone.

For whatever reasons they choose to work together, the social construction of the classroom is an important aspect of the authentic learning that takes place there. Ken Goodman and his colleagues (1987) have explained the importance of social arrangements in classroom learning by clarifying how individual inventions are influenced by social conventions. In the Sunshine Room, children come to individual understandings and unique inventions that they test against the understandings of others. Language and literacy are the media for sharing new ideas and the authentic language and literacy of a whole language classroom are especially critical for second language learners (Freeman & Freeman 1992).

Additive Bilingualism and Biliteracy

It is clear that Seaaira and Lolita's mutual interest in language intensifies their curiosity about each other and their attraction for each other. Seaaira expresses an explicit fascination with all languages, not just Spanish. One week a Canadian educator comes to visit Borton's whole language program. Her husband serves as her translator, since she is a monolingual French speaker. Seaaira inundates them with questions. Eventually, the man writes several words on the chalkboard at her request. Seaaira is particularly interested in the punctuation marks in written French and compares them with those in Spanish.

Lolita is also interested in language, but Lolita's bilingualism is easy for her, a natural part of her environment, and therefore more intuitive. As a sincerely curious but naive researcher, I have asked Lolita numerous questions she can't answer regarding her language abilities. I might wonder why she selects a book in one language or the other for example, or how she decides in which language to write. Sometime late in the year, I come to realize that the other features of the bilingual nature of Lolita's world drive her choices: topic and audience, for example, not Spanish or English. This is so true that Lolita is only mildly conscious of her biliteracy as she chooses. The result is that my questions are not only impossible for Lolita to answer, but in her view, silly for me to ask.

Susan Philips, the anthropologist who studied communication on the Warm Springs Indian Reservation, believes that language is an inherent part of a discussion about culture. Like other anthropologists she views language "as the key vehicle for transmission of cultural knowledge" (1983, p. 180). Shirley Brice Heath, in fact, argues that "all language learning is cultural learning" (1986, p.146).

All languages share similarities in that they have highly structured rules of sound and syntax and are used for interpersonal and intrapersonal communication (Cazden et al. 1981; Piper 1993). However, languages vary in their forms and include dialects and ideolects particular to groups of people and to individuals. They serve as a focal point for cultural identity. People who share a common language also share some common beliefs and behaviors (Chinn 1985). Thus language provides a common bond between individuals and serves to represent individuals' concepts of themselves as members of communities and cultures.

In the Sunshine Room, language difference is highlighted in a positive way. The children are very aware of who speaks which language and how well. The children's linguistic differences are accepted and respected. The bilingual play produced by Lolita and Seaaira is treasured by their classmates and spoken of with fondness and humor for the rest of the year. It deepens the sense of community in the classroom, further defining it as a bilingual community.

Although Lolita is certainly capable of communicating at any level of difficulty in English, the girls intentionally insert Spanish into their interactions, particular in academic situations. In the bilingual play, Seaaira's Spanish dialogue is fairly limited—single word utterances and simple, repetitive phrases. During the longest line in Spanish, a sentence, Seaaira is joined by Lolita's character in a choral reading technique. The girls have invented a bilingual zone of proximal development (Moll & Díaz 1987) for Seaaira that gives her opportunities to perform at a higher level with the cooperation of her bilingual best friend.

Historically, opinions about the value of bilingualism have ranged from positive to negative and have changed dramatically as research has contributed new information (Flores 1982). Gaardner (1977) expresses a political view that distinguishes between elite (academic) and folk (societal) bilingualism. In elite bilingualism, access to a second world of literature, ideas, and people is viewed as an advantage and enrichment for children who come from privileged backgrounds and choose to gain proficiency in a second language. Folk bilingualism, on the other hand, is not produced by choice, but by societal circumstances that dictate a need to use two languages. Folk bilingualism is frequently associated with a negative view of bilingualism as a language deficit. Classrooms like the Sunshine Room blur the distinction between questionably labeled "types" of bilingualism, advocating additive bilingual education for all learners.

I am very interested in the multiple advantages bilinguals have over monolingual language users. The positive effects of second language learning on young children's cognitive development as well as on affective and attitudinal development is well documented by many researchers. The process of becoming bilingual can and should be capitalized on by educators. I agree with Rafael Díaz (1983), who says, "I would like to present bilingual education not only as a right, but also as an excellent tool to enhance the academic and intellectual potential of our children, whether our children are native speakers of Navajo, Spanish, English, or Vietnamese" (p. 17).

Children's identification with a language or languages is an entry point to enlarge their ideas about the differences and similarities between people. Use of a variety of languages within a classroom increases children's self-worth with regard to differing individual languages and promotes an appreciation of the beauty and unique qualities of all languages through comparison. Additive bilingualism and biliteracy provides an opportunity for each of these friends to bridge their cultural differences.

The socially constructed nature of a whole language classroom provides many opportunities for bilingually organized groups of children to come together for mutual purposes. Be it a literature study group, a writing collaboration, or a theme-related research group, there are numerous chances for English-speaking, Spanish-speaking, and bilingual children to focus on making meaning as a group. In these situations, language differences are pushed into the background. They become procedural issues of translation and interpretation, while academic concerns are pushed to the forefront, creating authentic social conditions for learning language, learning through language, and learning about language (Halliday 1984).

There is no discounting the importance of native language literacy. Opportunities to develop native language literacy in school show children that their language has value in an academic setting and gives them a chance to draw on their strengths as language users. Reading involves the use of four cueing systems simultaneously—the semantic, syntactic, graphophonic, and pragmatic systems all come into play in helping a reader create a meaningful text (Y. Goodman, Watson & Burke 1987). Naturally, we are better able to make use of these systems in our native language. When a child begins to read in the second language, it's not necessary to learn to read again, because the reading process is the same (Barrera 1983; K. Goodman, Y. Goodman & Flores 1979).

When children in the Sunshine Room express an interest in reading and writing their second language, those requests are honored and celebrated. There are no prerequisites of oral language proficiency. Pat Rigg (1986) finds that children don't need oral control of their second language to construct meaning from a text in that language. They do, however, rely on semantic cues more than graphophonic or syntactic ones and are helped by knowing the schema, or story structure, of the text. The children developing biliteracy present me with frequent opportunities to better understand their second language reading throughout our regular days and weeks in the classroom.

When I observe Susana, a bilingual and biliterate student, reading books in English one day, I decide to complete a miscue analysis with her (Y. Goodman, Watson & Burke 1987). The books she is choosing to read involve extended texts, so I select "The Name of the Tree," an English folktale of some ninety-five sentences with many compound and complex structures.

Overwhelmingly, Susana works at making sense of the text. The opening sentence reads, "Once upon a time, in a faraway country, there grew a beautiful magic tree full of ripe, golden fruit." Susana reads "ripes," then changes to "grapes golden fruit", for the words "ripe, golden fruit." By the next occurrence of those words, she reads "grapefruit", a substitution that still does not work syntactically, but makes more sense than her earlier effort. Throughout her reading, Susana monitors herself, making new substitutions when her first miscue interferes with her understanding and allowing ungrammatical constructions that do not influence the meaning as much to stand uncorrected. Her scores on the story are 54 percent for syntactic acceptability and only 50 percent for semantic acceptability, scores that would be cause for concern among native English speakers. Testimony to her strength as a reader, though, is her near-perfect retelling in Spanish that includes every important event of the story in order, a considerable amount of detail, all of the characters, and an appropriate theme statement.

Susana once again shows us how complicated reading is. If I were to define reading as a "performance" or to evaluate second language readers according to their oral reading without a retelling, particularly a cross-language retelling, I would not have access to my students' real reading abilities. Susana illustrates, as Lolita and other bilingual children have, that reading is a transactive, constructive process of making meaning in two languages as well as one.

Inventing Whole Language Culture

The children in the Sunshine Room, including Seaaira and Lolita, are members of several communities. While they are part of the classroom that is inventing itself as a community, they are also members of families, local neighborhoods, and the southwestern city in which they live. In addition, they are part of the historical cultures represented in their school, which are predominately Mexican American, Anglo, or African American.

Educational literature is replete with vague and ambiguous terms such as *multiculturalism, cultural pluralism, cultural relativism,* and *multiethnicity* (Boutte & McCormick 1992; Bullard 1992; Gibson 1976; Reagan 1984; Schlesinger 1992). These terms have been so popularized and are used so easily and frequently that their power and purpose have been lost; as Arthur Schlesinger suggests, multiculturalism itself becomes ethnocentric. In 1981, Harry Wolcott contended that the terms are misused and abused by many educational authors who are not anthropologically informed. An anthropologist himself, he criticizes educators for thinking that the only locus of culture is in ethnic identities, for suggesting that multiculturalism is experienced by only a portion of the population, and for using "multiculturalism" as a catch-all slogan for many styles and types of teaching.

In the United States, classrooms like the Sunshine Room are filled with children from diverse cultural backgrounds. Multicultural education recognizes the ethnic pluralism within our schools; however, there is also a common limiting view that "education for the culturally different is basically a condescending approach that assumes that cultural differences cause school failure" (Bennett 1986, p. 53). A stronger multicultural perspective recognizes each person in the context of his or her cultural background and attempts to enlarge human potential by capitalizing on actual multicultural situations in classroom life (Macdonald 1976). This means that 'culture' consists of all the people, objects, and events that impart meaning to our lives, not only historically, but in our present everyday living experiences.

Recognition of cultural differences and human potential can be extended further, however, if multicultural education includes Ward Goodenough's (1957) definition of culture as "the process whereby a person develops competencies in multiple systems of standards for perceiving, evaluating, believing and doing" and recognizes "multiculturalism as the normal human experience" (p. 4). Such a view not only justifies but necessitates a multicultural experience for all children, mainstream and parallel cultures alike. It also recognizes the personal invention of culture within social conventions.

We know that racial and cultural awareness develops along with other values and attitudes as children learn from the significant people in their lives (Allport 1954; Banks 1992; Derman-Sparks 1989; Derman-Sparks, Higa & Sparks 1980; Galyean 1983; Seefeldt 1984). Children adopt and demonstrate the prejudices of their families in part because they are taught them by their parents and in part because they have little contact with people different from themselves. As children develop an awareness of race and culture during the early years of childhood, they are vulnerable to negative influences of inaccurate, stereotypic, or prejudiced information.

A quality multicultural program that has a theoretical fit with whole language is firmly based as a philosophy that encompasses and affects every interaction and every moment during the school day. Carole Seefeldt (1984) tells us that "multicultural education is not a set of activities, but an embodiment of a perspective" (p. 230). A teacher who upholds this perspective ensures that each individual is not only accepted and valued for her or his culture, but is helped to learn and develop greater understanding of other cultures and of culture in general.

In building multicultural curriculum, Caryl is a teacher who follows the guidelines of selecting topics that highlight similarities across groups of people (frequently universals) and approaching curriculum humanistically. She also calls attention more directly to cultural issues in the Sunshine Room through techniques that involve the physical environment, learning experiences, and the community. Some of these have been described throughout our story.

Multicultural literature, for example, provides children with specific information about cultures and stimulates children's language and cognitive growth (J. Goodman & Melcher 1984; Norton 1985; Harris 1992). Teachers like Caryl help students note details about culture in their reading of multicultural literature so that it provides vicarious experiences with other places and peoples and develops pride in students' unique heritages. "A well-balanced multicultural literature program includes literature that depicts people with a variety of aspirations, from different socioeconomic levels, with different occupations, and with a range of human characteristics" (Norton 1985, p. 107).

And yet Caryl does not encourage children to dip into multicultural literature without also taking a critical and political stance (Edelsky 1994; Shannon 1993). The war and peace literature study depicted in Chapter 6 shows how children are urged to sound a resounding why? to the historical and current U.S. policies in wartime. As children's understanding of innocence and power grows as they read engaging books, they become increasingly aware of their positions in a sociopolitical context. In the Sunshine Room, issues of politics, democracy, and power are centrally located in issues of culture and language.

Teachers in some geographic areas have a specific responsibility to meet the needs of children from local cultures (the Native American and Hispanic populations of the Southwest, for example). Leroy Ortiz and Guillermina Engelbrecht (1986) recommend that attention be given to the cultural relevance of materials used in the classroom, particularly in bilingual settings. They further suggest that communities and schools form partnerships for instruction in which the community represents the most meaningful and direct cultural setting for young children. The classroom work of the Community Literacy Project in Tucson, Arizona, develops curriculum that is built directly from the funds of knowledge in the community (Moll et al. 1992).

Curriculum designed by anthropologists, educators, and community members in Rough Rock, Arizona, provides another effective illustration of how these ideas can be developed. The social studies curriculum in Rough Rock is centered around the Navajo concept of *k'e*. It highlights inquiry and culture-centered ideals for inside the classroom using "the pattern of learning for Rough Rock children in natural situations *outside* the classroom" (McCarty et al. 1991, p. 50, emphasis in original). Teresa McCarty and her colleagues elaborate on the community's self-evaluation of the curriculum:

> The inquiry-based curriculum, teachers said, encouraged students to "make their own unique generalizations and conclusions." Teachers related this to the materials' clear social-cultural relevance, or content "that really interests the kids." "The kids think it's great," one teacher remarked, "because they're learning about things in their own community"—the people, places, and institutions that have meaning for them. (p. 49)

Another Southwestern example is described in *Literacy Events in a Community of Young Writers* (Y. Goodman & Wilde 1992), a study of written language development and instruction in the Tohono O'odham community of southern Arizona. In the foreword to the book, linguist Ofelia Zepeda recognizes that the study demonstrates that Tohono O'odham children learn the habits of writing and meet school expectations like all children in schools in the United States. Also, the Tohono O'odham children's writing reflects their cultural heritage and the oral tradition of their storytelling in their written products. Zepeda suggests that these children use the O'odham "power of words" as they write, "gathering insights from their own experience, from their community, home and family, to write what they felt made a good story" (p. xi).

Yetta Goodman (1992) places these Tohono O'odham children and their community in a broader contextual framework:

> Communities of students in schools cannot be separated from the communities of their homes, villages, towns, and cities. The social history

> children bring to school represents the language, beliefs, and knowledge of their community and affects both their writing and their views of themselves as writers. We can observe the similarities among all young writers and at the same time come to understand the unique individual and social differences among children and the communities in which they live. (p. xiv)

One important goal whole language teachers have for children centers around their students' development of positive self-concepts: that students become self-initiated critical thinkers, questioners, and problem solvers. These attitudes and characteristics of learners develop in children who believe in themselves, have confidence in their abilities and ideas, and are accepted warmly and sensitively by their teachers (Flores 1992). They develop as children encounter socialization experiences that help them learn a language and culture (Banks 1992). A strong self-concept is directly associated with culture as it is defined by Goodenough (1957): "whatever it is one has to know or believe in order to operate in a manner acceptable to its members" (p. 167). It is explained by Williams (1989):

> Children derive their identities as worthy human beings, as capable learners, as problem solvers, as aesthetic judges, from their own particular combinations of significant people, objects and events, some of which are expressive of a larger cultural perspective. Reflection of those people, objects and events in the classroom provides children with a recognizable context within which to display their knowledge and skills. (p. 3)

Multicultural education must occur every minute of every day, and teachers must be aware of the attitudes their students are developing about cultures different from their own. Friendships like the one between Seaaira and Lolita are real multicultural experiences. Teachers who sensitively apply their knowledge of culture and language in connection with their commitment to a multicultural philosophy may positively influence the cultural development of their students as they challenge the status quo positioning of various cultures in their classrooms.

Sigrid Heuck

8

Inventing a Classroom

The Tension Between Invention and Convention

FROM the first day of school through the critical events that occur during a year's time, Caryl and the children in this third-grade classroom work at becoming a community called the Sunshine Room. The process takes time, patience, care, and respect as the community members invent a negotiation process, a theme cycle, a literature study, and a friendship. Each of these critical events illustrates the specific conditions that are essential as the classroom invents itself: a high level of intellectual expectation, symmetric power and trust relationships, authentic language and literacy events, and additive bilingualism and biliteracy.

In this chapter, we review these issues across the critical events from each preceding chapter to weave a theory of learning. Two additional issues, the teacher as mediator and the role of play, are suggested as provocative when considering how classrooms invent themselves. Then Caryl and I take a moment to reflect separately on our experience in this research project. I describe my methodology and respond to questions that are generated by our work. Caryl looks at where the Sunshine Room children are today and considers the role of teachers in classroom research. We conclude by uniting our two voices to propose questions for ourselves and others.

Specific Issues Across the Year

Although educational experiences in transmission-style classrooms typically limit the learning potential of children, especially those of parallel cultures, children in the Sunshine Room are engaged in academic challenges as they develop. This *high level of intellectual expectation* greatly influences the potential to invent in this classroom. It validates children's existing funds of knowledge and their language, literacy, and thinking abilities. Caryl supports the children and the children support one another as they take risks with challenging materials, processes, and experiences. This in turn increases risk-taking possibilities for all the children and encourages authentic, not fabricated, zones of proximal development for individuals and the class as a collective.

No criterion is as important to the high intellectual level of instruction in the Sunshine Room as the issue of control, played out through *power and trust relationships.* Repeatedly, Caryl demonstrates her trust of children as learners, she shares control of virtually every aspect of the classroom with the children, and she helps children become responsible for their learning and behavior. Because individual children have power, they are more likely to experience success, and the group as a whole is more successful as a community.

These symmetric power and trust relationships between children and adults are unusual for elementary classrooms. Children have considerable voice in the experiences and activities they invent, and Caryl openly advocates their choices, in fact showing concern for children who are less confident in the inventive role she envisions for them. Children participate in areas of the curriculum usually reserved for teachers (like planning), they take uncharacteristic roles in discourse (like interrupting the teacher), and they invent unique forms of presentation for their learning with the support of their teacher.

Authentic language and literacy events are the norm in the Sunshine Room. Children use and produce whole, real texts for real functions and purposes and for real audiences. They choose the language for reading and writing, they select their own topics, and they determine the forms for their written products and other forms of presentation. Reading and writing are vehicles for children to become "literate thinkers" rather than isolated subjects in and of themselves. Reading and writing are viewed as pleasurable recreational activities, too, at school, just as they often are at home and in the real world.

Through all areas of the curriculum and the moments of each day, *additive bilingualism and biliteracy* creates positive contexts for second language development. Language choice for each moment of the day is made by the speakers, readers, and writers of the language, not solely by the teacher. English or Spanish is used when the audience, materials, or particular purposes of the user(s) warrant one or the other or a combination of the two, through either translation or codeswitching.

The use and value of the bilingual nature of this class is an important ingredient in its invention as a community. Reading and writing initially occur in first languages, but ventures into second languages are always supported. Second language learners invent systems for each language as their developing knowledge of the two orthographic systems influence each other. All children experience both Spanish and English in whole, real contexts, and many children become competent in both languages.

Learning as Invention and Convention

Each component of this ethnographic study illustrates how this classroom creates diverse opportunities for invention to develop and flourish within authentic conventional parameters. Figure 8-1 conceptualizes the tension between invention and convention, both real and important forces in the Sunshine Room. It demonstrates how a tension between invention and convention exists when natural learning is developed in an instructional setting like a classroom.

The issues in the center of the semicircle are the critical events described in this book. Each of these events carries the potential for

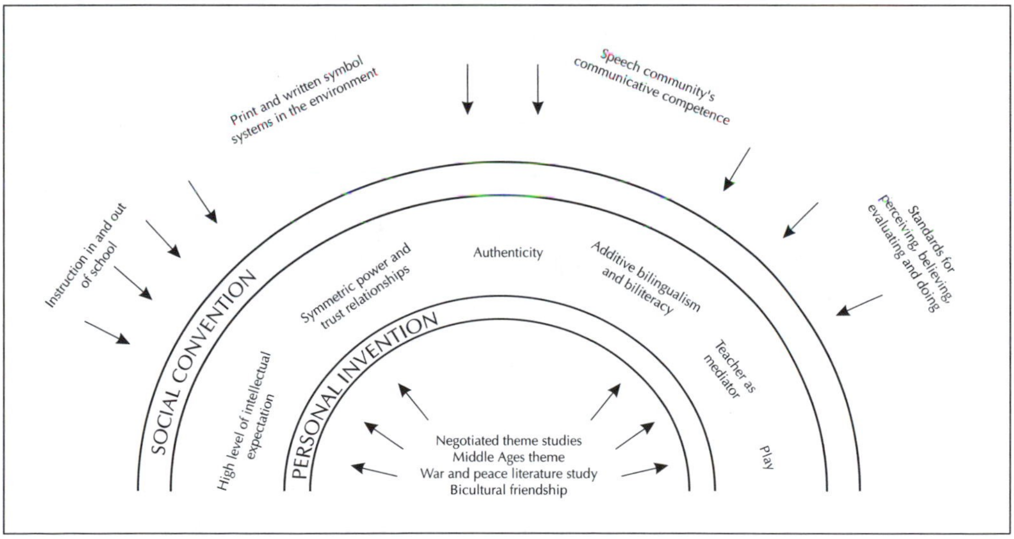

Figure 8-1. Conceptual framework for understanding the dynamics of learning in whole language classrooms.

the force of *personal invention.* The events are countered by the real world, on the outside of the semicircle, which pushes classroom events toward *social convention.* Inventions and conventions are both part of every learning experience; their presence in the Sunshine Room suggests they are positive necessities in whole language classrooms if personal inventions are to approximate social conventions through learning and development.

Directly on the semicircle are the specific conditions that are demonstrated during critical events. These criteria are necessary to create the tension between invention and convention that is natural in authentic learning outside of school and must be thoughtfully considered to create authentic learning in school. The role of the teacher as mediator and the role of play are also included here as additional influences on the tension between invention and convention in whole language classrooms. These implied criteria are discussed in the classroom issues section later in this chapter.

The Role of Convention

Professional literature about schooling acknowledges the strong role of convention across instructional components in typical transmission classrooms. It points to the dominating value of convention that characterizes classrooms where teachers (or perhaps more appropriately, publishers and school administrators) develop curriculum for children that is rote, decontextualized, and isolated for the sole purpose of instruction. In such classrooms, where children from parallel cultures are likely to be the students, it is rare to find challenging experiences for children; rather, children are powerless against the inauthentic learning forced on them. When more than one language is involved, such children are frequently working hard to learn English at the expense of their first language.

An overemphasis on the value of convention in learning at a theoretical level translates into a skills-and-practice focus in the classroom, creates untenable goals of accuracy and perfection, and systematically reduces community members' opportunities for invention. Overemphasizing convention suppresses the individual's desire or willingness to invent, indeed the knowledge of how to invent.

I ask the students in my undergraduate and graduate curriculum courses to select a topic that interests them and to pursue it as a personal inquiry project. My one constraint is that the topic can't be directly related to children or school, like the topics they usually study in their teacher education programs. They find this very hard, and it fascinates and disturbs me that this should be the case. Sometimes during discussions the (almost all female) students reveal that no teacher has ever asked them, What do you want to learn? in such a nonschool manner. These adults, who are usually products of thirteen years of public education and often four or more years of university courses, have *lost the ability* to invent their own learning. They are trained to ask, What do you want me to do? and What do you expect? It is frequently a painful process for them to have their inventive capacity restored. But at the end of the semester, if they have truly engaged in the process as I invite them to, they are often changed learners.

William Shakespeare invented an entire vocabulary that became part of conventional English language usage following the publication of his work (Bryson 1990, cited in Wasserman 1992). Selma Wasserman wonders:

> What would have happened if, for example, little Billy Shakespeare had given his Grade 6 teacher a paper with the words *majestic* or *hurry* or *radiance*—all words that he invented? The likelihood is great that his paper would have been returned slashed with red X's and an admonition to go to the dictionary and use proper vocabulary! (p. 135)

An increased value placed on convention quickly translates into a reduction of risk taking for some individual learners (Wasserman 1992; Harste, Woodward & Burke 1984). Constant attention to a mythical perfection for conventional reading, writing, and learning in all subjects reveals to children that their personal attempts to make meaning through inventions are not valuable, and they avoid taking continued risks. "Avoiding risk means becoming totally constrained by convention, by what others think is an acceptable response" (Short & Burke 1991, p. 18). Children in such situations quickly lose sight of their potential and, in essence, learn to fail at school (Moll & Díaz 1987). Or, as in the case of my college students, they learn to "do" school so well that they feel more comfortable doing *school* than doing *real learning*.

The Sunshine Room does not lack for attention to convention. Conventional spelling and punctuation, as well as conventional behavior, are held as goals for all the students. However, convention in whole language classrooms has an authentic role. The social force of convention is actively held against the personal force of invention, as if not to let convention overwhelm the strength of invention and take control. Whole language practice capitalizes on personal invention, trusting the natural role of convention in social learning experiences to provide the tension. It also recognizes and exploits the role of social invention against social and personal conventions.

In some cases, acceptable conventions are openly negotiated by the class, as on the first day of school when Seaaira asks Caryl whether to call the teachers by their first or their last names. Although Caryl could make an authoritarian decision, she places the burden of responsibility back on the students, leading them to invent the convention of name use for the year for themselves. At other times, the conventions of behavior naturally evolve out of rich learning experiences, as when the war and peace literature study group develops their own process for seeking answers to their questions about the effects of war. The convention of questioning that grows out of the discussions is neither planned nor negotiated, but literally invented by the members of the group as they interact. In these ways convention has an important role in the classroom. Its role is similar to the role of social needs in the real world.

The Role of Invention

In whole language classrooms like the Sunshine Room, the value given to children's inventions emphasizes children's strengths as learners. This different view of children and their role in the learning process creates a nearly balanced relationship between invention and convention. In reality, the balance is precarious; that's why it's conceptualized more realistically as a tension.

Valuing invention in elementary school classrooms removes the ceiling of potential for creativity, empowerment, and success for children from all cultures, communities, and histories. It incorporates the need for culturally specific instruction to achieve success (as is suggested by Vogt, Jordan, and Tharp [1987] and the results of the Kamehameha Elementary Education Program). But it capitalizes on "children's language, culture, or intellectual capacities" (Moll & Díaz 1987, p. 300) as they enter school and seeks to expand those capacities. Recognizing the value of invention supports risk taking and reduces the chance of failure. "Inventions of the new do not come from duplicating what is already there. They come from minds that are unafraid to take risks to try" (Wasserman 1992, p. 135).

Caryl says that "once the children assume the responsibility and power over their own learning, they are very reluctant to give it up." Children often revolt and complain about substitute teachers who challenge their expectations, for example. Caryl appreciates her students' determination in this regard, and she recognizes that their search for real learning may take even more initiative and perseverance in their future school experiences.

In the parallel example from my teaching, my adult college students also find it difficult to return to a transmission-style classroom once they recapture their inventiveness. By the end of the course, they often come to terms with their disequilibrium and recognize the value of having control of their own learning. In other courses they are more likely to challenge a professor who wants to assign a specific topic or requires a predetermined format for a paper. And they are more likely to seek experiences for evaluation that enable them to demonstrate their knowledge and learning, rather than completing typical comprehensive examinations, for example. Recognition of, and reflection about, the personal power of invention is exhilarating for learners of all ages.

Toward a Theory of Learning

The learning that occurs in the Sunshine Room does not characterize the theories of learning that have historically dominated the educational system in the United States. For instance, the students in the Sunshine Room are not the empty vessels or blank slates passively waiting to be filled or written upon as a behavioristic learning theory would suppose. The children can't be thus, because in their classroom they are responsible for creating their own curriculum, asking and answering their own questions.

Children involved in whole language, inquiry-centered learning are active constructors of their own knowledge, as Jean Piaget helps us understand. As they construct knowledge about the physical world around them, they build a meaning for what they know and understand. Piaget, however, presents invention in a light that is often criticized as solitary, so that children's constructions are seen as so independent of others that they lack sufficient influence from the social world surrounding them. A more realistic view, achieved by understanding learning in contexts outside of the classroom, recognizes that "the knowledge we construct is strongly influenced by others through the coordinated mutual interpretation of each other's intentions" (Wells 1989, p. 257). "We neither invent language and culture on our own nor have any options about learning them" (Wolcott 1982, p. 89).

Most critical of a solitary process of meaning construction are the Vygotskians, who support a strongly social learning theory. L. S. Vygotsky (1978) presents human learning as an internalization of the social world at the individual level; he writes about the central element of education as the cooperation between children and adults as they interact.

Luis Moll (1990a) presents the zone of proximal development as Vygotsky's most influential concept, remarking that it captures "the individual within the concrete social situation of learning and development" (p. 4). Evidence of both individual and collective zones of proximal development, both sign mediated and socially mediated, exists in the activity of the Sunshine Room. The zone of proximal development sheds light on the tension between personal invention and social convention as learners construct their own meaning through interaction with others. In Moll's words, "Vygotskian theory posits a strong, dialectic connection between external (i.e., social and, as we noted above, extracurricular) practical activity mediated by cultural tools, such as speech and writing, and individuals' intellectual activity" (p. 12).

The students in the Sunshine Room, and perhaps in all whole language settings (certainly the natural learning environments of the home and the community), are social constructivists: they invent their own knowledge and learning in a socially demanding context. Effective classroom practice, as seen in this classroom, points to the crucial role of creating a dynamic, transactive tension between the inventive forces of the personal and the conventional forces of the social.

Ideas for Classroom Practice

This story is a description of a classroom setting that includes demonstrations of practice that teachers may like to follow, but teachers and researchers who are eager to adapt the practices of the Sunshine Room need to recognize several realities as they proceed. It is important to place the Sunshine Room in its real context of the institution of public schooling. Although the children in the classroom community are certainly similar to children in any third-grade classroom, they are fortunate to attend a whole language school. Many of the battles whole language practitioners face in transmission-style schools and districts have already been won by the teachers and administrators at Borton. The central administration in the district and the parents in the community support the school's success and whole language goals (regardless of how they contrast with other schools in the district). Teachers who hope to emulate the practices we've described in the Sunshine Room must be aware of the need to be politically as well as pedagogically sophisticated in their theories and practices.

It is also important to state explicitly that this classroom includes all the regular trials and tribulations of classroom life in elementary school. There are days when activities don't work as smoothly as they are planned. There are students who are disruptive and difficult to channel into academic work. There are behavior problems with individuals and social problems in families and homes. In all these areas, Caryl responds as any whole language teacher might. She adapts to scheduling changes and material shortages. She discusses possibilities and solutions for problems with the children as partners in the community. Although it hasn't been the focus of this book, the problems that arise in classrooms, regarding discipline for instance, invite opportunities for invention. They create space for discussion and negotiation, and they provide real-life settings for problem solving in a variety of areas.

Lastly, my awareness of the most critical contributors to the emphasis on invention in this classroom grew out of my firsthand experiences with this classroom's life. These specific categories were not drawn out of thin theoretical air and "applied" to the data; I didn't enter the classroom with a theoretical hypothesis to prove. Although each category has been substantially documented in educational literature, the framework for my theoretical understanding followed my understanding of classroom practice from the inside. The practices that are theoretically explained in this analysis are real-life events, unaltered by the hopeful anticipation of a researcher's "findings." Therefore, they couldn't simply be "replicated" elsewhere. Classrooms are complicated places.

Two More Classroom Issues

The specific issues of classroom practice that have been discussed in detail so far emerged naturally from critical events and were also driven by my own questions, interests, and biases. Two additional issues, Caryl's role as a teacher who mediates and the notion of play, also have potential as vehicles for understanding the practice in this classroom, or any other, at a theoretical level. They deserve attention as potentially significant contributors to inventive classrooms because they propose additional areas for future research and further analysis of this data.

Role of the Teacher as Mediator

The role of the teacher is, of course, central to all classroom practice. The teacher is the hub of all activity, the leader and the orchestrator of active learning. Good teachers, regardless of the methods they employ or the philosophy they call their own, value children and their successes, demonstrating their expectations for learning to children and patiently nurturing their development. Caryl's various roles as the teacher in the Sunshine Room have been alluded to in each critical event.

My interest in the inventive processes in learning has focused my attention on individuals and groups of children during my descriptions of classroom life. My observations have often been drawn to the children's unusual independence and capability to operate on their own. This focus is not meant to negate the importance of Caryl in any experience. Rather, it applauds her ability to foster independence by planning and creating an environment in which this complex system can operate.

Caryl's visible role as a learner in the classroom is very important to the inventive nature of the Sunshine Room. When she joins the students in their search for new knowledge and learning experiences, she finds answers to her own questions about the world. She also effectively demonstrates real reading, writing, and researching, and her participation adds a notable measure of genuineness and authenticity to the children's questions and their attempts to find answers.

No two whole language teachers are alike, yet they share commonalities, like taking advantage of repeated opportunities to invent themselves as teachers. Whole language teachers play and experiment alongside their students, for example, discovering not only content areas that they enjoy and can get excited about, but areas of teaching in which they excel. They can find niches of expertise through the inquiry process, just as children do. Caryl has become aware of her expertise in bilingual and biliterate development, literature study, and thematic curriculum. She regularly shares her expertise with preservice and practicing teachers through workshops and conference presentations, as well as through published writing.

Teachers like Caryl mediate their students' learning without intervening or taking control (K. Goodman 1992). They realize that teaching and learning are not dichotomous, but that children must have responsibility for constructing their own knowledge and that frequently teachers' interventions will impede rather than promote real learning. This means they "arrange, change, improve, or modify social situations to teach at the highest level possible" (Moll 1988, p. 465).

Gordon Wells (1989) reconceptualizes teaching as "behaviour which has as its intention to facilitate the active construction of knowledge by the learner" (p. 257). Vygotskians present teaching as striving to create contexts for zones of proximal development for individuals and collectives (Moll & Whitmore 1993). In invention/convention terms, whole language teachers provide dynamic opportunities for children to develop strength as personal inventors while creating authentic conditions for social conventions. This keeps the tension of real learning alive in the classroom.

Whole language teachers are theoreticians. They attend conferences and ask presenters challenging theoretical questions, they read voraciously, they conduct their own classroom research independently or in collaboration with others, and they speak out for their professionalism in political forums. Now, more than ever because of the innovative teaching happening in whole language classrooms, we may learn from the theoretical practitioners who explore and understand learning in real classroom contexts every day.

Role of Play

Selma Wassermann (1992) describes a class of third graders examining bundles of fabrics in their classroom. One child, Andre, discovers that his fabrics make different sounds as he scratches them. As he investigates, Andre discovers a major concept in the world of music. Wasserman postulates that introducing what she calls "serious play" in classrooms will enable children to "have it all." She outlines the possibilities:

> . . . the development of knowledge, of a spirit of inquiry, of creativity, of conceptual understanding—all contributing to the true empowerment of children. Is it possible that serious play is, in fact, the primary vehicle through which serious learning occurs? (p. 133)

Cognitive and creative development of children is fostered through the generative nature of play that allows risks to be taken and reduces fear of failure. Play develops self-initiating autonomy, giving children a feeling of control. And play activates children's hands, engaging their minds at the same time.

Although play has not been a structured focus of my interpretation of the Sunshine Room, it is possible to predict, I think with confidence, that evidence of play exists in the critical events. The children play with language and ideas. They also play in a more conventional sense as they build with blocks and use manipulatives in creative, expressive ways. Attention to play is too frequently limited to discussions of very young children. Additional research that documents the role of play in the process of invention and convention in older children at school would be fascinating.

Inventing Classroom Research

In our introductions of ourselves and our project at the beginning of this book we promised a reflection on our research process and our collaboration. Reflection is an essential part of learning, and the students in the Sunshine Room are clearly not the only learners in this story. In this section, we consider how we've invented our classroom research.

As I present my work to varied audiences, I am sometimes questioned about the process of collecting, coding, and analyzing data. Data collection and analysis methods are insufficiently described far too frequently in anthropological and educational literature, presenting readers with a murky view of what researchers actually do while researching. This lack is logically explained by time and space constraints in the publication process, but it is a dilemma that warrants attention.

My work in the Sunshine Room began when I was an assistant in the Community Literacy Project. Therefore, I began collecting data in this setting with the goal of answering someone else's questions rather than my own. In retrospect, this was fortuitous, because it enabled me to hone my skills as a classroom observer and become saturated in the setting and the data before I was responsible for developing my own project and asking my own personal questions. It meant that by the second year of data collection, I was able to confidently predict a majority of particular behaviors and interactions in the classroom community given any event or combination of participants. This opportunity contributed validity to my analyses and conclusions. The three years that I spent, first in the Sunshine Room and then understanding what I had observed there, suggest a minimal period of time that qualitative, interpretive, ethnographic researchers should consider for field study.

The data available to me for analysis was triangulated (Denzin 1989) across several sources, as described in Chapter 1: field notes, interview transcripts, naturally occurring language transcripts, writing samples, and collaborative interpretations written by Caryl and me. At the conclusion of the first year of data collection I reviewed this data by reading through hard copies of each source with a yellow highlighter in hand. I marked any of the notes or quotes that struck me as significant and labeled them with descriptive phrases. "Use of Spanish," "authentic language," "codeswitching," "high level of intellectual work," and "teacher knowledge" are examples of the types of descriptions that fit these markings. I marked the texts in this way as completely as possible so as not to leave out any potentially important events or items.

These descriptions, over time, became the codes that helped me further understand the patterns of the data that are so important to ethnographers. They showed, through a simple tally, which descriptions were most frequent. This in turn allowed me to return to the classroom to confirm the patterns and examine their surrounding contexts, search for more detail, and ask Caryl, the children, and my university colleagues to respond to them. At this point, I was also confidently able to narrow my attention to the most salient codes, or categories. The five categories of intellectual level of instruction, power and trust relationships, authenticity, bilingualism, and role of the teacher were the categories that appeared most important and interesting at the end of the first year of the study, and they framed my research questions for the second year. The categories, while they remained significant, were fine-tuned with continued thought and observation, resulting in those in the preceding chapters.

At this point, one might ask how theory fits into this process, and how researcher bias affected my own data collection and analysis, as it does others'. All researchers enter research settings with biases and theories about how the world operates that affect the research process. Piaget taught us that we see what we know, meaning, in the research process, we most often find what we look for. My own experiences as a classroom teacher as well as my graduate studies certainly instilled in me a personal whole language perspective on teaching children.

As a whole language teacher, when I examine a student's work, perhaps a writing sample, I look for the strength of that work. I am far more interested in understanding what the child has done well than in what the child has done poorly. So, in Lolita's dual narrative (Figures 7-2 and 7-3), for example, I notice her sophisticated use of genre structures rather than incorrect, or invented, spelling. And I attend to the creativity of the biliterate format rather than the lack of appropriate punctuation within language. I tend to see the success of each child's accomplishments in order to provide a context that will build on that child's strength through the curriculum of the classroom.

I've come to realize that I approach the research process in a similar manner. That is, although there are plenty of examples of times that don't go well in the classroom (there were some tremendous disciplinary difficulties in the second year), I opt to focus my attention on the positives and the strengths of the children, of the teachers, and of the classroom as a system. Yes, this certainly means that the data is filtered through my selective attention as I gather and analyze it (as I feel all research is, regardless of paradigmatic differences). However, it also enables me to narrow my focus on the strengths so I can describe them in depth for others. It leads to my ability to see this classroom in a developmental frame of potentials for other classrooms, much as I see children's development (Whitmore 1992).

Some may criticize my view as one of building a mythical utopia where it didn't exist or creating a self-serving image of classroom life. I would counter that it is this perspective, itself, that enables me to see the inventive nature of the classroom and derive from that a theory of learning. I would also suggest that our story provides teachers and researchers with strong positive examples of the successes of schooling that are nearly impossible to find in our own literature and in the media.

Although I entered the Sunshine Room with a "whole language head" and was clearly attentive to strengths rather than weaknesses and solutions rather than problems, the theory truly evolved within the data. Ken Goodman's theory of invention and convention provided the theoretical frame for my work only after the categories described above were derived from a "grass roots" approach to analysis. And, through closer examination during a second year of data collection and analysis specifically geared to do so, his theoretical insights were expanded and confirmed at a new level. If there are findings that are "generalizable" from this process (although generalizability as a construct is not a part of my personal goals), it would be the theoretical understanding of the process of becoming that occurs in all classrooms and all settings, regardless of population, geographic location, size of the classroom or grade level, or languages spoken.

As Kathy has explained, we have chosen to focus on the positive aspects of whole language classroom life that distinguish it from typical transmission classrooms. Although we have mentioned the presence of discipline problems, the instability in some children's lives, and other realities that make learning difficult, we have not dwelt on these factors. Such children are present in every classroom, but I believe they have more opportunity to be successful in a whole language classroom such as the Sunshine Room. I would like to think that they leave Borton with more of their self-esteem intact.

Sometimes, I wish we could just hold onto our students for a while longer. At the end of third grade, they all move on to other schools. Many of the volunteer children continue in the magnet schools, where they find communities that create social learning experiences and provide support for innovative teaching. Seaaira continued in the intermediate magnet school until her family moved out of our district and she was no longer eligible to attend. Mark, Randy, Travis, Ethan, Paul, Jon, Ilinca, Aaron, and Brooke all went on in the magnet system. Mark has overcome his shyness and developed his artistic talents. In a note accompanying the permission to use his story "Cyndee," his mother attributes her children's school success to family support and the "wonderful foundation they received from all their teachers at Borton." Brooke even chose to stay in the bilingual program and wrote me a full-page letter in Spanish, with comprehensible invented spellings, during her fourth-grade year. A few of these children are now enrolled in middle school magnets.

Most of the Borton neighborhood children are bused across town to cope with very conventional intermediate classrooms. Their teachers are caring people with their own special strengths, but often they have not had an opportunity to reflect on how their teaching practices and their curriculums limit the children's opportunities to demonstrate their knowledge and to invent new learning for themselves. Despite the radical change the children experience as they move from one school setting to the next, most of the children are doing reasonably well. The children who are bilingual have managed, for the most part, to remain in bilingual programs, even though there are not enough bilingual teachers at their new school. Marisela is now fully bilingual and biliterate. Some children have obtained transfers to other schools closer to home. Lupita, Susana, Roberto, Antonia, Lolita, and her brother, Francisco, are all attending a bilingual middle school magnet program that was established voluntarily by the school district. David, the clever wolf in Seaaira and Lolita's play, graduated from sixth grade as an honor role student at another desegregation school. Marco moved to a neighboring school. His mom works at the school, and he is doing fine.

Unfortunately, a few of the students who were not yet firmly established in their uses of literacy, or who were choosing to act out inappropriately in school, have not fared as well. On my recent visit to one receiving school, a former Sunshine Room student who was barely emerging as a reader when he left third grade had been isolated within his own classroom. His desk had been pulled away from the others and surrounded on three sides with bookshelves and a divider, making it physically impossible for him to be a member of the classroom community. Another child, who was finally reaching independence as a reader and writer near the end of third grade and who, like Seaaira, raised many questions for our class to consider, had been referred to a pull-out ESL program at the beginning of fourth grade. She doesn't even speak Spanish.

I have been unable to locate some of the children. Elisabeth and Trevor moved with their families to other states, while Jaime and Azucena returned to Mexico. Daniel, Gabe, and Rachel have all disappeared. I hope their families have left the neighborhood in order to take advantage of new opportunities for stability, although I suspect they are continuing their patterns of mobility. I pray they take a bit of the Sunshine Room with them wherever they go. I know they will be better off for having spent a period of time, however short, at Borton.

Susana once wrote a story that captures the potential I envision at Borton for Daniel, Marco, Gabe, and others with similar struggles:

El oso malo

Una vez había un oso malo y vivía en el bosque con su mamá. Y la mamá era muy buena con su niño y con la gente. Un día la mamá le dijo que lo iba a apuntar a la escuela y él dijo -Yo no quiero ir a la escuela. Y la mamá le dijo -Tienes que ir a la escuela para aprender a ser bueno. Entonces, su mamá estaba tratando de convencerlo pero no pudo. Entonces lo convenció y quiso ir a la escuela de Borton. En Borton lo trataron muy bien y a él le gustaba ir a la escuela y su clase era el Sunshine Room. Su maestra era muy buena. Y él también se hizo muy bueno con su mamá. Cuando se hizo grande, se hizo un maestro y la escuela la llamó la Escuela

> *Susan Borton y su clase la llamó Sunshine Room. Y su mamá estaba muy contenta porque se hizo muy bueno y porque se hizo maestro y le puso el nombre de ella y luego Borton. En un tiempo se murió su mamá antes de que se hiciera principal. Pero nosotros estamos seguros que si estuviera viva, estuviera muy contenta con su niño. (Once there was a bad little bear who lived in the woods with his mother. And the mother was very good with her children and with the other people. One day, the mother told him that she was going to send him to school and the bear said, "I don't want to go to school." And the mother told him, "You have to go to school to learn to be good." Then the mother tried to convince him but she couldn't. Then she convinced him and he wanted to go to Borton School. At Borton, he was treated well and he liked to go to the school and his class was the Sunshine Room. His teacher was very good. He also became very good with his mother. When he grew up, he became a teacher and called his school the Susan Borton School and his class was called the Sunshine Room. And his mother was very happy because he was good and because he became a teacher and gave her name to the school and then Borton. After a while, his mother died before he became principal. But we are sure that if she were alive, she would be very happy with her child.)*

I wish Borton and the Sunshine Room could help every troubled child to the extent that Susana foresees, but such children are offered new opportunities to realize their potential every day within a supportive environment.

While I have been inventing myself as a teacher with these children, and other students over the years, I have also been inventing myself as a researcher. Like Kathy, I have been informed by the research of others. However, reading about their questions, their studies, and their answers has not been as valuable as my searching for answers to my own questions, even if my questions and conclusions are similar to theirs. Kathy is reluctant to assume any generalizability as a result of our study. I wholeheartedly agree; the Sunshine Room cannot be replicated from one year to the next, much less from one classroom to another. For this reason, I hesitate to transfer the findings from any research study directly into my own classroom. In much the same way as the children benefit from searching for answers even though I might be able to tell them the answers with considerably less work for us both, I own my learning by pursuing it myself.

This is not to say that I've ignored the conventions of research generated by others more experienced than myself. I followed the recommendations of others to tape and transcribe literature study discussions and to code different categories of talk as they emerged. Like other researchers before me, I collected every piece of paper connected to the groups, sifting and sorting with each new addition. My analytic categories were my own inventions, based on what I was observing and noticing.

During the first year that Kathy was in the Sunshine Room, she made use of the same pieces of data that I was collecting for my own study, but analyzed that data according to her criteria. The opportunity to be part of a mutual thinking community gave us an opportunity to hypothesize, to clarify our own ideas, and also to create a domain of shared knowledge. The event that brought Kathy and me together as researchers was the war and peace group's discussion of The Butter Battle Book. *During their talk about this book, the children identified the role that questions played in driving their discourse. At this point, Kathy and I began to ask the same questions and work together as learners.*

I cannot comment on my role as a teacher researcher without mentioning the support system that is integral to my success. Classroom research takes time and commitment. It implies trying new strategies that may not always be successful, a certain amount of disorganization and hesitancy, and at times not quite knowing what you will do tomorrow. It requires administrators who value teachers' pursuing their own professional growth and students who are willing to regard their teacher as a colearner. These are not earthshaking conclusions, but they are essential prerequisites that have been recognized by others as well (Patterson, Santa, Short & Smith 1993; Cochran-Smith & Lytle 1993).

I could not have maintained my investigative zeal without the sense of humor and support of my friend and principal, Bob Wortman. My teaching assistant, Halie Pence, has now endured years of expecting something new to happen at any moment, and I believe she actually looks forward to it. Most of all, my students have come to regard themselves as my informants and co-researchers. There were times when Kathy and I would find pieces of writing left in prominent places on my desk, with a sticky note attached reading,

"Ms. Crowell, make two copies of this—one for yourself and one for Kathy. She'll want to see it too."

The children's role in this research should not be underestimated. They were much more than subjects in a study. They took their own learning very seriously and saw a place for themselves in supporting our project.

Opportunities for teachers to confer with one another as an essential part of their professional work are limited. Even in places where inservice training is offered regularly, it usually centers on providing instructions for carrying out some new aspect of a mandated curriculum. Rarely do we have the luxury of investigating our own self-invented questions within our own mutually invented thinking community.

One place where such perceived indulgences exist is among university-based educators. Within the collegial atmosphere of a university department of education, it is appropriate to spend time each day perceiving, ideating, and presenting. The university professionals I know take time to read, write, think, and talk together. It is expected. Perhaps when such practices come in regular contact with public schools, similar behaviors will be legitimatized among classroom teachers.

University researchers can offer teachers their knowledge of the research conventions that are necessary to carry out research within a classroom, as well as provide another set of experienced eyes to observe and record the activity that teachers cannot always stop to document. Certainly, Kathy made it possible for me to learn more about my students by giving me access to her field notes and the data that she collected apart from my own. Through Kathy, I also gained access to research I had not been aware of through my own limited professional reading. At the university, I found an audience and support for my research and my writing that had not been available within my district beyond informal sharing with my school's faculty.

In turn, university researchers have much to gain from an association with public schools and teachers. As a teacher, I can assure you that theories of teaching and learning propounded by someone long removed from the classroom and real children are not always to be trusted. Researchers need to take advantage of the knowledge that teachers possess and the opportunity to observe children engaged in the process of learning. Classroom teachers may not always be able to cite the latest research that supports their understanding, but we have tremendous insights about our students and our work that can bring a sense of the real world to even the most conventional research. Naturally, I have a bias toward the more ethnographic research designs that recognize the inventive forces at work in the classroom, those that probe the complexities of life "at the chalk-face" and do not attempt to reduce it to a series of arbitrary numbers on a page.

Two Voices Become One

We end our story in one collaborative voice as we pose new questions for ourselves and others. Although we continue to maintain our separate insider and outsider perspectives on teaching and learning, we have also developed a new third voice that speaks as a teacher researcher team. It is from this voice that we suggest areas of research and thinking for future classroom and university teacher researchers to consider. Our questions, and many others relevant to particular settings and characters, are being tapped by our colleagues in teacher research—Fred Burton (1988, 1991), Gay Su Pinnell and Myna Matlin (1989), Marilyn Cochran-Smith and Susan Lytle (1993), Sarah Hudelson and Judith Lindfors (1993), and Leslie Patterson, Carol Santa, Kathy Short, and Karen Smith (1993), among others. We join their celebrations of understanding learning and teaching by understanding classrooms in action.

As a result of this classroom ethnography, the door is now open for another researcher (perhaps Caryl or another Borton teacher) to look beyond the classroom doors to those outer layers of the context surrounding the setting we have described. A series of questions come to mind when considering a second project, complementary to this work. How does the Sunshine Room fit within the school as a community? What is Caryl's role in the school? How does Borton Primary Magnet School, self-labeled as a whole language school, fit into the district, particularly in light of the fact that its curriculum and practice are not typical for its neighboring schools? How has the school evolved over time? What are the political ramifications of the whole language perspective in the community? How do these ramifications affect the families at Borton, not only during their time there, but as they frequent the corridors of other schools in fourth grade and beyond? What happens to the children after they leave the comfortable confines of a primary magnet school? What can be predicted about the futures of these children—will they continue to succeed through high school and move on to college careers, for example?

In another vein, an implied direction for continued research is to transplant the theory of learning we've developed as the tension between invention and convention into a new setting. A series of questions come immediately to mind here as well. How do invention and convention occur in other whole language classrooms, or in larger settings like whole language schools? How do invention and convention change over time, from preschool (or birth) through graduate school, in terms of a school context? What strategies might teachers use in classrooms to support the inventive nature of learning? How might parents become aware of the inventive nature of their children's learning?

Our collaboration has also led to new questions about relationships between university and elementary school teacher researchers. Answers may lie in the data we've already collected, or further information may be required. What is the role between the university setting and the school in the research process? How does the experience of research affect the teacher and the children involved in the "doing" of research, whether that research is initiated by the teacher or an outsider? What is the role of research in the classroom curriculum? How can the relationship between ethnographic research and interpretive evaluation be defined?

Questions like these bring us to the beginning of a new cycle of inquiry, just like the one children in the Sunshine Room experience as they move from one theme to another or from one literature study into the next. They are good questions, because, as Elizabeth taught us, they are hard to answer, we don't really know the answers, and they take a long time to find out. That's what makes them interesting. Ending with questions reminds us that we are learners. That all of us—children, teachers, and university researchers—invent our learning for ourselves and that together, we can become the convention that defines us as a *community* of learners.

Appendix A: Middle Ages Bibliography

Curriculum Laboratory, University of Iowa
Compiled by Donilee Popham
February 1994
From Serfs to Sir Gawain: Life in the Middle Ages
(for Elementary Grades)

An Overview

Adams, Brian. *Atlas of the World in the Middle Ages.* Watts, 1981.
Anno, Mitsumasa. *Anno's Medieval World.* Collins, 1980. ©1979.
Caselli, Giovanni. *Everyday Life of an Irish Pilgrim.* Bedrick, 1987.
Caselli, Giovanni. *The Middle Ages.* Bedrick, 1988.
Ellenby, Jean. *The Medieval Household.* Cambridge, 1984.
Gee, Robyn. *Living in Castle Times.* Usborne, 1982.
Hunt, Jonathan. *Illuminations.* Bradbury, 1989.
Lewis, Brenda Ralph. *Growing Up in the Dark Ages.* Batsford, 1980.
Macdonald, Fiona. *Everyday Life: The Middle Ages.* Silver Burdett, 1985, ©1984.
Morgan, Gwyneth. *Life in a Medieval Village.* Lerner, 1982.
Oakes, Catherine. *Exploring the Past: The Middle Ages.* Harcourt, 1989.
Ruis, Maria. *La Edad Media.* Barrons, 1988.
Sabbagh, Antoine. *La Europa de la Edad Media.* Ed. Luis Vives, 1988.
Sancha, Sheila. *The Luttrell Village: Country Life In the Middle Ages.* Crowell, 1982.
Sancha, Sheila. *Walter Dragun's Town: Crafts and Trade in the Middle Ages.* Crowell, 1989.
Scarry, Huck. *Looking into the Middle Ages.* Harper, 1985. (Pop-up book.)
Ventura, Piero. *There Once Was a Time.* Putnam's, 1986. (Pages 44–97.)

Castles, Cathedrals, and Architecture

Adams, Brian. *Medieval Castles.* Gloucester, 1989.
Cairns, Conrad. *Medieval Castles.* Lerner, 1989.
Ceserani, Gian Paola. *Grand Constructions.* Putnam, 1983. (Pages 29–47.)
Clements, Gilliam. *The Truth About Castles.* Carolrhoda, 1990, ©1988.
Goodall, John S. *The Story of a Castle.* McElderry, 1986.

Isaacson, Philip M. *Round Buildings, Square Buildings and Buildings That Wiggle Like a Fish.* Knopf, 1988. (Various pages.)
Macaulay, David. *Castle.* Houghton, 1977. *Castle* (videocassette). PBS Video, 1983.
Macaulay, David. *Cathedral: The Story of Its Construction.* Houghton, 1973.
Macdonald, Fiona. *A Medieval Castle.* Bedrick, 1990.
Monks, John. *The Great Book of Castles.* Rourke, 1989.
Seymour, Peter. *Crazy Castle: A Creepy Pop-up Book.* Barron's, 1989. (Pop-up book.)
Simmons, Dawn Langley. *The Great White Owl of Sissinghurst.* McElderry, 1993.
Smith, Beth. *Castles.* Watts, 1988.
Unstead, R. J. *See Inside: A Castle.* Warwick, 1986.
Van Zandt, Eleanor. *Architecture.* Steck, 1990. (Pages 18–22.)
Vaughan, Jenny. *Castles.* Watts, 1984.

Kings, Queens, and Other Members of the Royal Household

Brierley, Louise. *King Lion and His Cooks.* Holt, 1982, ©1981.
Demi. *Chingis Khan.* Holt, 1991.
Hutchins, Pat. *King Henry's Palace.* Greenwillow, 1983.
Jessop, Joanne. *Richard the Lionhearted.* Bookwright, 1989.
Kraus, Robert. *The King's Trousers.* Windmill, 1981.
Lasker, Joe. *The Great Alexander the Great.* Viking, 1983.
Pevear, Richard. *Our King Has Horns!* Macmillan, 1987.
Schertle, Alice. *The April Fool.* Lothrop, 1981.
Schurnberger, Lynn Edelman. *Kings, Queens, Knights, and Jesters: Making Medieval Costumes.* Harper, 1978.
Siekkinen, Raija. *Mister King.* Carolrhoda, 1987.
Wood, Audrey. *King Bidgood's in the Bathtub.* Harcourt, 1985.

King Arthur and Other Noble Knights

Aitken, Amy. *Ruby, the Red Knight.* Bradbury, 1983.
Black, Quentin. *Snuff.* Lippincott, 1973.
Byam, Michelle. *Arms and Armor.* Knopf, 1988.
Carrick, Donald. *Harald and the Giant Knight.* Clarion, 1982.
Carrick, Donald. *Harald and the Great Stag.* Clarion, 1988.
Corbin, Carole Lynn. *Knights.* Watts, 1989.
de Paola, Tomie. *The Knight and the Dragon.* Putnam, 1980.
Fradon, Dana. *Harold the Herald: A Book About Heraldry.* Dutton, 1990.
Fradon, Dana. *Sir Dana: A Knight as Told by His Trusty Armor.* Dutton, 1988.
Gerrard, Roy. *Sir Cedric.* Farrar, 1984.
Gerrard, Roy. *Sir Cedric Rides Again.* Farrar, 1986.
Gibson, Michael. *The Knights.* Arco, 1980.

Greer, Gery. *Max and Me and the Time Machine.* Harcourt, 1983.
Hastings, Selina. *Sir Gawain and the Green Knight.* Lothrop, 1981.
Hastings, Selina. *Sir Gawain and the Loathly Lady.* Lothrop, 1985.
Hazen, Barbara Shook. *The Knight Who Was Afraid of the Dark.* Dial, 1989.
Heller, Julek. *Knights.* Schocken, 1982.
Hindley, Judy. *The Time Travellor Book of Knights and Castles.* Usborne, 1976.
Hodges, Margaret. *The Kitchen Knight: A Tale of King Arthur.* Holiday, 1990.
Hodges, Margaret. *Saint George and the Dragon: A Golden Legend.* Little, 1984.
Hunter, Mollie. *The Knight of the Golden Plain.* Harper, 1983.
King Midas and the Golden Touch (videocassette). Rabbit Ears, 1991.
Lasker, Joe. *A Tournament of Knights.* Crowell, 1986.
Lister, Robin. *The Legend of King Arthur.* Doubleday, 1990, ©1988.
Mayer, Mercer. *Herbert the Timid Dragon.* Golden, 1980.
Mayer, Mercer. *Whinnie the Lovesick Dragon.* Macmillan, 1986.
McCaughrean, Geraldine. *Saint George and the Dragon.* Doubleday, 1989.
Miquel, Pierre. *The Days of Knights and Castles.* Silver Burdett, 1980.
O'Connor, Jane. *Sir Small and the Dragonfly.* Random, 1988.
Philip, Neil. *The Tale of Sir Gawain.* Philomel, 1987.
Pyle, Howard. *King Arthur and the Magic Sword.* Dial, 1990.
Pyle, Howard. *The Story of the Champions of the Round Table.* Scribner, n.d.
Pyle, Howard. *The Story of King Arthur and His Knights.* Scribner, 1984.
Ross, Stuart. *A Crusading Knight.* Rourke, 1987, ©1986.
Rutland, Jonathan. *Knights and Castles.* Random House, 1987.
Scieszka, Jon. *Knights of the Kitchen Table.* Trumpet, 1993.
Sutcliff, Rosemary. *The Road to Camlann.* Dutton, 1982.
Sutcliff, Rosemary. *The Sword and the Circle: King Arthur and the Knights of the Round Table.* Dutton, 1981.
Talbott, Hudson. *King Arthur—The Sword in the Stone.* Wonder/Morrow, 1991.
Windrow, Martin. *The Medieval Knight.* Watts, 1985.

Literature, Legends, and the Legendary

Ceserani, Gian Paola. *Marco Polo.* Putnam, 1982.
Cohen, Barbara, sel. *Canterbury Tales.* Lothrop, 1988.
Cole, Joanna. *A Gift from Saint Francis: The First Creche.* Morrow, 1989.
Creswick, Paul. *Robin Hood.* Scribner, 1984.
De Angeli, Marguerite. *The Door in the Wall.* Dell Yearling, 1949.
De France, Maire. *Medieval Fables.* Dodd, 1983.
dePaola, Tomie. *Francis, the Poor Man of Assisi.* Holiday, 1982.
Domanska, Janina. *What Happens Next?* Greenwillow, 1983.
Fujita, Tamao. *William Tell.* Gakken, 1971.
Gauch, Patricia Lee. *Once upon a Dinkelsbuhl.* Putnam, 1977.
Gies, Frances. *Joan of Arc: The Legend and the Reality.* Harper, 1981.
Grahame, Kenneth. *The Reluctant Dragon.* Trumpet, 1966.

Hastings, Selina, sel. *The Canterbury Tales.* Holt, 1988.
Hayes, Sarah. *Robin Hood.* Holt, 1989.
Hodges, Margaret. *Brother Francis and the Friendly Beasts.* Scribner, 1991.
McCaughrean, Geraldine. *Canterbury Tales.* Childrens, 1985, ©1984.
McKinley, Robin. *The Outlaws of Sherwood.* Greenwillow, 1988.
Ross, Tony, ret. *The Pied Piper of Hamelin.* Lothrop, 1978.

Art and Music

Brown, Laurene K. and Brown, Marc. *Visiting the Art Museum.* Dutton, 1986. (Pages 12–15, 29.)
Davidson, Marshall B. *A History of Art from 25,000 B.C. to the Present.* Random, 1984. (Pages 26–37.)
Glubok, Shirley. *The Art of the Vikings.* Macmillan, 1978.
Janson, H. W. and Anthony F. Janson. *History of Art for Young People.* Abrams, 1992. (Pages 126–95.)
Venezia, Mike. *Da Vinci.* Childrens, 1989.
Ventura, Piero. *Great Composers.* Putnam, 1989, ©1988. (Pages 16–23, 112.)

Miscellaneous

Aliki. *A Medieval Feast.* Crowell, 1983.
Brookfield, Karen. *Book.* Knopf, 1993.
Cosman, Madeleine Pelner. *Medieval Holidays and Festivals.* Scribners, 1981.
Day, James. *The Black Death.* Bookwright, 1989.
Fradin, Dennis Brindell. *Medicine: Yesterday, Today, and Tomorrow.* Childrens, 1989. (Pages 20–25.)
Lasker, Joe. *Merry Ever After: The Story of Two Medieval Weddings.* Penguin, 1976.
Machines, Power and Transportation. Arco, 1984. (Pages 14–19.)
Murphy, Wendy. *The Future World of Agriculture.* Grolier/Watts, 1984. (Pages 41–43.)
Perl, Lila. *From Top Hats to Baseball Caps, from Bustles to Blue Jeans: Why We Dress the Way We Do.* Clarion, 1990. (Pages 25–32, 75–79, 91–94.)
Weil, Lisl. *New Clothes: What People Wore, from Cavemen to Astronauts.* Atheneum, 1987. (Pages 15–18.)

Additional books can be found in the Card Catalog under these headings:

Arms and Armor
Art, History
Art, Medieval
Castles

Civilization, Medieval
Crusades
King Arthur
Kings and Rulers
Kings, Queens, Rulers, etc.
Knights and Knighthood
Middle Ages
Middle Ages, Fiction
Robin Hood

For teaching resources, including curriculum guides and nonprint materials, look in the Curriculum Materials Card Catalog under Middle Ages.

Reference books used: *Best Books for Children; Elementary School Library Collection; Children's Catalog; World History for Children and Young Adults.*

Appendix B: War and Peace Bibliography

Adler, D. 1989. *We Remember the Holocaust.* New York: Trumpet Club.

Bunting, E. 1990. *The Wall.* Illustrated by Ronald Himler. New York: Clarion Books.

Cohen, B. 1985. *The Secret Grove.* New York: Union of Hebrew Congregations.

Durell, A. & Sach, M. (Eds.). 1990. *The Big Book for Peace.* New York: Dutton's Children's Books.

Eco, U. & Carmi, E. 1989a. *The Three Astronauts.* New York: Harcourt Brace Jovanovich.

———. 1989b. *The Bomb and the General.* New York: Harcourt Brace Jovanovich.

Finkelstein, N. H. 1985. *Remember Not to Forget.* New York: Franklin Watts.

Gauch, P. L. 1975. *Thunder at Gettysburg.* New York: G. P. Putnam's Sons.

Greene, C. 1987. *Elie Wiesel—Messenger from the Holocaust.* Chicago: Children's Press.

I Never Saw Another Butterfly . . . Children's Drawing and Poems from Terezin Concentration Camp 1942–1944. New York: McGraw Hill. Originally published in Czechoslovakia in 1962.

Innocenti, R. 1985. *Rose Blanche.* Mankato, MN: Creative Education, Inc.

Kellogg, S. 1973. *The Island of the Skog.* New York: Dial Books.

Morimoto, J. 1987. *My Hiroshima.* New York: Viking Children's Books.

Seuss, Dr. 1984. *The Butter Battle Book.* New York: Random House.

Slater, D. 1988. *Why Do Wars Happen?* New York: Gloucester Press.

Tennyson, A. (Lord). 1964. *The Charge of the Light Brigade.* New York: Golden Press.

Tsuchiya, Y. 1988. *Faithful Elephants.* Boston: Houghton Mifflin.

Appendix C: Individual Whole Language Check Lists

Whole Language Checklist
Borton Primary Magnet School
Caryl Crowell

KEY:
1 - rarely observed
2 - sometimes observed
3 - often observed

Name: Seaaira
Year: 1990–1991
Grade: 3rd

Oral Language Development	**1**	**2**	**3**	**4**	**Comments**
Listens attentively in one-to-one interactions	3	3	3	3	1. Seaaira routinely participates in discussions of all kinds. She enjoys listening to stories, too.
Listens attentively in small groups	3	3	3	3	2. Seaaira really enjoyed listening to Matilda. She joined the group in making predictions as we went along.
Listens attentively in large groups	3	3	3	3	3. Seaaira listened intently to Bridge to Terabithia and Island of the Blue Dolphins. She was amazed that I cry over books.
Listens to stories read aloud	3	3	3	3	
Participates appropriately in conversations	3	3	3	3	
Elaborates responses	3	3	3	3	
Explains thinking	3	3	3	3	
Engages in language play	3	3	3	3	
Demonstrates understanding of oral directions	3	3	3	3	

Literacy Development - Reading Strategies	**1**	**2**	**3**	**4**	**Comments**
Selects own reading material	3	3	3	3	1. Seaaira needs to become more aware of the strategies she uses as a reader so she can use them consistently.
Initiates reading promptly	3	3	3	3	2. In her self-evaluation, she still sees herself as sounding out. This next quarter we'll be constructing stories based on clues. Perhaps this will help. At home, when she miscues, ask her to guess what it could be without looking at the text. Mad Libs are fun and help kids use syntax cues.
Reads for a sustained period	3	3	3	3	
Reads a variety of material	3	3	3	3	
Reads for a variety of purposes	3	3	3	3	
Uses library for enjoyment and research	3	3	3	3	
Attempts to make meaningful substitutions	3	3	3	3	
Uses language sense and meaning to predict	3	3	3	3	
Monitors own reading and self-corrects	3	3	3	3	

Literacy Development - Literature Response	**1**	**2**	**3**	**4**	**Comments**
Retells and summarizes stories	3	3	3	3	1. Seaaira has a good sense of story and freely shares her ideas.
Relates reading to personal experiences	2	2	3	3	2. Seaaira and her group wrote a delightful, bilingual play to share what they learned about different versions of fairy tales.
Demonstrates awareness of story elements	3	3	3	3	3. Seaaira was a catalyst in our literature study group. Her sincere questions generated a lot of discussion. She learned a lot about World War II and the Holocaust.
Recognizes a variety of genre	2	2	3	3	
Discusses reading with others	3	3	3	3	
Extends reading through other reading and projects	-	3	3	3	
Writes thoughtfully in log	-	3	2	2	

Whole Language Checklist
Borton Primary Magnet School
Caryl Crowell

KEY:
1 - rarely observed
2 - sometimes observed
3 - often observed

Name: Seaaira
Year: 1990–1991
Grade: 3rd

Literacy Development - Writing	**1**	**2**	**3**	**4**	**Comments**
Self-selects writing topics and ideas	3	3	3	3	1. Seaaira has some wonderfully creative ideas for writing. I'm anxious to hear how "The Magic School Bus Goes Back in Time" turns out!
Engages in writing promptly and sustains writing	3	3	3	3	2. Seaaira has done some nonfiction writing as part of our Middle Ages study. She is at her creative best in collaboration with others on some self-initiated project.
Writes for a variety of purposes and audiences	3	3	3	3	3. She tried some new genres: poetry, and a script for a shoebox theater presentation. She is so innovative and spontaneous!
Uses a variety of styles, forms, literary devices	3	3	3	3	
Ideas/story are cohesively and sequentially developed	3	3	3	3	
Writing shows character and theme development	3	3	3	3	
Uses a variety of vocabulary and sentence structures	3	3	3	3	
Shares and discusses writing with others	3	3	3	3	
Revises for clarity and meaning	3	3	3	3	
Self-edits for conventions	3	3	3	3	
Uses appropriate resources to support writing	3	3	3	3	

Literacy Development - Writing Mechanics	**1**	**2**	**3**	**4**	**Comments**
Explores uses of punctuation	3	3	3	3	1. Seaaira is aware of punctuation usage and usually edits for final drafts. It's obvious her first concern in writing is meaning—as it well should be.
Uses end punctuation appropriately	2	3	3	3	2. Final drafts show her understanding of these conventions.
Uses other punctuation appropriately	2	2	2	2	3. I must confess to having difficulty reading Seaaira's handwriting at times. Maybe it's because I now need bifocals!
Uses capitals and lower case letters appropriately	2	3	3	3	
Uses age-appropriate handwriting	3	3	2	2	

Literacy Development - Spelling	**1**	**2**	**3**	**4**	**Comments**
Uses invented spelling freely	3	3	3	3	1. Seaaira's overriding concern for meaning makes her spelling hard to read at times. She's aware of the need to edit and often consults the dictionary.
Invented spellings are easily read	2	3	3	3	2. I do see growth, especially with regard to visualization. It's easier to read her inventions.
High frequency words show standard spelling	3	3	3	3	3. I still see signs of growth. However, on at least a couple of occasions, Seaaira had ready access to standard spellings from maps and charts that were at a center and chose not to use them as a resource.
Invented spelling shows awareness of spelling patterns	3	3	3	3	
Spelling shows visualization of words	2	3	3	3	
Many words show standard spelling	2	3	3	3	

Whole Language Checklist
Borton Primary Magnet School
Caryl Crowell

Key:
1 - rarely observed
2 - sometimes observed
3 - often observed

Name: Seaaira
Year: 1990–1991
Grade: 3rd

Math Problem Solving	**1**	**2**	**3**	**4**	**Comments**
Uses manipulatives effectively	3	3	3	3	1. Seaaira is such a positive person. She persists in problem-solving situations.
Uses representational drawings appropriately	3	3	3	3	2. Rounding-off and mental math practice has helped with estimating. She's made some perceptive observations with regard to multiplication patterns, square and prime numbers.
Solves problems at an abstract level	3	3	3	3	
Attempts to solve problems in an organized way	3	3	3	3	
Estimates answers and considers reasonableness	2	3	3	3	
Discusses problem-solving strategies	3	3	3	3	
Keeps working when answer is not immediately apparent	3	3	3	3	
Makes mental calculations	3	3	3	3	

Learning in a Social Environment	**1**	**2**	**3**	**4**	**Comments**
Is organized and has necessary materials	3	3	3	3	1. Seaaira works diligently at centers. Her enthusiasm is wonderful. She works well with everyone.
Begins work promptly and continues working	3	3	3	3	2. I love watching Seaaira create. She always surprises me with novel and interesting ideas.
Completes work appropriately	3	3	3	3	3. I wish all my students could be risk takers like Seaaira. She tries her hand at everything. We all take delight in her creations.
Self-directed and self-motivated	3	3	3	3	
Uses room resources for information and clarification	3	3	3	3	
Uses other children as resources	3	3	3	3	
Collaborates effectively with others	3	3	3	3	
Values ideas and contributions of others	3	3	3	3	
Takes risks as a learner	3	3	3	3	
Interactions show respect for safety and feelings of others	3	3	3	3	
Assumes responsibility for solving problems verbally	3	3	3	3	
Behaves appropriately in a variety of situations	3	3	3	3	
Self-evaluates	3	3	3	3	

Second Language Development	**1**	**2**	**3**	**4**	**Comments**
Demonstrates interest in learning a second language	3	3	3	3	1. Seaaira is very interested and takes advantage of second language activities.
Listens attentively when second language is used	3	3	3	3	2. Growth in this area is a self-stated goal.
Attempts purposeful communication in second language	2	3	3	3	
Builds/draws upon knowledge of native language	2	2	3	3	
Demonstrates ongoing development of literacy in second language	2	3	3	3	

Whole Language Checklist
Borton Primary Magnet School
Caryl Crowell

Name: Seaaira
Year: 1990–1991
Grade: 3rd

First Quarter

Teacher comments: Seaaira throws herself into everything with such enthusiasm and energy! She's imaginative and conscientious about her work. She takes risks freely as a learner, enabling her to take advantage of many opportunities for learning.	*Parent comments:* This checklist is wonderful. Thank you for all your effort. I would like some direction as to how to make Seaaira more aware of her reading strategies. Any suggestions would be greatly appreciated.

Second Quarter

Teacher comments: Seaaira's growing interest in bilingualism found expression in a bilingual play performed by her group, but written mostly by Seaaira and Lolita. They are an interesting pair. They seem to bring out the best in each other. It's a truly wonderful friendship. Seaaira's own interests and self-initiated projects consume her. Once she starts something, she develops it with a passion and sees it through to the end. Her wonderings about the multiplication rectangles we explored were the catalyst for an extra day of exploration.	*Parent comments:*

Third Quarter

Teacher comments: Seaaira and her compatriot were truly innovative with their ocean study presentation, behind Seaaira's leadership. She threw herself into her work with a fervor and used a most unusual format for presentation—poetry and songs about coral. We have it on tape. She began her study of Puerto Rico in a similar way. Without waiting for direction from me, she was off to the library and returned with a stack of materials. Then she arranged with Kathy Whitmore to interview Dr. Moll. Need I say more!?!	*Parent comments:*

Fourth Quarter

Teacher comments: Seaaira finally took on the challenge of reading with a Spanish literature study group and she enjoyed the experience. Throughout the year, I have awaited each surprise from her with anticipation and delight. She has kept me on my toes. Knowing her has been wonderful. She is the kind of creative, questioning thinker that I would love to clone, but I'd never have enough energy. I will miss Seaaira a lot!	*Parent comments:*

Lista de cotejo de lenguaje integral
Borton Primary Magnet School
Caryl Crowell

Clave:
1 - Se observa rara vez
2 - Se observa de vez en cuando
3 - Se observa frecuentemente

Nombre: Lolita
Año: 1990–1991
Grado: 3ro

Desarrollo del lenguaje oral	**1**	**2**	**3**	**4**	**Comentarios**
Escucha con atención durante interacciones de uno a uno	3	3	3	3	1. Lolita usa su bilingüismo como un recurso dependente en la situación social.
Escucha con atención en grupos pequeños	3	3	3	3	2. Dentro del grupo de sus amiguitas habla mucho pero es muy callada en el grupo de estudios de literatura.
Escucha con atención durante reuniones del grupo entero	3	3	3	3	
Escucha cuando se lee en voz alta	3	3	3	3	
Participa adecuadamente en conversaciones	3	3	3	3	
Explica sus respuestas con detalles	3	3	3	3	
Explica sus ideas y razonamientos	2	3	3	3	
Participa en juegos de lenguaje	2	2	3	3	
Demuestra entender instrucciones dadas oralmente	3	3	3	3	

Desarrollo de la lectoescritura	**1**	**2**	**3**	**4**	**Comentarios**
Auto-selecciona material para la lectura	3	3	3	3	1. Lolita demuestra habilidad de lectura en ambos idiomas. Este año puede escoger libros por interés y no solo por lenguaje. Está participando en la clase de recursos de la biblioteca.
Comienza a leer con prontitud	3	3	3	3	2. Le gustó mucho el estudio de cuentos de hadas. Leyó muchos en ambos idiomas.
Lee por un período prolongado	3	3	3	3	3. Lolita usa estrategías muy efectivas y reconoce que se usa la lectura para aprender. Ella dice que no lee de una manera diferente en el inglés que en el español.
Lee una variedad de materiales	3	3	3	3	
Lee con una variedad de propósitos	3	3	3	3	
Usa la biblioteca para el entretenimiento y la investigación	3	3	3	3	
Hace sustituciones de palabras desconocidos	3	3	3	3	
Use el sentido y el significado del lenguaje para predecir	3	3	3	3	
Se auto-corrige mientras lee	3	3	3	3	

Reacción a la literatura	**1**	**2**	**3**	**4**	**Comentarios**
Narra y resume los cuentos	3	3	3	3	1. Participa bien en el grupo de estudios literarios. Comparte sus ideas.
Relaciona la lectura con sus experiencias personales	2	2	2	3	2. Sus apuntes en su diario de literatura son muy pensativos. Participó en la presentación de una versión original de Caperucita Roja.
Demuestra discernimiento de los elementos del cuento	3	3	3	3	3. Lolita reconoce que necesita hablar más en las discusiones de libros que leemos en común. Estaba muy callada en los grupos. Necesita poner más atención a su diario.
Reconoce una variedad de géneros	2	2	3	3	
Discute la lectura con otros	3	3	2	3	
Extiende la lectura a otras lecturas y proyectos	-	3	3	3	
Escribe con atención en su diario de literatura	-	3	2	2	

Lista de cotejo de lenguaje integral
Borton Primary Magnet School
Caryl Crowell

Clave:
1 - Se observa rara vez
2 - Se observa de vez en cuando
3 - Se observa frecuentemente

Nombre: Lolita
Año: 1990–1991
Grado: 3ro

Desarrollo de lenguaje escrito	1	2	3	4
Auto-seleciona tópicos e ideas para escribir	3	3	3	3
Inicia los escritos con prontitud y sostiene el proceso de escribir	3	3	3	3
Escribe con una variedad de propósitos y para varias audiencias	3	3	3	3
Usa una variedad de estilos, formas, y recursos literarios	2	3	3	3
Desarrolla las ideas y el cuento con consistencia en sucesión	3	3	3	3
El texto escrito demuestra desarrollo de personajes y temas	3	3	3	3
Usa una variedad de vocabulario y estructuras en sus oraciones	3	3	3	3
Comparte y discute sus textos escritos con otros	2	3	3	3
Revisa sus borradores buscando significado y claridad	2	3	3	3
Se auto-edita en busca de las reglas convencionales	3	3	3	3
Usa recursos apropriados para apoyar el proceso de la escritura	3	3	3	3

Comentarios

1. Lolita ha escrito cartas, cuentos, artículos. Usa ambos idiomas, a veces dentro del mismo escrito para que su mamá pueda leerlo también.
2. Hizo revisiones extensos en su cuento de hadas.
3. Exploró una variedad de estilos en su presentación acerca del coral, incluyendo la poesía.

Lenguaje escrito - Reglas convencionales	1	2	3	4
Explora el uso de los signos de puntuación	2	2	2	2
Hace uso apropriado de los signos de puntuación al inicio y al final	3	3	3	3
Hace uso apropriado de otros signos de puntuación	2	2	2	2
Utiliza apropriadamente las letras mayúsculas y minúsculas	2	3	3	3
Utiliza una letra clara y apropriada para su edad	3	3	2	2

Comentarios

1. Se nota. ? !
2. Después de editar con un adulto usó " ". Está usando cursivo.

Lenguaje escrito - Ortografía	1	2	3	4
Hace uso de la ortografía inventada libremente	3	3	3	3
La ortografía inventada se puede entender con facilidad	3	3	3	3
Demuestra ortografía convencional en palabras de alta frecuencia	3	3	3	3
Su ortografía demuestra conocimiento de modelos ortográficos	3	3	3	3
La ortografía demuestra el uso de la memoria visual	3	3	3	3
Muchas palabras demuestran la ortografía convencional	3	3	3	3

Comentarios

1. En español se confunde nada más que ll/y y b/v. Su ortografía en inglés tiene mucho de lo convencional con algunas influencias del español.
2. Progreso notado.

Lista de cotejo de lenguaje integral
Borton Primary Magnet School
Caryl Crowell

Clave:
1 - Se observa rara vez
2 - Se observa de vez en cuando
3 - Se observa frecuentemente

Nombre: Lolita
Año: 1990–1991
Grado: 3ro

Solución de problemas matemáticos	1	2	3	4	Comentarios
Manipula objetos efectivamente	3	3	3	3	1. Lolita fue parte de un grupo que se organizó muy bien y resolvió un problema bastante trabajoso.
Usa dibujos efectivamente	3	3	3	3	2. El saber redondear y hacer cálculos mentales le ha ayudado mucho a predecir sus respuestas.
Resuelve problemas a un nivel abstracto	3	3	3	3	3. Demuestra uso del pensamiento lógico para resolver problemas.
Intenta resolver problemas de una manera organizada	3	3	3	3	
Predice posibles respuestas y examina su viabilidad	2	3	3	3	
Discute las estrategías que utiliza al resolver problemas	2	3	3	3	
Sigue trabajando cuando no encuentra una respuesta de inmediato	3	3	3	3	
Hace cálculos mentales	2	3	3	3	

Aprendizaje en el ambiente social	1	2	3	4	Comentarios
Se organiza y tiene los materiales necesarios	3	3	3	3	1. Lolita fue elegida como representante del Consejo de Estudiantes (Student Council). Aunque es callada, otros le ven bien responsable y capaz.
Empieza el trabajo con prontitud. Se mantiene ocupado(a)	3	3	3	3	2. Siempre espero algún proyecto muy individuo y original de Lolita. Es especialmente creativa en colaboración con Seaaira. Es una amistad tremenda.
Termina su trabajo apropriadamente	3	3	3	3	3. Empezó su estudio de Puerto Rico independientemente.
Se auto-dirige y se auto-motiva	3	3	3	3	
Utiliza varios recursos en busca de información y para aclarar dudas	3	3	3	3	
Hace uso de los otros niños como recursos	3	3	3	3	
Colabora efectivamente con otros	3	3	3	3	
Valora las ideas y contribuciones de otros	3	3	3	3	
Se toma riesgos en el aprendizaje	3	3	3	3	
Sus interacciones demuestran respeto hacia otros	3	3	3	3	
Acepta responsabilidad para resolver problemas sociales oralmente	3	3	3	3	
Se comporta apropriadamente en una variedad de situaciones	3	3	3	3	
Se auto-evalua	3	3	3	3	

Desarrollo de segundo idioma	1	2	3	4	Comentarios
Demuestra una actitud positiva hacia el uso del segundo idioma	3	3	3	3	1. El inglés está bien desarrollado. Mueve facilmente entre ambos idiomas oralmente y escrito.
Escucha con atención cuando se usa el segundo idioma	3	3	3	3	
Intenta comunicarse en el segundo idioma	3	3	3	3	
Utiliza el conocimiento de su primer idioma	3	3	3	3	
Demuestra un desarrollo continuo de la lectoescritura	3	3	3	3	

Lista de cotejo de lenguaje integral
Borton Primary Magnet School
Caryl Crowell

Name: Lolita
Año: 1990–1991
Grado: 3ro

Primer Periodo

Comentarios de la maestra: Lolita es un buen ejemplo del poder del bilingüismo. Usa ambos idiomas como un recurso para su aprendizaje. Es capaz de escoger cuál idioma debe usar basado en el contexto social, los materiales, y audiencia.	*Comentarios de los padres de familia:*

Segundo Periodo

Comentarios de la maestra: Lolita inicia mucho trabajo por su propio interés. La presentación que hizo su grupo fue una creación de Lolita y Seaaira. Ellas escribieron la historia, haciéndola bilingüe porque fue importante a ellas mismas. Dirigieron la producción hasta los disfraces. Me queda muy impresionada. Ella, sí, ha tomado responsabilidad por su propio aprendizaje.	*Comentarios de los padres de familia:*

Tercer Periodo

Comentarios de la maestra: Lolita sigue con buen progreso en todas áreas. Se reune una vez por semana con la maestra de recursos de GATE y los demás niños del programa. Necesito saber si Uds. quieren que se vaya a Roberts al programa bilingüe para el próximo año.	*Comentarios de los padres de familia:*

Cuarto Periodo

Comentarios de la maestra: Ha sido un verdadero placer conocer a Lolita y observarle aprender. Tiene mucha confianza en sus habilidades y ha tomado responsabilidad por su propio aprendizaje. Ella puede reflejar sobre su proceso de aprender y explicarse a otra persona. La Kathy Whitmore y yo les llamaremos durante el verano para discutir nuestro estudio con Uds.	*Comentarios de los padres de familia:*

Appendix D: Excerpt from the Little Red Riding Hood Script

ANTONIA: One day, Little Red Jennifer and Little Blue Jenny's mother called them and said,

ANGÉLICA: I want you to go over to your grandma's house and bring her these goodies. She is very ill.

LOLITA AND SEAAIRA: Bueno.

LOLITA: Vámonos antes de que se haga tarde.

SEAAIRA: Bueno.

ANTONIA: They were about to go when their mother called them and said,

ANGÉLICA: Wait! Don't fool around and don't talk to strangers.

LOLITA AND SEAAIRA: O.K. Mommy.

ANTONIA: So they went. While they were walking they came upon a wolf and he said,

MARCO: Buen día, niñas. ¿Para dónde van?

LOLITA AND SEAAIRA: We are going to our grandma's house to bring her some goodies. She is very ill.

MARCO: ¿Dónde vive?

LOLITA AND SEAAIRA: En el bosque.

MARCO: ¿Qué no van a ir a agarrar flores para tu abuelita?

LOLITA AND SEAAIRA: We ain't gonna pick no flowers, no flowers, no flowers. We ain't gonna pick no flowers, no flowers for a stinky, stinky grandma.

ANTONIA: But they were lying. So they went and picked some flowers. While Little Red Jennifer and Little Blue Jenny were picking flowers, the wolf was at the grandma's. Listen to him now.

MARCO: (Knocks on the door) Knock, knock.

ANGÉLICA: Who's there?

MARCO: Why it is us, Little Red Jennifer and Little Blue Jenny.

ANGELICA: Why come in darlings.

ANTONIA: So the wolf went in and chased her around and ate her.

While back in the woods, Little Red Jennifer and Little Blue Jenny were picking flowers, Little Red Jennifer said to Little Blue Jenny,

LOLITA: Vámonos a la casa de abuela.

SEAAIRA: Bueno.

ANTONIA: They went to grandma's. When they got there, they knocked.

LOLITA AND SEAAIRA: Knock, knock.

MARCO: Come in.

ANTONIA: They screamed. It was the wolf. They ran. The wolf caught them and ate them. He was so tired, he fell asleep. A while later, a woodsman came along and heard the wolf snoring and said,

RANDY: That is not grandma.

ANTONIA: And he came in and he said,

RANDY: I've been looking for you for years and now I found you. (The wolf dies.)

SEAAIRA: Let's go get some stones. We'll sew him up with stones in his stomach.

ANTONIA: As for Little Red Jennifer and Little Blue Jenny, they remembered what their mother said, "Do not talk to strangers."

References

Allen, V. 1989. Literature as a support to language acquisition. In P. Rigg & V. Allen (Eds.). *When They Don't All Speak English: Integrating the ESL Student into the Regular classroom.* Urbana, IL: NCTE.

Allport, G. W. 1954. *The Nature of Prejudice.* Garden City, NY: Anchor Books.

Anyon, J. 1980. Social class and the hidden curriculum of work. *Journal of Education* 162(1):67–92.

——— 1981. Social class and school knowledge. *Curriculum Inquiry* 11(1):3–42.

Atwell, N. 1987. *In the Middle: Writing, Reading, and Learning with Adolescents.* Portsmouth, NH: Boynton/Cook.

Banks, J. A. 1992. Multicultural education: For freedom's sake. *Educational Leadership* 49(4):32–36.

Barrera, R. 1981. *Reading in Spanish and Insights from Children's Miscues.* Linguistics and Literacy Series: Learning to Read in Different Languages. Washington, DC: Center for Applied Linguistics.

———. 1983. Bilingual reading in the primary grades: Some questions about questionable views and practices. In T. Esocbedo (Ed.). *Early Childhood Bilingual Education: A Hispanic Perspective.* New York: Columbia University Press.

Barrs, M. 1991/92. Genre theory: What's it all about? *Language Matters* (CLPE) 1:9–16.

Bennett, C. L. 1986. *Comprehensive Multicultural Education Theory and Practice.* Boston: Allyn and Bacon.

Bird, L. B. 1991. Supporting real research. In Goodman, K. S., Bird, L. B. & Goodman, Y. M. (Eds.). *The Whole Language Catalog,* 296. Santa Rosa, CA: American School Publishers.

Bishop, R. S. 1982. *Shadow & Substance.* Urbana, IL: NCTE.

Bloome, D. 1981. Reading and writing in a classroom: A sociolinguistic ethnography. Paper presented at the Annual Meeting of the American Educational Research Association, Los Angeles.

———. 1986. On the nature of events, classrooms, classroom literacy, and procedural display: An interactive sociolinguistic perspective. Paper presented at the American Educational Research Association Meeting, San Francisco.

Board, P. E. 1982. Toward a theory of instructional influence: Aspects of the instructional environment and their influence on children's acquisition of reading. Ph.D. thesis, University of Toronto.

Boutte, G. S. & C. B. McCormick. 1992. Authentic multicultural activities. *Childhood Education* 68(3):140–44.

Breen, M. P. 1985. Authenticity in the language classroom. *Applied Linguistics* 6(1):60–70.

Bullard, S. 1992. Sorting through the multicultural rhetoric. *Educational Leadership* 49(4):4–7.

Burton, F. R. 1988. Reflections on Strickland's "Toward the extended professional." *Language Arts* 65(8):765–68.

———. 1991. Teacher-research projects: An elementary school teacher's perspective. In Flood, J., Jensen, J. M., Lapp, K. & Squire, J. R. (Eds.). *Handbook of Research on Teaching the English Language Arts,* 226–30. New York: Macmillan.

Cairney, T. 1992. Mountain or mole hill: The genre debate viewed from 'down under.' *Reading* 26(1):23–29.

Calkins, L. M. 1986. *The Art of Teaching Writing.* Portsmouth, NH: Heinemann.

Cambourne, B. & Brown, H. 1987. A grounded theory of genre acquisition: Learning to control different textual forms. *Australian Journal of Reading* 10(4):261–66.

Campbell, J. 1988. *The Power of Myth,* 235. NY: Doubleday.

———. 1990. *The Flight of the Gander.* NY: Harper Perennial.

Cazden, C. B. 1988. *Classroom Discourse: The Language of Teaching and Learning.* Portsmouth, NH: Heinemann.

———. 1989. English for academic purposes: A hidden curriculum in ways of speaking. In Garcia, O. & Otheguy, R. (Eds.). *English Across Cultures Cultures Across English: A Reader in Cross-cultural Communication,* 103–16. Berlin: Mouton de Gruyter.

Cazden, C. B., Baratz, J. C., Labov, W. & Palmer, F. H. 1981. Language in day care. In Cazden, C. B. (Ed.). *Language in Early Childhood Education.* Washington, DC: National Association for the Education of Young Children.

Chinn, P. 1985. Language as a function of culture. *Social Education* 49(2):101–3.

Cochrane-Smith, M. & Lytle, S. 1993. *Inside Outside: Teacher Research and Knowledge.* New York: Teachers College.

Collerson, J., Ed. 1988. *Writing for Life.* Rozell, AU: Primary English Teaching Association.

Crowell, C. G. 1991. Becoming biliterate in a whole language classroom. In Goodman, Y. M., Hood, W. J. & Goodman, K. S. (Eds.). *Organizing for Whole Language,* 95–111. Portsmouth, NH: Heinemann.

———. 1992. A whole language checklist. In Goodman, K. S., Bird, L. B. & Goodman, Y. M. (Eds.). *The Whole Language Catalog: Supplement on*

Authentic Assessment, 112–13. Santa Rosa, CA: American School Publishers.

———. 1993. Living through war vicariously with literature. In Patterson, L., Santa, C. M., Short, K. S. & Smith, K. (Eds.). *Teachers Are Researchers: Reflection and Action,* 51–59. Newark, DE: International Reading Association.

Crowell, C., Crites, A. & Wortman, B. 1991. Borton Primary Magnet School: Winner of IRA's exemplary reading program award. *Arizona Reading Journal* 20(1):15–17.

Cummins, J. 1978. Metalinguistic development of children in bilingual education programs: Data from Irish and Canadian Ukrainian-English programs. In Paradis, M. (Ed.). *The Fourth Locus Forum 1977.* Columbia, SC: Hornbeam Press.

———. 1986. Empowering minority students: A framework for intervention. *Harvard Educational Review* 56(1):18–36.

———. 1989. *Empowering Minority Students.* Sacramento, CA: California Association for Bilingual Education.

Denzin, N. K. 1989. *The Research Act: A Theoretical Introduction to Sociological Methods.* Englewood Cliffs, NJ: Prentice Hall.

Derewianka, B. 1990. *Exploring How Texts Work.* Rozell, AU: Primary English Teaching Association.

Derman-Sparks, L., Higa, C. & Sparks, B. 1980. Children, race, and racism: How race awareness develops. *Bulletin* 11(3–4):3–9.

Derman-Sparks, L. & the A.B.C. Task Force. 1989. *Anti-Bias Curriculum: Tools for Empowering Young Children.* Washington, DC: NAEYC.

Dewey, J. [1916] 1961. *Democracy and Education.* New York: Macmillan.

———. 1990. *The Child and the Curriculum.* Chicago: University of Chicago Press. (originally published by the University of Chicago Press in 1902)

Díaz, R. M. 1983. The intellectual power of bilingualism. Paper presented at the New Mexico Humanities Council, Albuquerque, N.M.

Díaz, S., Moll, L. C. & Mehan, H. 1986. Sociocultural resources in instruction: A context-specific approach. In *Beyond Language: Social and Cultural Factors in Schooling Language Minority Children.* Los Angeles: Evaluation, Dissemination and Assessment Center, California State University. ERIC Document Reproduction Service No. ED 304241.

Dyson, A. H. 1989. *Multiple Words of Child Writers: Friends Learning to Write.* New York: Teachers College Press.

Edelsky, C. 1982. Writing in a bilingual program: The relation of L1 and L2 texts. *TESOL Quarterly* 16(2):211–28.

———. 1986. *Writing in a Bilingual Program: Habia una Vez.* Norwood, NJ: Ablex.

———. 1994. Education for democracy. *Language Arts* 71(4):252–57.

Edelsky, C., Altwerger, B. & Flores, B. 1991. *Whole Language: What's the Difference?* Portsmouth, NH: Heinemann.

Edelsky, C. & Smith, K. 1984. Is that writing—or are those marks just a figment of your curriculum? *Language Arts* 61(1):24–32.

Eeds, M. & Peterson, R. 1990. *Grand Conversations: Literature Groups in Action.* Toronto: Scholastic-TAB.

———. 1991. Teacher as curator: Learning to talk about literature. *Reading Teacher* 45(2):118–26.

Eeds, M. & Wells, D. 1989. Grand conversations: An exploration of meaning construction in literature study groups. *Research in the Teaching of English* 23(1):14–27.

Ferguson, C. 1978. Talking to children: A search for universals. In Greenberg, J. H. (Ed.). *Universals of Human Language.* Vol. 1, 203–24. Stanford, CA: Stanford University Press.

Flores, B. 1982. Language interference or influence: Toward a theory for hispanic bilingualism. Ph.D. diss. University of Arizona.

Flores, B., Tefft Cousin, P. & Diaz, E. 1991. Transforming deficit myths about learning, language and culture. *Language Arts* 68(5):369–79.

Flores, H. G. 1992. Please do bother them. *Educational Leadership* 49(4):58–59.

Freeman, D. & Freeman, Y. 1992. *Whole Language for Second Language Learners.* Portsmouth, NH: Heinemann.

Freire, P. & Macedo, D. 1987. *Literacy: Reading the Word and the World.* South Hadley, MA: Bergin and Garvey.

Gaardner, A. B. 1977. *Bilingual Schooling and the Survival of Spanish in the United States.* Rowley, MA: Newbury House.

Galyean, B. 1983. Teaching social themes in kindergarten and the primary grades. *Social Education* 32:269–71.

Gamberg, R., Kwak, W., Hutching, M. & Altheim, J., with Edwards, G. 1988. *Learning and Loving It: Theme Studies in the Classroom.* Portsmouth, NH: Heinemann.

Garcia, O. & Otheguy, R. 1987. The bilingual education of Cuban-American children in Dade county's ethnic schools. *Language and Education* 1(2):83–95.

Gibson, M. A. 1976. Approaches to multicultural education in the United States: Some concepts and assumptions. *Anthropology and Education Quarterly* 7(4):7–18.

Goodenough, W. 1957. Cultural anthropology and linguistics. In Garvin, P. (Ed.). *Report of the Seventh Annual Round Table Meeting on Linguistics and Language Study,* 167–77.

———. 1976. Multi-culturalism as the normal human experience. In M. Gibson (Ed.). Anthropological perspectives on multi-cultural education. *Anthropology and Education Quarterly* 7(4):4–7.

Goodman, J. & Melcher, K. 1984. Culture at a distance: An anthroliterary approach to cross-cultural education. *Journal of Reading* 28(3):200–207.

Goodman, K. S. 1986. *What's Whole in Whole Language.* Portsmouth, NH: Heinemann.

———. 1988. Language and learning: Toward a social-personal view. Paper presented at Brisbane Conference on Language and Learning, Brisbane, Australia.

———. 1990. Whole language at the chalk-face. In Goodman, K. S., Bird, L. B. & Goodman, Y. M. (Eds.). *The Whole Language Catalog,* 281–83. Santa Rosa, CA: American School Publishers.

———. 1991. The whole language curriculum. Plenary Session III. In Hydrick, J. (Ed.). *Whole Language Empowerment at the Chalk Face. Proceedings of the 1989 NCTE Day of Whole Language,* 191–211. New York: Scholastic.

———. 1992. Why whole language is today's agenda in education. *Language Arts* 69(1):34–43.

Goodman, K. S., Goodman, Y. M. & Flores, B. 1979. *Reading in the Bilingual Classroom: Literacy and Biliteracy.* Rosslyn, VA: National Clearinghouse for Bilingual Education.

Goodman, K. S., Smith, E. B., Meredith, R. & Goodman, Y. M. 1987. *Language and Thinking in School: A Whole-language Curriculum.* New York: Richard C. Owen.

Goodman, Y. M. 1992. Preface. In Goodman, Y. M. & Wilde, S. (Eds.). *Literacy Events in a Community of Young Writers,* xiii–xiv. New York: Teachers College Press.

——— (Ed.). 1990. *How Children Construct Literacy: Piagetian Perspectives.* Newark, DE: International Reading Association.

———. 1989. Roots of the whole-language movement. *The Elementary School Journal* 90(2):113–27.

———. 1986. Writing development in young children. *GNOSIS* (8):8–14.

———. 1978. Kidwatching: An alternate to testing. *National Elementary Principal* 57(4): 41–45.

Goodman, Y. M. & Goodman, K. S. 1990. Vygotsky in a whole-language perspective. In Moll, L. C. (Ed.). *Vygotsky and Education: Instructional Implications and Applications of Sociohistorical Psychology,* 223–50. Cambridge, MA: Cambridge University Press.

Goodman, Y. M., Watson, D. J. & Burke, C. L. 1987. *Reading Miscue Inventory: Alternative Procedures.* New York: Richard C. Owen.

Goodman, Y. M. & Wilde, S. (Eds.). 1992. *Literacy Events in a Community of Young Writers.* New York: Teachers College Press.

Goodwin, C. 1981. *Conversational Organization: Interaction Between Speakers and Hearers.* New York: Academic Press.

Graves, D. H. 1983. *Writing: Teachers and Children at Work.* Portsmouth, NH: Heinemann.

Hakuta, K. 1986. *Mirror of Language: The Debate on Bilingualism.* New York: Basic Books.

Hakuta, K. & Diaz, R. M. 1984. The relationship between bilingualism and cognitive ability: A critical discussion and some new longitudinal data. In Nelson, K. E. (Ed.). *Children's Language.* Vol. 5. Hillsdale, NJ: Lawrence Erlbaum.

Halliday, M. A. K. 1975. *Learning How to Mean.* London: Edward Arnold.

———. 1977. *Exploration in the Functions of Language.* New York: Elsvier North-Holland.

———. 1984. Three aspects of children's language development: Learning language, learning through language, and learning about language. In *Oral and Written Language Development Research: Implications for Instruction.* Urbana, IL: NCTE.

Harste, J. C., Short, K. G. & Burke, C. 1988. *Creating Classrooms for Authors.* Portsmouth, NH: Heinemann.

Harste, J. C., Woodward, V. A. & Burke, C. L. 1984. *Language Stories and Literacy Lessons.* Portsmouth, NH: Heinemann.

Heath, S. B. 1983. *Ways with Words: Language, Life and Work in Communities and Classrooms.* Cambridge, MA: Cambridge University Press.

———. 1986. Sociocultural contexts of language development. In *Beyond Language: Social and Cultural Factors in Schooling Language Minority Students.* Los Angeles: Evaluation, Dissemination and Assessment Center, California State University. ERIC Document Reproduction Service No. ED 304241.

Hubbard, R. S. & Power, B. M. 1993. Finding and framing a research question. In Patterson, L., Santa, C. M., Short, K. G. & Smith, K. (Eds.). *Teachers Are Researchers: Reflection and Action,* 19–25. Newark, DE: International Reading Association.

Huck, C. S., Hepler, S. & Hickman, J. 1987. *Children's Literature in the Elementary School.* 4th ed. New York: Holt, Rinehart & Winston.

Hudelson, S. 1981/82. An introductory examination of children's invented spelling in Spanish. *NABE Journal* 6(1–2):53–67.

———. 1984. Kan yu ret and rayt in Ingles: Children become literate in English as a second language. *TESOL Quarterly* 18(2):221–38.

———. 1986. ESL children's writing: What we've learned, what we're learning. In Rigg, P. & Enright, S. (Eds.). *Children and ESL: Integrating Perspectives, 25–53.* Washington, DC: TESOL.

———. 1987. The role of native language literacy in the education of language minority children. *Language Arts* 64(8):827–41.

Hudelson, S. J. & Lindfors, J. W. (Eds.). 1993. *Delicate Balances: Collaborative Research in Language Education.* Urbana, IL: NCTE.

Juliebo, M. & Edwards, J. 1989. Encouraging meaning making in young children. *Young Children* 44(2):22–27.

Kidder, T. 1989. *Among Schoolchildren.* New York: Avon Books.

Krashen, S. 1982. *Principles and Practice in Second Language Acquisition.* Oxford, UK: Pergamon.

———. 1985. *Inquiries and Insights.* Haywood, CA: Alemany Press.

Langacker, R. 1968. *Language and Its Structure: Some Fundamental Linguistic Concepts.* New York: Harcourt, Brace & World.

Lansky, B. 1989. *Free Stuff for Kids.* Deephaven, MN: Meadowbrook.

Littlefair, A. 1991. *Reading All Types of Writing.* Milton Keynes, England: Open University Press.

McCarty, T. L., Wallace, S., Lynch, R. H. & Benally, A. 1991. Classroom inquiry and Navajo learning styles: A call for reassessment. *Anthropology and Education Quarterly* 22:42–59.

McDermott, R. P. 1988. Inarticulateness. In Tannen, D. (Ed.). *Linguistics in Context.* Norwood: Ablex.

McLaren, P. 1994. *Life in Schools: An Introduction to Critical Pedagogy in the Foundations of Education.* White Plains, NY: Longman.

Macdonald, J. B. 1976. Living democratically in schools: Cultural pluralism. In *Multicultural Education: Commitments, Issues and Applications,* 6–13. Washington, DC: Association for Supervision and Curriculum Development.

Martin, J. R. 1991. Critical literacy: The role of a functional model of language, *Australian Journal of Reading* 14(2):117–32.

Meek, M. 1988. *How Texts Teach What Readers Learn.* Stroud, England: Thimble Press.

Mehan, H. 1979. *Learning Lessons.* Cambridge, MA: Harvard University Press.

Miller, R. 1990. Pioneers. In Goodman, K. S., Bird, L. B. & Goodman, Y. M. (Eds.). *The Whole Language Catalog.* Santa Rosa, CA: American School Publishers.

Moll, L. C. 1988. Some key issues in teaching Latino students. *Language Arts* 65(5):465–72.

———. 1990a. Introduction. In Moll, L. C. (Ed.). *Vygotsky and Education: Instructional Implications and Applications of Sociohistorical Psychology,* 1–27. Cambridge, MA: Cambridge University Press.

——— (Ed.). 1990b. *Vygotsky and Education: Instructional Implications and Applications of Sociohistorical Psychology.* Cambridge, MA: Cambridge University Press.

Moll, L. C., Amanti, C., Neff, D. & Gonzales, N. 1992. Funds of knowledge for teaching: A qualitative approach to connect households and classrooms. *Theory into Practice* 31(2):132–41.

Moll, L. C. & Díaz, S. 1987. Change as the goal of educational research. *Anthropology and Education Quarterly* 18(4):300–311.

Moll, L. C., Vélez-Ibáñez, C., Greenberg, J., Whitmore, K., Andrade, R., Tapia, J., Saavedra, E., Dworin, J. & Fry, D. 1990. Community Knowledge and Classroom Practice: Combining Resources for Literacy Instruction. Final report. Tucson, AZ: University of Arizona. OBEMLA Contract No. 300-87-0131.

Moll, L. C. & Whitmore, K. F. 1993. Vygotsky in classroom practice: Moving from individual transmission to social transaction. In Forman, E., Minick, N. & Stone, A. (Eds.). *Contexts for Learning: Sociocultural Dynamics in Children's Development,* 19–42. New York: Oxford University Press.

Moll, L. C., Tapia, J. & Whitmore, K. F. 1993. Living knowledge: The social distribution of cultural resources for thinking. In Salomon, G. (Ed.). *Distributed Cognitions,* 139–63. Cambridge, MA: Cambridge University Press.

Newkirk, T., with McLure, P. 1992. *Listening In: Children Talk About Books (And Other Things).* Portsmouth, NH: Heinemann.

Norton, D. E. 1985. Language and cognitive development through a multicultural literature. *Childhood Education* 62(2):103–8.

Oakes, J. 1985. *Keeping Track: How Schools Structure Inequality.* New Haven: Yale University Press.

Ortiz, L. I. & Engelbrecht, G. 1986. Partners in biliteracy: The school and the community. *Language Arts* 63(5):458–65.

Otheguy, R. 1982. Thinking about bilingual education: A critical appraisal. *Harvard Educational Review* 52(3):301–14.

Paley, V. G. 1981. *Wally's Stories: Conversations in the Kindergarten.* Cambridge, MA: Harvard University Press.

———. 1992. *You Can't Say You Can't Play.* Cambridge, MA: Harvard University Press.

Patterson, L., Santa, C. M., Short, K. G. & Smith, K. (Eds.). 1993. *Teachers Are Researchers: Reflection and Action.* Newark, DE: International Reading Association.

Philips, S. U. 1983. *The Invisible Culture: Communication in Classroom and Community on the Warms Springs Indian Reservation.* New York: Longman.

Phillips, D. C. & Soltis, J. F. 1991. *Perspectives on Learning.* New York: Teachers College Press.

Pinnell, G. S. & Matlin, M. L. (Eds.) 1989. *Teachers and Research: Language Learning in the Classroom.* Newark, DE: International Reading Association.

Piper, T. 1993. *Language for All Our Children.* New York: Macmillan.

Reagan, T. 1984. Multiculturalism: An educational perspective. *Educational Studies:* A Journal in the Foundations of Education 15(2):101–4.

Rigg, P. 1986. Reading in ESL: Learning from kids. In Rigg, P. & Enright, S. (Eds.). *Children and ESL: Integrating Perspectives.* Washington, DC: TESOL.

Rosebery, A. S., Warren, B. & Conant, F. R. 1992. *Appropriating Scientific Discourse: Findings from Language Minority Classrooms.* Working Paper 1–92. Cambridge, MA: TERC Communications.

Rosenblatt, L. 1978. *The Reader, the Text, the Poem.* Carbondale, IL: Southern Illinois University Press.

———. 1982. The literary transaction: Evocation and response. *Theory into Practice: Children's Literature* 21(4):268–77.

Ruiz, R. 1984. Orientations in language planning. *NABE Journal* 8(2):15–34.

Saville-Troike, M. & Kleifgen, J. A. 1989. Culture and language in classroom communication. In Garcia, O. & Otheguy, R. (Eds.). *English Across Cultures, Cultures Across English: A Reader in Cross-cultural Communication,* 83–102. Berlin: Mouton de Gruyter.

Schlesinger, A. M., Jr. 1992. *The Disuniting of America: Reflections on a Multicultural Society.* New York: W. W. Norton.

Searle, J. R. 1969. *Speech Acts: An Essay in the Philosophy of Language.* Cambridge, UK: University Printing House.

Seefeldt, C. 1984. *Social Studies for the Preschool-Primary Child.* Columbus, OH: Charles E. Merrill.

Shannon, P. 1992. Reading instruction and social class. In Shannon, P. (Ed.). *Becoming Political: Reading and Writings in the Politics of Literacy Education,* 128–38. Portsmouth, NH: Heinemann.

———. 1993. Developing democratic voices. *The Reading Teacher* 47(2):86–94.

Short, K. G. 1986. Literacy as a collaborative experience. Ph.D. diss., Indiana University.

Short, K. G. & Burke, C. 1991. *Creating Curriculum: Teachers and Students as a Community of Learners.* Portsmouth, NH: Heinemann.

Short, K. G. & Pierce, K. M. 1990. *Talking About Books: Creating Literate Communities.* Portsmouth, NH: Heinemann.

Sloan, G. D. 1984. *The Child as Critic: Teaching Literature in Elementary and Middle Schools.* New York: Teachers College Press.

Smith, F. 1989. Overselling literacy. *Phi Delta Kappan* 70(5):352–59.

———. 1977. The uses of Language. *Language Arts* 54(6):6 38–44.

Spradley, J. P. 1980. *Participant Observation.* New York: Holt, Rinehart & Winston.

Taba, H. & Elkins, D. 1966. *Teaching Strategies for the Culturally Disadvantaged.* Chicago: Rand McNally.

Taylor, D. & Dorsey-Gaines, C. 1988. *Growing Up Literate: Learning from Inner-city Families.* Portsmouth, NH: Heinemann.

Vogt, L. A., Jordan, C. & Tharp, R. G. 1987. Explaining school failure, producing school success: Two cases. *Anthropology and Education Quarterly* 18(4):226–86.

Vygotsky, L. S. 1962. *Thought and Language.* Cambridge, MA: The MIT Press.

———. 1978. *Mind in Society*. Cambridge, MA: Harvard University Press.

Wasserman, S. 1992. Serious play in the classroom. *Childhood Education* 68(3):133–39.

Wells, G. 1989. Language in the classroom: Literacy and collaborative talk. *Language and Education* 3(4):251–72.

Whitmore, K. F. 1990a. Jean Piaget. In Goodman, K. S., Bird, L. B., & Goodman, Y. M. (Eds.). *The Whole Language Catalog*. Santa Rosa, CA: American School Publishers.

———. 1990b. Amos Comenius. In Goodman, K., Bird, L. B., & Goodman, Y. M. (Eds.). *The Whole Language Catalog*. Santa Rosa, CA: American School Publishers.

———. 1992. *Reaching Potentials: The Personal and Social Language and Literacy Histories of 3- to 8-Year-Olds*. Occasional paper no. 22. Tucson, AZ: Program in Language and Literacy.

Whitmore, K. F. & Crowell, C. G. 1992. You learn the most when you can talk. In Goodman, K. S., Bird, L. B. & Goodman, Y. M. (Eds.). *Whole Language Catalog Supplement: Authentic Assessment*, 145. Santa Rosa, CA: American School Publishers.

Whitmore, K. F. & Goodman, Y. M. In press. Reaching potentials: Language and literacy development of 3–8-year-old children. In Bredekamp, S. (Ed.). *Reaching Potentials: Developmentally Appropriate Content and Assessment in Early Childhood*. Washington, DC: National Association for the Education of Young Children.

Wiggins, G. 1989. The futility of trying to teach everything of importance. *Educational Leadership* 47(3):44–59.

Wilcox, K. 1982. Differential socialization in the classroom: Implications for equal opportunity. In Spandler, G. (Ed.) *Doing the Ethnography of Schooling*, 269–308. New York: Holt, Rinehart & Winston.

Williams, L. R. 1989. Diverse gifts: Multicultural education in the kindergarten. *Childhood Education* 66(1):2–3.

Wolcott, H. F. 1981. Anthropology's "Spoiler Role" and "New" Multicultural Textbooks. *The Generator* 12(2):1–12.

———. 1982. The anthropology of learning. *Anthropology and Education Quarterly* 13(2):83–108.

Wong Fillmore, L. & Valadez, C. 1985. Teaching bilingual learners. In Wittrock, M. (Ed.). *Handbook of Research on Teaching, 3rd ed.*, 648–85. New York: Macmillan

Wortman, R. C. 1991. Authenticity in the writing events of a whole language kindergarten/first-grade classroom. Ph.D diss., University of Arizona.

Yolen, J. 1981. *Touch Magic*. New York: Philomel.

Zepeda, O. 1992. Foreword. In Goodman, Y. M. & Wilde, S. (Eds.). *Literacy Events in a Community of Young Writers*, ix–xi. New York: Teachers College Press.

Children's Literature Mentioned in the Text

Capdevila, R. & Company, M. 1988. *Las tres mellizas y Cenicienta.* Barcelona, Spain: Editorial Ariel, S. A.

Dahl, R. 1982. *The BFG.* Illustrated by Quentin Blake. New York: Farrar Straus.

Martin, B., Jr. & Archambault, J. 1987. *Knots on a Counting Rope.* Illustrated by Ted Rand. New York: Henry Holt

Munsch, R. N. 1982a. *The Paper Bag Princess.* Illustrated by Michael Martchenko. Toronto: Annick Press.

———. 1982b. *Love You Forever.* Illustrated by Sheila McGraw. Toronto: Firefly Books Ltd.

O'Brien, R. C. 1971. *Mrs. Frisby and the Rats of NIMH.* Illustrated by Zena Bernstein. New York: Atheneum.

Steig, W. 1969. *Sylvester and the Magic Pebble.* Illustrated by William Steig. New York: Windmill.

———. 1985. *Solomon the Rusty Nail.* Illustrated by William Steig. New York: Farrar Straus.

Van Allsburg, C. 1985. *The Polar Express.* Illustrated by Chris Van Allsburg. Boston: Houghton Mifflin.

———. 1984. *The Mysteries of Harris Burdick.* Illustrated by Chris Van Allsburg. Boston: Houghton Mifflin.

———. 1981. *Jumanji.* Illustrated by Chris Van Allsburg. Boston: Houghton Mifflin.

Index